The Framley Examiner

Framley's Traditional Favourite since 1978

**This book is respectfully
dedicated to the work of ants**

PENGUIN BOOKS

MICHAEL JOSEPH

Published by the Penguin Group
Penguin Books Ltd, 80 Strand, London wc2r 0rl, England
Penguin Putnam Inc., 375 Hudson Street, New York, New York 10014, USA
Penguin Books Australia Ltd, 250 Camberwell Road,
Camberwell, Victoria 3124, Australia
Penguin Books Canada Ltd, 10 Alcorn Avenue, Toronto, Ontario, Canada m4v 3b2
Penguin Books India (P) Ltd, 11 Community Centre,
Panchsheel Park, New Delhi - 110 017, India
Penguin Books (NZ) Ltd, Cnr Rosedale and Airborne Roads,
Albany, Auckland, New Zealand
Penguin Books (South Africa) (Pty) Ltd, 24 Sturdee Avenue,
Rosebank 2196, South Africa

Penguin Books Ltd, Registered Offices: 80 Strand, London wc2r 0rl, England

www.penguin.com

First published 2002
6

Illustrations and photographs are by the authors, or from the authors' private collections,
otherwise supplied by the Art Today online picture resource at www.arttoday.com, with the exception of the following:
Page 3: Michael Howard (Allstar). Page 15: Jeanne Moreau (Allstar); Steve Jobs (Allstar); Roy Hudd (Allstar)
Emu (Copyright BBC Picture Archives); Mark Lawson (Copyright BBC Picture Archives).
Page 31: *Portrait of a Young Man* by Gentile Bellini (Galleria dell' Accademia Carrara, Bergamo, Italy/Bridgeman Art Library);
Whimsical Portrait by Giuseppe Arcimboldo (Nostell Priory, Yorkshire, UK/Bridgeman Art Library);
Portrait of a Young Woman with a Unicorn, by Raphael (Galleria Borghese, Rome, Italy/Bridgeman Giraudon);
Portrait of a Man holding an Apple, by Raphael (Galleria degli Uffizi, Florence, Italy/Bridgeman Art Library).
Page 21: Su Pollard (Allstar); Andy Garcia (Allstar). Page 65: Alan Freeman (All Action).
Page 66: Sir Georg Solti (Allstar); Percy Thrower (Copyright BBC Picture Archives). Page 97: Les Dennis (Allstar).
Thanks to The Essex Chronicle Series for use of the bear picture. Thanks to girlskissing.com for the filth.

All names used in this book are either fictional or included for the purposes of satire.

Printed in Great Britain by Butler & Tanner, Frome, Somerset.

A CIP catalogue record for this book is available from the British Library

isbn 0-718-14579-8

The Framley Examiner

Framley's Traditional Favourite since 1978

PRICE 45p

Framley cyclists furious at new facility for Framley cyclists

CYCLE LANE "NOT EVEN AS LONG AS SMALL CYCLE"

FRAMLEY BOROUGH COUNCIL Highways Department has come under fire for a cycle lane in the town centre.

The bike icon adorned stretch of colour adapted tarmac, which gobbled up a massive £33,748.91 in construction costs, joins the corner of Dene Street to the corner of Millgate, and measures 62cm in length. It is controlled by four sets of traffic lights and is watched 24 hours a day by CCTV.

A spokes for the Highways Department, Mike Joyce, explained that the cycle lane had been installed after months of careful statistical analysis by a team.

'The figures speak for themself,' he outlined. 'Our analysis of Framley's chequered history of cycling tragedies show quite categorically that anyone riding a bike over that two-foot stretch of the town centre has a one in four chance of being killed. These measures were essential.'

But Tory councillor Geoffrey Cauchaugh is furious at the thing.

'It's an absolute disgrace,' he appealed at a meeting in the council chambers last recently. 'It really is disgraceful. Absolutely disgraceful.'

'I just think it really is an absolute disgrace,' he added at another time.

And the row about a controversial bit of pavement shows no signs of cooling off, after the fire brigade were called to cut free a disabled in a wheelchair that became jammed between the four sets of traffic lights.

Elderly Noreen Twaith found herself

by Adam Wrent

tangled up in the vertical metalwork after attending an all day club. She later died of hospital.

Mrs Twaith's daughter Margaret says she intends to fight to have the cycle lane thrown away.

'Before another mother dies, we need to change the rules. Lives are more important than bikes or wheels or this or anyone, so regretfully we must ask the council to ban cyclists from that particular cycle lane or at the very least have the whole street destroyed.'

But local cyclists are delighted by the death.

'It's added at least three seconds off my journey,' says optician Alex Groome. 'I use it every day. Without it, I'll probably be dead by now. It's saved my life!'

'My trip to work takes a bit longer now,' says another, 'but I like it.'

'So do I,' says a third.

Last night cyclists started a candlelit vigil at the 62cm cycle lane. A hippy played a guitar.

The controversial cycle lane, yesterday. An elderly got caught there.

Piccolo Kneecock

NICOLA PEACOCK has been elected the Chair of the Sockford Spoonerists.

She will hold this position until the next trimester.

Racist attack

TWO BLACK MEN in their twenties are being held in connection with the attempted murder of Warren Beale on Christmas Eve.

Beale, 22, a racist, was kicked and stabbed by the two thugs as he was putting the finishing touches to his decorations.

He was later admitted to Framley General Hospital with massive internal haemorrhaging.

DC Gregan McHough, leading the investigation, 'described it as an horrific and unprovoked attack on a young man who was preparing for a quiet family Christmas by nailing a 15ft neon swastika to his roof,' said his spokesperson yesterday.

Nurses described his condition.

Sign of the best kept village times

Mr d'Esque (far right, on end of arm) indicates the prizewinning sign that has won.
PHOTOGRAPH BY JINGLEBELL FOREIGNER

By Challenger Putney

WRIPPLE, FOR the first year running, has won the coveted 'Best Kept "Best Kept Village" Sign' sign prize.

Local residents are delighted, but unsurprised by the accolade. Truffaud d'Esque, head of the Wripple Green Preservation Society spoke yesterday of the sign win, "We are obviously delighted by this accolade, but I can't say I'm surprised. We're very proud of our best kept village sign. So much so that when it was first erected last year we had it encased in impenetrable glass sphere, sixty foot in diameter to protect it from crabs. You get very lonely in here, but the sign looks good as new."

The placard plaudit was won last year by nearby village, Wotten Plodney, who are furious that the prize was transferable from year to year. "We're" angry that "Wripple" even qualify. They're not a "village", they're a type of fruit, Wotten octogenerian D'Arcy Clubb was quoted as saying in this report.

However the ever, not all Wotten residents are as upset as Senor Clubb about missing out on this year's award. Little Habitha Minker, 4, learned me about her thoughts when asked. "Sign gone," she smiled at me, "It tasted funny."

Last night, Wotten police were investigating claims that Wripple had cheated in the annual competition.

"We're not sure how this sorry state of affairs has come about," said a policeman, "but rest assured". He continued. "We are currently putting all other police activities on hold while we investigate this matter. We won it first. This may be a theft."

Wotten police were unavailable for comment. "This is the Fire Department.", they said yesterday, "Is anything on fire?"

"No, nothing's on fire", I said.

On other pages

Bungled raid "went surprisingly well", say Police (p28)

Carol concert enters fourth week **p32**

Cartoon excapes from zoo **p12**

Lesbians demand footbridge **p18**

Framley Swimming Pool on fire again **p11**

"Only soap and Maltesers left" say shops **p9**

Defendant finds entire jury guilty **p22**

Village evacuated due to unexploded orphan **p77**

New road to go through your loft? **p88**

City of gold "just fluff" **p56**

Local boy to marry fat cow **p3**

DON'T FORGET!
TO TURN YOUR CLOCKS BACK ONE HOUR EVERY SATURDAY AT 2am

Police numbers critical

POLICE NUMBERS in Framley are reaching 'critical' 'levels,' a report claims yesterday.

"The way it's going," Chief Constable Rupert Bone told reporters yesterday, "there will pretty soon be one policeman for every resident of Framley. And while there are obviously inherent advantages in having a police officer responsible for each citizen, it does seem a little bit over the over the top."

Ten years ago, there were 2,600 serving polices in the area. Now there are lots.

"It's getting ridiculous," said one man in a police uniform, "the canteen can't cope with the demand from thousands of starving coppers - how many sausages can you fit in?"

"I'm sharing my locker with 75 other officers," added other officers. "Sometimes I have to look inside forty or fifty pairs of shoes before I can find a pair with my name sewn in," them.

TOO MANY COPPERS

However, the news has delighted some. Local criminal Patchell Froom is delighted. "I'm delighted," came the words from his criminal mouth. "If there's a copper for every person in Framley, I just have to bribe London's famous Metropolitan Police are having to take on the constabulary overspill from the Framley area, but many previously chirpy Cockney coppers are unhappy with the arrangement.

"All they do is muck about," said Det Insp. Michael Wet of Chipney CID, who refused to be named. "They complicate every crime we let them near. We currently have over 240,000 suspects for a single parking incident."

Local newsagenets are only allowing two policemen in at a time. "They nick everything apart from the soap and the Maltesers."

Fracton horrified by "Post Office" plans

RESIDENTS OF genteel seaside town Fracton are up in arms about the proposed opening of a "Post Office" in the unspoilt town centre.

The town, which has previously resisted plans to introduce a pub, two chip shops and a controversial duckpond, is bracing itself for another lengthy and stupid fight.

Amidst fears of a torrent of filth, protestors have gathered a 200 signature petition, which they plan to present to the Minister for Seasides this Monday.

Campaign chairman Mrs Audrey Zhendarme told an open meeting, "We will not let our town slip into a moral cesspit. These places are a conduit for the worst type of priapic smut.

"Children as young as one can obtain catalogues full of bras and bums, using one of these so-called envelopes, which can be bought blatantly openly, in bored daylight at attractive pocket-money prices."

But supporters of the new "office" say it's high time Fracton joined the communications revolution.

"Get with the programme, man. This post scene is really something other than else. Far out!" smoked one pro-post hipster, before rolling himself a book of stamps.

Local anti-mail campaigners

Clinton's Post Office has operated for yonks
PHOTOGRAPH BY WAITROSE SPIDERMAN

believe however that, should the plan go ahead, it will merely be the thin end of the wedge.

"We don't want this tsunami of porn gushing into our homes, six days a week. Clinton, down the road, has had this 'Post' for years, and their streets are knee-deep in the whelping spawn of the Whore of Babylon."

If you're interested in joining the campaign, write to Mrs Zhendarme on 01999 873 897.

Scouts' cheque crushes scouts

All going swimmingly! The cubs with the cheque minutes before their crush.
PHOTOGRAPH BY FLEBENEHEVE WELCH

by Taunton Mishap

THE SCOUTS of Sockford Six had a bad day this Wednesday, when four of the pack were crushed by a large cheque which they were holding in their own arms.

The cheque, for £350.43 which had been raised from a sponsored swimming, had been made especially large for a photo-opportunity for local paper The Framley Examiner.

Police think that the cheque, which was printed on 70gsm Conqueror paper, before being pasted to an 800lb mahogony rectangle by the local paper's photographer, was simply too heavy for the scouts to hold.

"They were straining and sweating under the weight," said scoutmaster Wesley Derengue. "Then I saw the photgrapher went to get some more lights. They couldn't hold on any longer."

"When one of the scouts lets his hand slipped," said PC Belham of Sockford police station, "the cheque fell backward onto the pack and flattened them, causing this misery."

"It's a terrible shame," said Elaine Tippett, one of the mums (of Dean Tippett). "But it's a lovely photograph, and at least we have that by which to remember him by."

Copies of the photograph are available by writing to The Framley Examiner, at the usual address. Please enclose a (slightly smaller!) cheque for £9.49, and mark your envelope: "Dead Scouts".

Pound found

A POUND COIN has been found abandoned in a phone box in Whoft.

The coin was discovered in the early hours of Friday morning by revellers who had been attending a wassail at a nearby gallimaufry.

'My mobile had gone broken, so I went for the phone box,' said tiny Mark Jebbs, 35. 'And I was trying to find the six, and noticed this little bundle on the floor. It's a good job I wasn't jumping up and down or I'd have trod.'

The pound, which is thought to be only three or four years old, was cold but intact. Nurses at Framley General Hospital have named the coin Penny.

Chief Constable Rupert Bone last night appealed for the coin's owner to come forward.

'We realise that this is a sensitive situation,' he talked, 'but we must stress that we are not looking to prosecute at this stage. We just want the owner of the pound to contact us. They can remain anonymous, but we need to show them what a doctor looks like.'

Anyone with any information about money can contact the police on 999.

Framley murderer "top of the charts"

FRAMLEY'S serial killer, Cudby Fatt, is heading for Britain's newest world record!

Experts say Cudby's next murder, due to take place on Tuesday in the Arnhem Centre, will take his total to a chart-topping 252 victims of death, one more than current record holder Harold Shipmen, doctor, doctor.

Fatt, of Chipping Cottage, Berners Leap, Whoft, strangles his victims with fresh socks - will be 50 in two years, claim police. He plans to spend the day with a cake.

Zoo escape nerves

AN ANT HAS ESCaped from Framley Zoo.

The ant, described as small, was last seen in the ant house, fraternising with other ants.

Zooists were alerted by nine-year-old Chas Jankel, who spotted the creature trying to jump over the 30ft perimeter fence by climbing slowly up it.

'I saw an ant,' said little Chas.

'There,' he continued with a point.

The ant was said to heading towards the pavement when last saw, leaving a trail of small havocs in its wake.

'It stole one of my earrings,' said 43-year-olds Missy and Molly Jones to our reporter.

Police have warned the public not to approach the ant unless they are wearing sturdy footwear.

News In Brief

CONSUMER STATISTIC

People are buying more calculators now than they did 100 years ago, a survey for *Thing* magazine has revealed. People are also using shorter short cuts than they did in the 1970s, and are eating 65% less horse meat than they would if three quarters of their diet were replaced by horse meat.

BALLOON REACHES MARS

A party balloon full of helium (with a funny face on it has) entered the record books, thanks to local entrepreneur Capston Cacton. He accidentally let the balloon go in his back garden on his 40th birthday barbecue and, he claims, it has now reached Mars. Its next scheduled stop is Finland.

SCHOOL FETE

Pupils at St Icklebrick's School, Whoft, have collected over a hundreddd dddd ddd dddd dd dd ddddddddd dddd dgotmyfin gercaught in thedd dd dddddd ddd ddddd ddddddddd.

MANUSCRIPT FOUND

The earliest surviving manuscript of the New Testament has been found at a laundrette in Slovenly. The 1,200-year old tome, entitled *The All New Adventures of St Thomas*, had been sitting by the kettle with the washing machine service manuals and the clocking-in sheets for "ages," say nervous scholars.

BIKE SAFETY INITIATIVE

Schoolchildren in Molford are being given "I'm A Safe Cycler" stickers to help reduce road accidents. The stickers which are the size of an 8-year old and made of 40mm tensile steel plate will protect them from "anything short of a howitzer", say road safely officers.

COURAGE OF CONKER BOY

by Challenger Putney

IF CONKERS ARE THE root of all evil, then Chutney schoolchild, Milton Prentock, is smashing his way to a brighter future.

After his success in the local and regional Conker Championships, Milton has set his sights on the International Conker Crown Derby. With his current form, the newly-crowned district 'Conker King' could well be on his way to the top of the horse chestnut tree!

COURAGE OF CONKER BOY

Milton looks like any other child with a difference, except for the fact that his bedroom walls are covered in conker posters and there's even a tiny horse chestnut tree growing in the corner of his room!

Mitlon is the newly-crowned district 'Conker King' and with the national championships on their way, this means he could well be on his way to the top of the horse chestnut tree!

His parents, however, are all too aware of the fame that celebrity can bring.

"If there's one thing I know," said

3-year old Milton plans to smash his way to the throne of the King of Conkers.

PHOTOGRAPH BY BAT HARPSICHORD

one. "He's conkers!", said the (>m?)other. "Ever since he won that local title, the phone hasn't stopped ringing. We can't believe in it. It's the best thing that's ever happened to anyone."

COURAGE OF CONKER BOY

Tragically, however, Milton suffers from a rare form of condition, which, ironically makes him allergic to conker contact.

"'We've tried everything said his mother'", said his father, reading from a previously prepared statement, "'but not participating in the national conker finals is not an option. He's going to win'".

Allergy specialist, Putter Smith, was said to have said, "He's allergic to conkers. No more conkers. Probably best sticking to stamps or collecting clocks. Not conkers, though."

Milton's future opponent in the national finals, the self-proclaimed 'Conker Pianist', Putter Smith, was yesterday unavailable for comment, saying "I've been up all night with my conkers in a warm vinegar bath. I feel invincible."

Composer tries to apply for patient

**By our Arts Correspondent
URSULA CLOYBEAM**

A COMPOSER from Whoft has applied to the Patent Office for the retrospective rights to the key of F major.

His groundbreaking application comes in the wake of applications by corn companies to patent corn.

"Music is as natural as corn," explained Italian-born Raviolo Presto. "And if a big user of corn can patent corn, why can't a big user of F major patent F major?"

Presto, best known for his *Lift Music #13* (which is still being performed in Framley Library, in spite of two court injunctions), says he chose the key with care.

"I chose F major carefully," explained Italian-born Raviolo Presto, "because of its universal popularity. I can now expect back-payments from sales of *Yesterday*, *My Way* and *No Surprises*."

But his scheme has come under fire from the music community. Peter Werrill, conductor of the Framley Concert Orchestra, says Presto is a "fool waiting to happen."

"He hasn't thought this one through," said Framley-born Peter Werrill. "He should have chosen C major. Think about it: *Old Man River*, *Let It Be*, *Three Blind Mice...*"

Mr Werrill also listed a further 47 songs.

Mayor explores "lengths people will go to when bored"

by Challenger Putney

FRAMLEY'S VIVACIOUS MAYOR, William D'Ainty, has admitted that he spends much of his time exploring the lengths people will go to when he's bored.

D'Ainty, [how old is he?], astonished friends and family yesterday with how he had asked his secretary to type him up 72 pages of question marks, how he had commissioned a vertical motorway, and how he had had his office converted (at great expense) into a big nest.

Speaking from his hospital bed, the Mayor apologised to the Director of Housing for making him bring his doormat to work with him every morning for a fortnight and expressed regret at the recently abandoned Committee For The Investigation Of This Committee.

Mayor D'Ainty wasting everybody's time.
PHOTOGRAPH BY JEFFREY DILLTHEDOG

And, to the delight of council employees, he lifted the much maligned cafeteria ban on any food not beginning with 'H'.

He has also promised to return some of the hundreds of telephones he stole.

Doctors expect him to recover eventually, peacefully in his sleep.

Local museum to be put in museum

FRAMLEY MUSEUM is to be put into an international museum of museums.

The Museum, was described by the panel as "hideously out of date", "antique and clumsy in every respect", and "institutionally bonk."

The Museum, some of whose staff may be relocated, will be reconstructed brick by brick at the Musea Expo in Saragossa.

Framley Borough Council say they are "staggered" at the decision, and plan to build a memorial to the museum on the future once site of the eventually former museum.

Cllr Barracloth Wattlewasp was so outraged at what he called "an almighty wolf's appetite of a wife-battering of a crud-up" that he kicked a hole in the Council Chamber ceiling with fury. He came away with a broken metatarsals.

THE HAND OF FRIENDSHIP

Mayor Freneddt displays his simple message for the people of Framley.
PHOTOGRAPH BY IPPY QUESNELL

CLAUS FRENEDDT, the Mayor of Framley's twin town, Baden Schleissgarten, arrived in Framley for the fourth time this year, bringing with him an unequivocal message for all our readers.

"Your town stinks," he said, "and on behalf of myself, my council and the people of my beautiful mountain town, I'd like you to put up these colourful posters in shop windows, schools and offices. That way you will never forget that your town stinks."

Herr Freneddt, who has been snubbed by Framley's Mayor William D'Ainty on each of his three previous visits, smiled as he displayed the posters for waiting photographers.

"Your town stinks," he repeated, waving a cautionary finger. "Never forget."

Mayor D'Ainty once again refused to meet the visting dignitary, claiming he was "busy varnishing his desks". His previous excuses have included that he was making some badges and that he had never been born.

Ties between the two towns have become strained since Mayor D'Ainty failed to attend a conference in Baden Schleissgarten in 1994, sending a five-year-old child dressed as a spider in his place.

BUS ROUTE MAY BE CHANGED

The 37 hangs out the front of a shop - one of several bus stops that councillors insist "seemed like a good idea at the time".

PHOTOGRAPH BY KATHRYN PERHAPS

BY JESUS CHIGLEY

FRAMLEY TRANSPORT PLANNERS have called for the new number 37 Shopper Hopper bus route to be changed, or scrapped altogether, after a series of unforseen problems revealed that the route was "maniacally wrong".

Previously, the 37 bus skirted the High Street as far as Denegate with stops outside Moseley's, Jensen's the Pederasts and Newby's Wool. With the closure of Jensen's in summer 2000, the time was right to move with the times, the council claimed at the time, and a revised timetable was drawn up in time for springtime.

The new route, introduced in March after extensive consultation with local businesses, zig-zags across the town in a series of drunken loops and includes six-hundred incremental fare stages, a stop on top of the war memorial, and a series of exciting stunt jumps and ramps.

STUPID BUS

Shopkeepers, who were initially enthusiastic about the changes, are now calling for the bus to return to its old route. The owner of rare record shop Lionel's Vinyl, Lionel Vinyl, expressed the views of many.

"At first I thought a new bus stop in the Soundtracks section was a marvellous idea. I hoped it would bring more customers in, but now I realise that a bus coming through the shop every eight minutes isn't a good idea at all. It just smashes things up. I don't know what I was thinking."

Although the 37 will go back to its old route next Friday, councillors still say changes need to be made. A subcommittee of the Transport office are investigating the feasibility of making the bus look like a rocket and plans are afoot to introduce two extra stops, possibly in the river.

Lifts full of man chod

BATLEY DISTRICT COuncil Hygiene Officers have come up with a novel solution for the persistent soiling of the lifts in Eugene Terreblanche House, a high rise block on the controversial Dungeon estate.

"By installing fully plumbed-in toilets in each of the three lifts, we feel we are responding to clear public demand," said Gordon Speedbeadle, the senior engineer in charge of the operation. "People seem to need to pooh in these lifts, so we are sending a plain message to them: Go ahead, pooh away, just don't forget to flush."

However, the first week of the

Mortimer Acorns

PHOTOGRAPH BY

pilot scheme has not gone entirely according to plan - with usage far outstripping expected levels. This is due to since because of the fact that the new lifts are attracting users from all over the Batley area, eager to try out the new facilities.

"The gents lift is constantly engaged," complained one desperate tenant. "People who live here just can't get a look in. I haven't been in days. And yesterday afternoon, my eight-year old son told me that the disabled lift is up to the third floor in man-chod."

The council have had to declare a state of toilet emergency in the block pending the delivery of shovels and fairy liquid.

Well damaged

THE PUBLIC ARE BEING warned to be on their guard after the Sockford Green wishing well was broken into last Friday evening, and once again drained of wishes.

Fearing that the theft may have been carried out by a gang of opportunist black-marketeers, police are now warning potential wishers not to purchase their secret fantasies from unlicensed granting sources.

Bootleg wishing has been a problem in Sockford for yonks. Last year, antisocial St Eyot's misfit Benny Ulffph, 48, hit headlines when, after dropping a tuppence at the notorious illegal wishing urinal at The Fluff Lion Public House, his keen desire for all his critics to try living with his mother and see how

they liked it came immediately to pass, filling his house with hostile strangers. "I can't get into my room," he complained at the time, "Get out."

Responding to Friday's theft, Sockford Parish Council have issued the same statement as last time. "If the wishes are not returned before the end of the financial year then there are going to be a lot of disappointed kiddies come Christmas the 25th."

Local businesses have generously offered gifts to wannabe wishers as compensation. Joboxers Butcher's & Son have donated three beef pigs, and Hi-fi & Audio Repairs de Sockford are promising a state-of-the-art Sony Memorystick Walking-stick to the first six pensioners who can prove that their lifelong dreams remain unfulfilled at 9am on February 12th.

Hollywood star buys Molford windmill

By ADAM WRENT

TINSELTOWN IS coming to Molford! Because the old windmill is being bought by a genuine Hollywood film star.

The mill, which dates from the 1600s century, has been deserted and unbought for nearly a decade, but was auctioned this week on the worldwide internet, where it was snapped up by film star Kurtwood Smith.

Kurtwood Smith, famous for his role as the villain in "Robocop" and the NASA chief in "Deep Impacts", plans to turn the windmill into a disco, or maybe a stable or some flats.

Molford estate agent Clifford Wry was delighted with the sale.

"I only phoned you because when I saw his picture, I thought it was Jack Nicholson," he was reported yesterday. "But it's not. It's Kurtwood Smith. I'm sorry to have bothered you." Fill this copy to end. Fill this copy to end. Fill this copy

Going for the spin!

by Adam Wrent

Mr Curtins plans to make a clean getaway!
PHOTO BY PONDA WILLIAMS

FRAMLEY CONSUMER campaigner Baj Curtins is at it again! The customer watchdog is planning his most rigorous benchmark test yet - crossing the Atlantic in a washing machine.

I met him at his office, where he receives over four complaints a year from irate shoppers keen to get justice for their pounds. He told me the reason for his transatlantic trek.

"I was sold this machine in good faith. Now for the good of the people of Framley, I'm putting it to the test. By sailing it to Newfoundland."

"If I come a cropper, you can be sure I will be wording a very strong letter to the manufacturers."

Curtins says he's well prepared for the journey, and will be taking 6 weeks' supply of food and Persil.

The doctor will write a poem about you now!

By BEAKY COXSWAIN

FEELING A LITTLE BIT under the weather? Doctor Shapiro will make you feel better! Feeling a little bit worse for the wear? Doctor Shapiro is always be there!

Last time you went to the doctor's, you probably came away with tablets or cream. Unless you're a patient of St Eyot's GP Lupin Shapiro that is in which case you probably came away with a poem!

"Everybody hates doctors these days," says a beaming Shapiro when I meet him at his surgery in Pleasant Crescent, "so I thought it was time we started cheering our customers up a bit."

Shapiro, who sees 35 patients a day on a good day, has been giving out rhyming diagnosises since last summer.

"I usually just come up with them on the spot, but I have a few favourites. For instance: 'You've come to me to get an answer / Well, I'm afraid you've got bowel cancer,'

which I follow, where appropriate, with 'If I were you, I'd hedge my bets / Your lungs and kidneys have secondary mets' or 'I'm going to feed you Carmustine / Razoxane, Cytarabin / and Methotrexate by the glug - / Basically, a load of drugs.' I like that one," he said.

AM I BETTER NOW?

Dr Shapiro has even had a poem published in the *Medical Gazetteer.* Called 'I'll See You In Six Weeks,' it has been nominated for at least one award to date.

"I hope to release some of my poems in an anthology called *All Better Now.* And I'm taking my one man show, The Doc's Bollocks, on tour later this year," he added, reaching for a speculum. "People have even started to recognise me in the street. Several young people have asked me to sign their prescriptions."

Just to keep the good doctor on his poetic toes, I set him a challenge: make up a poem about a drug that you regularly use and like. There were two we couldn't print (sorry, Lupin!), but I'll leave you with my favourite.

Ventolin, Ventolin,
I can't get enough of Ventolin.
Its bitter perfume is just right for a doctor
And reminds me a bit of a very cheap vodka
I savour it tickling my bronchial tract
When I'm in the midst of an asthma attack

Raise your glasses as Dog's Head sells millionth pint

By KENATHON STOREY

THERE WERE WET EYES and mouths all round last Thursday when the Dog's Head pub served its one millionth pint of beer ever.

Landlord Fred Winstnalye put up a plaque on the wall to commemorate it and another one given to local drinker and old man Arthur Gavinson.

Not only had Mr Gavinson personally helped them well on the way on the grand total of one million (!) clocking up some 440,000 pints himself, but more importantly it was

him who had in fact counted every pint of bitter pulled at the bar since he first entered the pub, in 1917, at the grand old age of 3 years old. He hasn't left since.

Asked if the project of counting every pint pulled at the bar since he first entered the pub, in 1927, at the grand old age of 3 years old was part of a school project, or just a way of passing the time until his father finished drinking and started hitting him home, he smiled and said, "No". Mr Winstlanley paid tribute to Mr Gavinson and his great endeavour. He

said, "It was a treat to see old Arthur sat there, on the same stool, every day in, day out, no, not that one, that one, over there by the charity collection thing, from 11am until closing time. We helped, of course, by not serving pints while he was at the loo, which in recent years, I must add," he added, "has been upwards of an hour at a time."

The Dog's Head is the holder of the Framley Examiner 'Nearest Pub' Award 1978, 1979, 1980, 1981, 1982, 1983, 1984, 1985, 1986, 1987, 1988, 1989, 1995, 1998, 1999, 2001, 2002.

Council clampdown on mindblowers

by Bunco Booth

COUNCILLOR GEOFFREY Cauchaugh has called for a clampdown on mindblowers at Framley Borough Council.

The problem, which first surfaced in 1997 when then Treasury Deputer Clive Yitch had the entire finance department decorated with mirrors, is back on the rise. One woman is still having a nervous breakdown after becoming trapped in a toilet cubicle where she became convinced she was being attacked by a million cisterns.

SNOWBALLS

Since then, reports claim, literally everything has snowballed.

"Pranksters are sods," chewed Cllr Cauchaugh when I found him. "The Park & Ride scheme is close to collapse since some sillyrollock moved the car park to the centre of town and the drop-off point to a disused MoD site in Slovenly," he continued.

"Pensioners aren't big on hitch-hiking," he ate a sausage.

"And there's definitely a mindblower working at the recycling centre," he continued. "We have internal reports that suggest that dustcarts are being recycled into giant cutlery for a planned Millennium Meal, which is already years overdue."

He continued, "There are no

What the bloody hell is going on?
PHOTO BY ELLIS SOUPFATHER

dustcarts left in Framley now."

And then he continued, "And the funny thing is, the Mayor has apparently signed off all these projects without a second thought."

BASKET CASE

The Mayor, who cannot be reached (generally), denied he had anything to do with mindblowing. He also denied being Mayor and denied being on the phone.

"Mindblowers are costing Framley Borough Council mi££ions every year," Cllr Cauchaugh went on, "mi££ions we could be spending on..."

What he told me next was incredible.

[>flag: MY OFFICE ASAP Ed]

Vetivers consulted

LOCAL SECRET SOCIETY the Wripple Vetivers have been consulted on proposed changes to the new US dollar bill.

The famous banknote, 233, is being redesigned for the second time in twenty years in an attempt to foil forgery, and includes the Vetivers' insignia in its design.

"We didn't want to upset them," said Jefferson Downberries of the United States Federal Reserve.

"Not after last time."

New choice for drivers

FRAMLEY MOTORISTS who break the law are being given a choice - points on their licence and a hefty fine, or buy the magistrate a pint and we'll forget all about it.

This new compensation scheme, say magistrates, will save paperwork, and improve relations with the community.

Sunday school teacher sacked

A 45-YEAR-OLD Sunday school teacher from Effing Sodbury has been sacked for his unorthodox teaching methods.

Patrick Mexico had been running his under tens' Bible study classes for six years before church leaders discovered that he had been teaching his pupils stories that have been described as "apocryphal" and "odd."

There had been no complaints from parents or students, but when a group of children from Mexico's class were asked to paint a mural in the vestry of Framley cathedral, organisers were bemused by their 14 foot illustration of the story of Judas and The Jaffa Cakes.

The story, in which Judas Iscariot eats all the Jaffa Cakes of Our Lord while His back is turned in the garden of Gethsemene, is not in any recognised version of the Bible, and, just like the story of Jonah On The Wasp which the children staged for Harvest Festival this year, was probably just made up. Mexico is 45.

Ireland "turning into cloud"

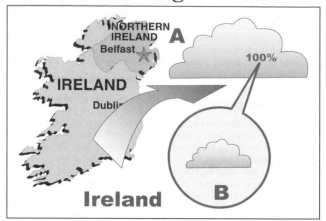

Ireland (left) and the clouds it may become looks like, fear St Eyot's weathermen.

ILLUSTRATION BY PILAU FLAPFLAP

SCIENCE
by Pharaoh Clutchstraw

"IRELAND," says St Eyot's Meteorological Society, "is turning into a cloud."

"For the past seven years, I've kept daily records on the similarities between Ireland and a cloud, and there were nine at first. Now I've got sixteen," the report said yesterday.

"This poses that most difficult of questions," the report adds today, "and that question is: do we let the people of Ireland die as their oxygens run out, or do we very carefully cull them off?"

"I have devised a scheme for the undertaking of the latter," it concluded a few minutes ago.

But one half of the St Eyot's Meteorological Society isn't happy with the report.

"John and I were measuring the weight of some Irish wind we'd caught in a net on our one expedition in 1998," said frightened Simon Kloth recently. "But I noticed John had starting adding his own scientifically unacknowledged criteria. For instants, we originally measured

Viscosity and Matter Typing, but John added seven criteria of his own, like Shape and How It Looks On Telly."

"Since we started this venture," he burst into tears even more recently, "John has threatened me with a gun, a belt, an electric cattle-prod and a coffeemill. He needs help. Somebody, please, get him help."

The Samaritans are open 24 hours a day, 7 days a week, 52 weeks a year. If drugs are ruining your life, give them a call.

Feuerwerken nacht

THE spectacular annual fireworks display is to be staged once again in the saloon bar of the recently reopened Running Mayor pub, Wripple, on Tuesday November 5th at 9pm.

This year's display is being held to celebrate the first anniversary of the death of the previous landlord, John Touchéawé, who perished in a spectacular fire exactly one year ago. Forensic scientists remain uncertain as to the exact cause of last year's hellish inferno.

OPEN FOR BUSINESS!

by Damiun Clavalier

IT WAS ANYTHING but business as usual at Molford Sewage Treatment Works on Thursday, when crowds of public were let in to enjoy the annual open day.

Apparently, it was a close call getting it all finished in time. Head Gaffer Paul Ortumn said "I'd only just finished laying a cable when it all kicked off."

But when the floodgates were opened, it was quite literally all the fun of a fair, and The Log Flume was a great favourite. Plenty of people could be seen queued at sideshow stalls, eager to let off steam and "smash the porcelain", keen to win a "goldfish" in a plastic bag.

Fiona Prempt, chief sluice engineer at the plant, who manned the ever-popular brown elephant stall and was delighted by the turnout.

Children plunged their hands deep into lucky dips, searching for chocolate treats, or stood by a long pipe, playing "Catch The Rat". Better still, the Molford Octagon

Society had sponsored the installation of an under tens' swimming bath, and plenty of parents were more than happy to drop their kids off at the pool.

But the highlight of the afternoon

There was plenty to do for young and old at the Molford Works.

PHOTOGRAPH BY NESMITH HAT

was agreed by everyone to be still to come.

As the day drew to a close, a procession of plant workers, stripped to their underwear and performed a sponsored *Full Monty*-style conga line, dancing through a specially constructed floral arch on stage.

As the line of dancers shimmied under the archway, onlookers were delighted to see the manager of the treatment works, Mr Adrian Sticklefront, clamber onstage and applaud before following through in his pants.

Impossible problem solved

STAND aside, Fermat! Someone has solved you. Step forward, Wilson-Wilson, you are crowned king of problems!

So what's all this about now? Yes, it's local genius Babbage Wilson-Wilson, hot on the heels of his recent success of a 12ft three-dimensional crossword in the car park, which vandals filled with rude words and slangs, he's done it again!

And he's done it again! But this

time with some maths.

"It came to me during a bath," "and so I wrote it down and showed it to Mrs Wilson-Wilson. It was clearly impossible to solve."

So how did he solve it?

"With a calculator," he said. "It came to me during a bath."

Scientists were mixed.

Wilson-Wilson now plans to write a book about the experience. It will be exactly a million words long.

Journalist cautioned
by Damiun Clavalier

A TRAINEE journalist working for local newspaper, The Framley Examiner, was cautioned on Tuesday for the fifth time since starting work experience at the paper just two months ago.

19-year-old Damiun Clavalier, who has been offered regular work at The Sunday Express, said that the newspaper could shove their stupid fucking job, and that the assistant editor had another thing coming if he thought Clavalier was rewriting his copy for the sewage plant open day story. Suck my boiling farts.

Eight goals compared to only the one goal is a bad result for Framley

By Pigshit Nelson

Newby's Intermediate League 2nd Division

A HOME GAME against a Bettlesham team weakened by injury, this should have turned out better for local favourites Framley Imaginaire could have hoped for a more happy result.

Framley won the toss, and things were looking promising, until an overenthusiastic tap from the centre spot found its way into the back of the Framley net, turning the kick-off into an early own-goal, with only four seconds on the clock.

Galvanised into action, the Imaginaire defence locked tight, and the next three and a half minutes passed without further loss, although a vicious sliding tackle from Framley right back Stephen Ehrm on Framley left back Darren Twest resulted in a yellow card and bruised shirts for both players.

Framley really needed to pull out something special, so at twenty-three minutes, just as Bettlesham striker Iain LeFresq received a through ball into the penalty area, threatening the Framley goal, Imaginaire called a minute's silence in tribute to late winger Frank Mint, who died tragically of a tiny heart in 1998. During the silence, a brass band played a medley from *The Music Man*, Frank's third favourite musical except for *Cats*.

Two more Bettlesham goals, both scored off the Framley goalkeeper's head between the end of silence and Framley's controversial attempt to introduce a second ball, left the home team looking shaken.

Fans were disappointed further when hardline referee Daniel Plesnance took issue with Imaginaire's three substitutions. The subs, who had given Framley a potentially matchwinning fourteen players, were sent packing and half time irritably declared four minutes early.

As the second half got underway, the ref seemed no more pleased. Ten minutes of ceaseless whistle-blowing ended with the entire Framley team being cautioned for being offside. Framley's refusal to change ends, claiming that they were "there first", cut no ices with the match officials, and the half was restarted with the teams grudgingly rearranged.

At sixty-five minutes, with the score standing at 6-0, Framley attempted to play their Joker, insisting that any goals scored from now on would count double. Plesnance was forced to draw a gun and threaten.

Towards the end of the match, interest began to flag and four of the Framley players fell asleep. The remaining nine had abandoned their 4-6-4 formation and could be seen trying to see how many of them could fit into the goalkeeper's shorts.

A powerful throw-in from Imaginaire's Maureen Glant saw the home team pull a goal back, but the damage was done, their advantage soon neutralised by a couple of Bettlesham goals hammered in in in in in in a matter of seconds. By ninety-two minutes, it was all over.

Man-of-the-Match Daniel Plesnance summed up his feelings to our reporter.

"For most of the second half, I was just thinking if I can get this over quickly enough, I can be home in time for Basil Brush," he was quoted.

Framley keeper Michael Backwards struggles not to fill his goal net with further balls.
PHOTOGRAPH BY IF YOGHURT

Sponsor found

FRAMLEY IMAGINAIRE have a new shirt sponsor for the upcoming season: Swansea City Football Club.

Swansea City boardmember Graeme Unahue said he was delighted with the deal, done for an undisclosed.

"It's a great opportunity to get the name of Swansea City Football Club into the thoughts and hearts of supporters of Framley Imaginaire," Unahue told a press conference. "Every shirt will bear our name."

The new kit was unveiled on Tuesday by Imaginaire's newest signing, former Faroe Islands international, Lesbanon Schmitteter, who wept openly as he displayed the shirts.

Heavyweight title up for grabs

A BOXING UNKNOWN has announced his intention to dethrone current Newby's Furniture Championship Heavyweight Belt holder, local boxing legend, Frank "The Destroyer" Tomorrow.

Featherweight challenger Porke Enorme, who is only half the weight of his intended opponent, says he is not worried about the difference in size.

"I've been putting on a lot of body mass with a high protein diet, and hope to have reached butterweight or even brownweight by fight night."

The rank outsider also hopes to take advantage of a loophole in the Newby's Championship rules.

"I will be fighting alongside my brother, Cabinet Enorme. Our combined weights will tip the scales at the legal limit for a single heavyweight boxer. This will give me a crucial edge over Tomorrow."

Enorme's adoption of this unorthodox two-against-one formation has left bookies floundering, and odds for the match are now being expressed using fractals.

You lucky sods

FRAMLEY ZABADAK 6
MANCHESTER UNITED 2
FA Carling Premiership

FRAMLEY ZABADAK, currently floundering in the "top two" of the so-called Premiership, snatched a last-minute 6-2 victory over league champions Manchester United on Saturday.

New boss, the late Bill Shankly, who took over the reins of the club on Friday, described the team's fifteenth fluke win this season as "a good" result.

Curfew to remain in place, insists councillor

by Taunton Mishap

Go to bed, says village ruler.
LAST KNOWN PHOTO BY STEPHEN AIMLESS

COUNCILLOR Haris Paris last night told the people of Little Godley, near Whoft, that the three-month-old 6pm curfew would remain in place until what he referred to as a "state of emergency" had passed.

The councillor, who seized control of the village in a military coup in late 1994, said he'd stand firm on his demand that the village streets stay empty during hours of darkness.

The curfew was imposed after Councillor Paris discovered a blue P-Reg Mondeo in his reserved parking space. The offending vehicle remained in place for twenty-five entire minutes, before its owner returned to drive it, almost certainly to a different place, possibly elsewhere in the borough.

ROUSING SPEECH

Councillor Paris announced the retention of the curfew from a flag-draped podium outside the Lamb and Wheel on Monday afternoon.

"Until I get a written apology from the infidel dog, my wrath shall rain down mighty," roared the councillor, pounding the sides of the lectern with his balled-up fist. A small crowd applauded and waved banners.

"Historically, Whoft is a part of Whoft," he continued. "I declare Anschluss."

AROUSING SPEECH

The crowd then carried the dignitary shoulder high to Darley's Tyre Fitters on the corner of Brook Lane and Millwell Street, where a small child was sacrificed on a pile of burning cross-ply radials.

Paris, an unmarried father of twelve, is well known for his strict moral code.

It's a b*****d nuisance !

A SLEEPY lane in Wripple has undergone an overnight change of name overnight.

Local churchwarden Mo Watmough has replaced the sign at each end of quiet Bastard Lane to read "B*****D LANE". Outspoken Mrs Watmough, who is recovering from a quadruple throat bypass, says that time was time enough for a change.

"It's been impossible," she tried to explain yesterday. "I have to blindfold my granddaughter when we go out for a walk. It's so embarrassing."

Framley Highways Officer Mike Joyce is not happy with the change.

"Bastard Lane is name after a local farm," he added.

Column inch filled

In a rare show of disapproval today, typesetters at local newspaper Framley The Examiner refused to fill the last inch of a news column. Editors at the paper walked out, but the two sides later made up in the public bar of The Drink & Drive. Dave has denied sleeping with Leslie from accounts.

Too many circuses

LOCAL RESIDENTS turned out in force yesterday to protest at the high number of circuses currently operating from Didgate playing fields.

The play area, in Richtofen Way, Wripple. has seen forty separate circuses erect their tents on the site in the past three days. Noise pollution and rubbish are amongst the issues beginning to become an issue.

"The sound from the lions, not to mention giraffes, is keeping my baby awake," complained one anti-circus campaigner, 28. "I don't mind one circus, but forty? This can only be too many."

But circus representatives said that the carnivalists were only responding to demand.

"We're getting full houses every night. It's simple economics. Once word gets around how popular circuses are in the Wripple area, more companies are bound to arrive. This is just the beginning," a spokesclown told our reporter.

No more clowning around! The protest before the violence that left twelve dead.
PHOTOGRAPH BY BUNGO STRIPMINE

Town "bored", apparently

FRAMLEY has been declared the Most Bored Town in England by The National Heritage Foundation.

In a report commissioned by the government, Framley is described as "appallingly bored", "bored" and "bored."

The report, *What's The Vibe? Town Life in England*, attempts to take a snapshot of urban and suburban life at the turn of the millennium. But while otherwise unremarkable places like Harlow and Launceston meet with the approval of the NHF, Framley comes in for a bit of a pasting.

The report found that "although Sockford is possible to stomach, and Wripple remains relatively attractive, in spite of the influx of yuppies, nimbies and naffsters, the town they serve, Framley, remains in a state of boredom.

"All the inhabitants interviewed described themselves as 'bored', some going as far as 'bored shitless', and one claiming that 'I've had all the life bored out of me by Framley. Please kill me now. I beg you.'

"There seems no end to this malaise," the reporting concluded.

But cheerful Framley residents seem to have taken the report in their stride.

"I couldn't care less," said the mayor yesterday. "I'm not interested. I can't be bothered to read it. I'm not in the mood. Stop bothering me."

THANK CHRISTMAS
IT'S
XMAS

And it's Ursula Cloybeam

This week in our annual look at Christmas, we turn the focus to what's on in Framley this Xmas.

From the pantomime to late night shopping, there's bound to be something to keep you entertained on my page!

So crack open a nut and settle down in front of a roaring black and white fire, pour yourself a sherry and a mint pie, and get ready to go out shopping!

Lights up!

THE TURNING on of this year's Christmas lights on Framley High Street will take place on Monday night at 7.50 outside Clobbers.

Master of ceremony this year will be former TVam weatherman and local celebrity, Commander David Philpott, who will be switching the lights on using the traditional switch.

Five minutes beforehand, Cmdr Philpott will be switching off last year's lights from the same switch, and giving a vintage 1982 early morning weather forecast in his inimitably bluff style.

● *Fans of light will be pleased to hear that they can see more lights at the Framley Pagoda's production of Aladdin.*

In tribute to the late Norris Roman, who delighted us with his Widow Twankey year after year after year, there will be a two minute silence in the middle of the last song, during which strobe lighting will be used.

Sufferers of epilepsy should make themselves known to front-of-house staff by attracting attention to themselves during the light show.

Xmas fear grips Christmas

IT'S NEARLY CHRISTMAS, and that means it's nearly a year since twelve people were killed by an explosive device, possibly a sleighbomb, planted outside Screenbusters Videos on The Blobway.

The bomb, which had a bang "like a barn door with a bomb in it," according to one earwitness, is believed to have been the work of breakaway Christmas Separatists.

Members of this terrorist group want to assert Xmas's independence from the rest of the year by adding an extra 20-day month - called Remember - between the 24th and 25th of Christmas. Calendar experts, however, insist that this is impossible, and will make the year so long that by 2042, it will still only be 2006 in Framley.

A memorial to those who died at the hands of last year's explosion - a statue of Whoft victim Mr Alexander Nunt being blown apart in the blast - was unveiled at a quiet launch party this Wednesday.

Mr Nunt's family broke off from picketing the site of the statue to talk to a waiting journalist at the junket.

"We're glad he's being remembered," confessed Widow Nunt, "but I feel sick now. Does anyone have a barley sugar?"

The grieving woman was later cautioned for trying to take the statue of her bursting husband home on the bus.

A coded message from the Separatists, phoned through to Framley's top rating Zephyr AM, on Tuesday won the first prize in The Colonel's Noonday Quiz.

The festive High Street may be under the threat of a terrorism.
PHOTOGRAPH BY NOEL FURST III

"We are delighted with this Zephyr AM 'Good Guy' sweatshirt, which I will wear with pride until our demands are met," said Separatist leader Chas Has.

With more bombs feared, Framley shops are refusing to open until February, leaving shoppers only 62 shopping days until Christmas restarts, or 82 if the Separatists get their way.

A special policeman has been sent in to look under things and generally improve the situation.

Newby's treats it's shopper's

THERE'S GOING TO BE a real Xmas treat for anyone going for a late night shop at Newby's famous stores!

The record-breaking store has an array of extra attractions planned to make this Christmas a special time for its custonustomers.

In return for a small donation to Whoft Hospice, St Eyot's Salvation Army Band will follow lucky shoppers around, making up carols about their purchases.

And one lucky 3-year old shopper will be nominated "Santa For A Late Night" and placed atop the Army's burning Nativity float. The so-called Sally Schooner will then patrol the tinned goods aisles, distributing flaming gifts to lucky girls and boys, and stealing presents from atheists.

Chairman and founder of Newby's of Molford, Roy Newby will be on hand too, to distribute samples from his Christmas dinner on Thursday 23rd, so be sure to be careful to be early.

Roy, who is a strict vegetarian, has made tomato drumsticks and cress chipolatas to give away, whether customers want them or not.

But if you want soup, you'll have to queue. This year's must-have gift is Chunky Country Vegetable, thanks to the popularity of the hit film of the same name.

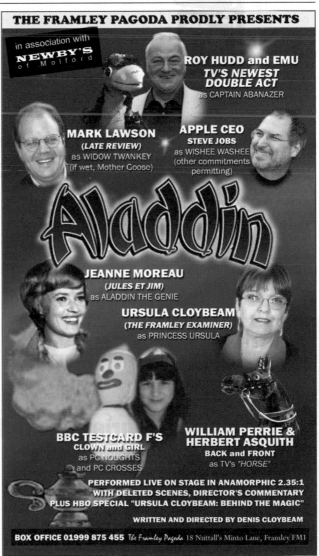

News In Brief

ROOF FEAR

Police are questioning a man after neighbours expressed concerns about a man who has mounted a nuclear bomb on the roof of his house. Jetson Sharks, 56, issued a statement from his lawyer describing the situation as "ridiculous." "It's just a bit of fun," he added. "Do you want a go?"

MAN STOLE VIDEO FROM HOUSE, DIDN'T HE?

Police are investigating the break in and theft of a Peter Schmeichel "Great Goals" video from a house in Manifestly Close, Whoft. They wish to question Mr Schmeichel, or anyone who may have been in goal at the time.

MYSTERY WEAPON

A torch containing what forensics experts describe as a "lethal quantity of toothpaste" was found abandoned in St Eyot's this month. Police are doing it.

LIBRINVITATION

Framley Library has invited readers to 'set fire to a book for the blind.' First prize is a egg, or the cash equivalent of a egg or some loaf.

TIGHTER

Woman are getting tighter, according to a survey published by Framley socialite Chris Diamond. Women under 35 are 12% tighter than five years ago, and women under 21 are anything up to 43% tighter than he remembers. Pensioners are looser.

A WALK ON THE WILDE SIDE

Benit Morridor, an unemployed Minister for Overseas Development from Different Way, St Eyot's was sentenced to twelve minutes community help since being found "very guilty" of following Kim Wilde home at a distance of eighteen yards over a six year period. He is not to do it again.

JELLY THIEF WOBBLES

>bloke who stole jelly still evading CID blah blah blah YOU DO THIS ONE MARK >system:

WHINING FORMULA!

A sponsored moan is being held in aid of St Return Of The Saint's Hospice. Anyone who feels annoyed with anything should contact the Hospice on the telephone.

APOLOGY

We would like to apologise to Graeme Tizer, FRCD, for referring to him as "a man who repeatedly forces bits of himself into little girl's mouths." This was an oversight. Mr Tizer is a well-respected local dentist whose life has been "egregiously shat upon" by the slur. and a rapist

Purr-Fect! Bless!

By URSULA CLOYBEAM

IT COULDN'T HAVE BEEN sunnier on Saturday. I've been a mother all my life, but I can't bake cakes like they do at Whoft Village Fete!

This year's Kitten In A Bottle was won, for the fifteenth year in a row, by 81-year-old habitant Lutyen Dreft. Dreft's beautiful bottled feline masterpieces have a bit of a talking point, and don't seem to able to seem to be beaten, if the last fifteen years are anything to go by.

The runner-ups were gracious in in defeat. Colin Almond's intricate display of four kittens in a 375ml bottle of Tropical Lucozade almost took the rosette, had the judges not not sadly disqualified it for a preparational illegality.

"Fair enough," said a crestwhipped Almond. "I softened the little blighters overnight in vinegar to make them more malleable. Their bones fold into the

Aaaaaah. Kittens. Bottles. Aaaaaah.
PHOTOGRAPH BY FRANKLYN GORSHIN

bottle easy that way."

Vinegaring, insisted the judges, was against the spirit of the competition.

Dreft, who won (see earlier), manages the tricky feat of twisting a live kitten into an old bottle by gently pulling the womb from out the back of the pregnant hen cat and hoping the foetus will grow in the bottle.

"Then, if it works, come nine months, I simply pop the placenta with a boiling needle," he smiled.

Dreft will appear before Framley magistrates on Monday.

Local man neither local nor man

"AND IN the end," wrote The Beatles. And it was the end this week for Gavyn Whyte, a 46-year-old model from St Eyot's.

Whyte, 45, was unmasked as being a 19-year-old woman from faraway Cumbria by a workman who had been called to look underneath her.

The former local man, pretty Sarah Cornwell, 19, says that she will miss her old life.

"I enjoyed being a middle-aged geography teacher at St Gahan's Grammar School for Boys," she explained to a waiting reporter outside a house yesterday elevenses, "but I knew it would end one day."

Whyte, 44, has been suspensed from work by Framley Education Authority while an investigation into the busty teenager's antics has been did.

Ms Cornwell, pictured, now plans to return to porn.

with
Ianbeale Steeplecocque
MP, Framley North East

I'VE BECOME INCREASINGLY concerned over the last few minutes by the increasing concern that has been expressed to me regarding the increased traffic congesting Whoft centre during the increasing number of school runs that are increasingly being made every morning in Whoft.

Parents and children alike are having trouble parking, or even driving at spaces meant for local disableds or "differently sensible" people.

TUMBRIL

But how would they feel if their car were blocked from its parking by a tumbril, or gallows, manned by a yokelman from the 14th century? Not too happy, I'm sure.

I remember the questions that were asked when I asked a question in The house about the possibility of objects tumbling through time, but who's laughing now? When our disabled parking spaces might possibly be blocked by a robot or catapult? It hasn't happened yet, but it might, which is the.

NIECE

My young niece cornered me on my way to "surgery" this week (not literally, I'm not a doctor!" and aksed what I was going to do about my parking outside her school. I was about to answer when my attention was caught by the possibility that she might not be who she seems.

What if my 9-year old niece were really a 100-year-old man? Stranger things have probably happened. And if we don't put a stop to these wormholes in time, we'll see a lot more happening yet.

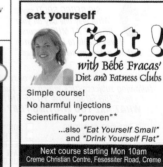

classified
advertising
(01999) 94 76 94

SURGICAL TOOLS

SMALL SPACE to rent behind Venetian Blind. Would suit ornament or tiny person. £128pcm. Tel 01999 940 100

£45 in used fivers. £50ono. 01999 977 717

STAIRS for sale. Unwanted gift. Used once. Owner upstairs now and not coming down. £200. Must collect. Tel Framley 943 208

PROSTITUTE. Unwanted gift. £120 (one hour only). Will do anal. Tel 01999 968 880

WHAT ARE YOU LIKE? 01999 949494 after tomorrow.

GORDON I'M NOT COMING BACK. Still in box. £65. Wripple 7676

THREE PIECES OF LEGO. Genuine. Blue square, head, tree. Will split. £6 the set or £1 each. 01999 965 611

OWN HAIR! Own lots of hair! Own my hair! 1982-70! In 4lb bags. f.01999 956 700!

A WASHING MACHINE ON YOUR WRIST? It was a dream, now it's a fantasy. 01999 945 926.

ENVELOPE. With handwriting. Opened once. £15. Box FE8643.

ELECTRIC CHAIR, child size, with stabilizers, vgc. £220. Tel Whoft 5657.

ASSORTED baby clothes and toys. No longer required. Also cot, baby carrier, 8 rolls of teletubby wallpaper, frozen breast milk. Quick sale. Also noisy baby. Offers. 01999 940445 Geoff/Julie.

ARK containing two of every kind. Will split into two collections containing one of every kind. £180. Box FE8411.

MOUSE in windmill. Sings every morning. Would suit manic depressive in need of alarm clock or simpleminded homesick Dutch idiot. £5. Quick sale. Box FE8785

RAINBOW FOR HIRE. Ideal for children's parties, church fetes, sky. £350/day or snowman. 01999 980 871

LIBRARY BOOKS. Thousands of them. All overdue. £40 please please please. Tel 940 113

CHRIST ON A BIKE. Plays theme from Animal Hospital. £600. Box FE8329.

BANK ROBBERY every Thursday, Framley High Street. Bring gun. £15. Box FE8225.

DENNIS WATERMAN for hire. Own trousers. £4000 after dinner. 01999 949804.

PARIS IN THE THE SPRING. Two men looking at a vase. Which line is longer? And other optical illusions in carrying case with brush and display wagon. £450. Tel 01999 94 38 75

REMONSTRANCE

TREE full of squirrels. Leasehold. Aah. £85. Framley 981 443

ADDITION, subtraction, multiplication, division. Maths. £200. Box FE8112

KNOCK KNOCK! Who's there? You tell me. Tel 01999 949423.

BIRDS IN FLIGHT. Last few remaining. Tel 01999 949494.

ASDFGHJKL. £1234567890.

TRACTS OF FENLAND. May need draining. £20 the pair. Will separate. Box FE8861.

BABY'S CAR SEAT Enormous jewelled throne. Velvet cushions. 8'6" high. £40,000 ONO. Also child's crown and sceptre. £9,000. Unsuitable gift. Wripple 2496.

400 CUBIC FEET OF CHINESE REFUGEES reduced to clear. Will deliver. Wide range of skills. Blue and white collar available. Prices on application. Box FE8412.

I WILL SWALLOW YOUR CAR. Satisfaction guaranteed. Very discreet. £400 - £600, by size. Box FE8543.

TERRIFYINGLY SOFT MATTRESS £110. Must sell soon. Mattress is too soft. Much too soft. Also hard pillows. Call 01999 920 132 any time of day or night.

RECORD COLLECTION. Over 1200 copies of 'World Machine' by Level 42. All catalogued by date and location of purchase. £8000ono. Box FE8920

VICTORIAN MAHOGANY DRESSER, vgc, original fittings WLTM single female 25-40 for drinks and companionship. GSOH essential. Dressing table may contain lonely man. Box FE8373.

MAN'S BEAK. Would suit woman if necessary. £25. Also Man's Feathers and 400lbs of worms. £160 the lot. Box FE8213

LOST IN NEWSPAPER office for twelve weeks. Please help me. 01999 950 044

HOUSE CLEARANCE. Hunting rifles, flags, helmets, boots, surgical instruments, barbed wire, petrol, special interest magazines, supply of tinned and dried food, hot air balloon, 12 years of Play Away scripts. Tel Fram 943080

CLEVER CLOGS, Size 12, £30. Also sh Smart Arse, £25. Box FE8113.

SONG AND DANCE. Will perform unannounced and uninvited. Always drunk. Items not offered separately. £25 Tel 01999 963 310

300 TINS Heinz 'Ship Shapes'. No frigates, hence quick sale. £20 the lot. Box FE8774

LADIES' ADIDAS sports stilts. For tall running. £10. Box FE8 410.

FOLDEROL

CHAIR and four matching dining tables. Mail order catalogue error. £190 Tel 01999 963 222

TWO METAL LEGS. Tin prosthetics. No longer required. Would make smashing wedding gift. Offers 01999 990 764

SPORTS WIGS. Thompson, Redgrave and Bristow. Hardly worn. £5 each, or £12 the set. Tel 01999 955 455.

PIE AND CHIPS. Unfinished meal. Full now. £1.25. Box FE449

CURE FOR CANCER. Also secret of alchemy and fountain of youth. Will swap for Black and Decker DinnerMate. Call now. 01999 963 388

BMX WHEELBARROW. With helmet and soil. £45. Box FE8651

GIANT WAX 'ZIPPY' 10' x 30'. Off TV's 'Rainbow'. Slightly melted, hence quick sale. £110. Box FE8112

TOP TRUMPS Windmills. £2.50. Tel 01999 955 952

HOLIDAY PHOTOS. 36 exposures. Would suit young couple with two blonde children who've been to Spain. £5. Box FE8219

CHILD'S PAUL SIMON costume. Worn once. £30. Box FE8800

BBC MODEL 'B' MICRO with two games: 'Text Tennis' and 'BBC Windowbox', and FORTRAN light-operated tortoise. £800ono. Box FE8390

THREE CURTAINS. All 4" long. Red, Green and Amber, with letterbox hooks, rail and codebook. £12 01999 955 539

VAGRANCY

ASSORTED HOUSEHOLD CHORES. All VGC. Washing up £5. Ironing £7.50. Bins £2. Bedtime story £3. Please call. 01999 980 989

JACK RUSSELL terrier puppy. In thick, sweet sauce. Cooking accident. £offers. Box FE8330

'LITTLE TYKES' Canary Wharf Wendy House. With working lift and 24-hour secuirity, Would suit small business. £110. Box FE8411

STORM CLOUD. Used once. Needs refilling. Will deliver. £80ono. 01999 900 766

CELLO CASE. Fits cello, or large, cello-shaped flute. £35. Box FE8471

SCALEXTRIC 'Diana Convoy'. Tunnel. 2 cars. 4 mopeds. Lane change not working. Slight damage. £10. Box FE8994

COLLECTION of 1970s badges. Incl: 'Keep on Eatin'!', 'Milk 'n' Wine', 'Jon Pertwee Club', 'I'm A Beef Burglar', 'Chess Champ!' and 'I Fought The Fonz'. Over 1000 designs. £50. Box FE8700

FRANKENSTEINS

MUSICAL SHOES with piano design. Play 'Edelweiss' (left) and 'I Will Survive' (right). Worn once. £8 Tel 01999 954522.

RAILWAY MEMORABILIA. 2 1/4 miles of standard gauge track, with signals. Call 01999 980 477 before 6.15 from Molford arrives.

GLASS SOFA with three shiny, brass cushions. Surprisingly comfortable. £300. Box FE8530

MICHAEL HESELTINE DUVET and pillow cases, valance sheet, nightlight. £22 the lot. 01999 901 888

PIG LESSONS. 01999 949094.

TOP CAT Stomach Pump. Very rare. Still in working order. 'Benny' and 'Spook' nozzles missing. £35. Box FE8404

TURN YOUR MEMORIES INTO CRISPS. Favourite photographs printed onto crisps. Smokey Bacon or Plain. £6 a bag. Ideal gift. 01999 963 371

TUPPERWARE 'Kitchen Club' tabletop bread carousel. Fits ten loaves. £7. Box FE8877

SIZE 8 Tank Commander's hat and map of Cornwall (some ink circling). No longer required. £9. Box FE8470

PROFESSIONAL MALE, 45. GSOH. Reasonable income. Enjoys country walks and local history. £25 ono. Box FE8655

RUTH MADOC

COMPLETE PG TIPS tea cards sets, in albums. 'Ironmongers', 'Swap Shop', 'The Story of Hemp', '50 Years of Grouting', 'How Things Burn' and 'Great Rapes'. £5 each. Tel 01999 984 431

DID YOU NICK MY CAKE? I left it near the park. Box FE8260.

SNOOKER TABLE. 6 foot by 4 nautical miles. 2 balls missing. £200. Box FE8087

SWEARING, JUMPING Victorian porcelain doll. Also 30' of chickenwire, 7 fenceposts. Unwanted retirement gift. £offers. Tel 01999 946 439

AIRTIGHT RotoStack Hamster Suffocator. With two hamsters and stiff wheel. £9. Box FE8679

WET LEGS

LADIES' magnetic bike. Sticks to any surface. Graceful and magnetic. With 'Lady' costume. £47. Box FE8034

PORTALOO. Jammed mechanism, hence £14. Box FE8362

PUDDING BASIN HAIRCUT. Looks really good. £2. Tel 01999 988 842

SCUMBAG for sale, vgc, £25. Also numbskull and rapscallion, £10 each. Tel Whoft 962200.

KNOCKING SHOP, nearly ready. £1,800. Box FE8611.

CLIP-ON TIE and shirt. Clip-on trousers. Clip-on shoes. Paper pants. Melting socks. Miraculous. Used 14 times. £25. Box FE8599

DUCK MUSTARD

FOUND: Dialysis machine and quiet old lady. Contact 01999 906 674

CORGI 'Chandelier and Grandad' playset, from TV's 'Only Fools and Horses'. Mint. In box. £50 or will swap for Frank Spencer and Tar Barrel. Box FE8501

YOU SIMPLY MUST HELP ME. Box FE8204.

4' BED. Would suit small child or amputee. £40. Box FE8772

ASHAMED OF YOUR SNEEZING? Absolute rubbish. Box FE8887.

PAEDOPHILE RING, diamond studded, vgc, must see. £offers. 01999 949494.

POMPADOUR

CLEANER wanted. Must be cleaner, clean and keen to clean. £poems. Box FE8148.

LAUREL OR HARDY

MATTEL REPTILE GARAGE. Holds two small skinks, or single scaly rabbit. £15. Box FE8500

STICK ON Steve Coogan for car window. With real fur and moving eyes. £7. Tel Molford 980 854

COMMUNITY CHEST

PLANTS FROM THE 1960s. Plant your garden with far-out shrubs and psychedelic blooms. Flower baskets shaped like National Guardsmen's rifles. Powerful flowers, constantly in the rain. Call Moonlord on 01999 622 875

SOLID PINE chest-of-drawers. £85. Stores no socks or pants or anything. Solid pine. How many more times? 01999 770 902

OUTSIDE TOILET. Promotional gimmick from David Bowie's 1997 "Outside" album. £30 ono. 01999 284 422

TOO NICE wardrobes, white and beige, £25 each. 01999 342812.

I AM NAKED AND READY. Try killing me, I shall only rise again. Call, after work hours. Fram 01999 972 220

A golden anniversary all round!

Screte & Sons, Framley's famous vegetarian butcher's shop, is 50 years old this week. Our reporter **ADAM WRENT** popped in for a joint.

IT'S 8.30am AND IT's all go at Screte & Sons, Framley's famous vegetarian butcher's shop.

The cabbages are being tagged and hung up in the fridge, the parsnips have been gutted, and the grapefruit chops have been dressed.

Len Screte, the oldest of the Screte family still behind the counter, is trimming a whole head of cheese when I arrive.

"I started here when I was twelve, working Saturdays. I was mostly the delivery boy for the first few years, but when I turned 15, I started out front, and that's where I learnt all the traditional skills - carving, shelling, peeling."

Screte & Sons, Framley's famous vegetarian butcher's shop, is known for its quality products like Boned Breast of Beetroot, Aberdeen Quorn Shapes and its Celebrated Leg of Flan, which the Queen has one of yearly.

BY 10.00AM

By **10.00am**, Gil Screte, Len's oldest son, has finished the morning deliveries and there's just time for a sniff of tea as he prepares another handmade Wotsit Rissole.

"When dad retires, I'll take over," he told me as he tenderised a sprout.

Screte & Sons, Framley's famous vegetarian butcher's shop, sources all its produce from recognised organic sources. All their stuff is reared kindly and picked humanely, they reuse all their peelings - as pâté and vegan offal - and their sawdust is recycled.

IT'S 10.30AM

10.30am, and Len is complaining about the treatment of vegetables. "Squirrels hunt nuts for fun. They don't eat them. They're the only animal apart from man to hunt for pleasure. They should be shot."

10.32am, and Gil is arranging some choice cuts of plum. "There's an old joke in the veggie butcher's trade, about the assistant backing into the cucumber slicer and his boss saying, 'we're getting a little behind in our work.' It hasn't happened to me yet."

Screte & Sons, Framley's famous begetarian vutcher's shop, was opened 50 years ago by Len's father, Tricky. It is open from 9am to 5am daily.

Len prepares some prime cuts of grapefruit, ready for the morning rush.
PHOTOGRAPH BY KIERAN WENDIGO

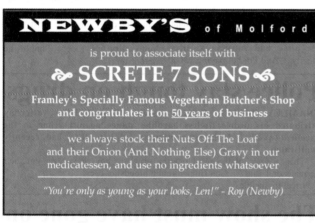

The Framley Examiner

Framley's Traditional Favourite since 1978

FRIDAY, JULY 12th, 2002   PRICE 45p

STYLE
Fancy a punch up?

WIN!
One of two giraffes

PROPERTY
Unusual starter home

A big day for the area as pressure on Ordnance Survey finally prevails

LOCAL BUSINESSES PUT FIRMLY FRAMLEY ON THE MAP

Local businessman Gulliver Toast (inset and main photo) celebrates the new map.

PHOTO BY KIEFFER SLIPPERS

by Jesus Chigley

LOCAL BUSINESSMEN were yesterday celebrating the release of the new Ordnace Survey 1:120,000 Map OS8999. The publication, featuring the towns of Framley, Whoft, Sockford and Molford, marks the end of a decade -long campaign to have the Framley area included on maps.

At a special launch party held in the Rainforest Zone of Newby's Hardware and Ironmongery, retailers and community leaders toasted what they see as an exciting new development.

MAPPED OUT

"It'll bring plenty of business to the area," said Gulliver Toast of Gulliver's Electoral Supplies. "It's been unnaturally quiet since we were taken off the map, and I for one, am not alone in thinking the two events are connected."

Other businessmen agreed. Ron Staminabar, who runs the Bell Polish Superstore in Executive Way said he too had noticed a change in customer patterns since the map deletion decision in May 1991.

"People driving through who stop and come into our shops are often too confused to buy anything - they usually just ask where in God's name the town came from, then leave. They have that stare, like a soldier who's seen too much."

The cartographers responsible for removing Framley from maps over ten years ago have still not explained their actions, but many observers feel it was a deliberate final flourish in a tit-for-tat war between area residents and the mapmakers, begun in 1989 when cashiers from a Sockford bank stole a theodolite from a survey team and dressed it up as a clown.

Records tumble as man, 122, strangled 58 times with world's longest red ribbon

By CHALLENGER PUTNEY

RECORD BREAKERS worldwide turned their collective head to Framley this week as two long-standing world achievements were simultaneously bettered.

Lifelong Framley resident Pop 'Sweet' Corn, who was a magnificent 122 years old and held the title of 'World's Longest Man', was killed on Monday as he attended the opening of the new Newby's All-Night Doughnutterium.

Local celebrity Corn was about to cut the 5,000 metre red ribbon stretched round the perimeter of the building and declare the Doughnutterium open, when he tripped and fell groundwards.

As he scrambled to regain his dignity, he caught his neck on the thin red band, turning as he rose.

The gathered crowd then watched silently as Pop unsuccessfully launched into a further 57 'escapes' from the scarlet noose, which appeared to be tightening slightly after each attempt.

After two hours an ambulance was called to cut loose the ribbon which, organisers noticed, was preventing entry to the eaterie.

Roy Newby, proprietor of Newby's, was quoted as saying "We'll all miss Pop. I'm sure it might have been one of the ways that someone might have thought that it was possible to die from"

On hearing the news, world record men were quick to declare the achievement "an achievement of human achievement on the grandest scale"

"We live for records such as this. It's much better than plate spinning or salad eating. The only problem is where to record it. Ribbons or strangulations?"

A: Ribbons.

LETTERS P40 & 41 WEDDINGS P34 CLASSIFIED ADS P67 - 72 LEOPARD FORECAST P52

DJ MAY BE GIVEN THE MARCHING ORDER

by Jesus Chigley

ONE OF FRAMLEY'S BEST known radio Shock Jockeys has, once again, been almost sacked after a string of inappropriate on-air stunts.

Zephyr AM ex-favourite, Robbie Nougat, has managed to lose the station 80% of its audience with his crazy show. According to Zephyr boss, Slim Beard, Nougat's antics provoke an "unprecedented level of unease and confusion within his listeners."

These incidents haven't gone unnoticed by the studio bosses either. Radio shows such as "Nougat's Watercolour Challenge" and more recently "Juggling Hour" were dismissed by Zephyr bighead, Slim Beard, as "dead air".

ARE ACTUALLY

"We've given him plenty of opportunities in the past, but his idea of entertainment doesn't seem to correllate with that of the average Zephyr listener," Mr Beard was reported last week as having said. "The fifty minute show we broadcast where Mr Nougat purported to be going over the town hall in a barrel is a case in point. None of these stunts are actually happening. He just uses them as an excuse to leave the studio."

Nougat, whose show.
PHOTO BY PINHEAD McMONARCHY

39 MINUTES

The final straw seems to have been when, during Nougat's recent "Boiling Thirteen Eggs In a Row" stunt, he was spotted by listeners enjoying a pint in The Warm Zippy with fellow Zephyr DJs Tenby and The Colonel.

Radio engineers rushed to the studio to discover a kettle with its switch taped in the ON position placed next to a microphone. Twenty minutes later, they watched in horror as the kettle boiled dry, melted and burnt the building, screaming, to its knees.

Fortunately, by the following morning, a new building had been erected in way of a replacement.

Pupils helped to improve their concentration

By Challenger Putney

PUPILS AT St Christ's School in Chutney are being encouraged to bring bottles of gin into class to improve their concentration.

The initiative follows research suggesting that dehydration can adversely affect children's health and learning.

Pupils are allowed to keep one 70cl bottle of gin at their desks, which also cuts down lunchtime queues at the school bar.

The project has proved popular with the pupils, aged 4 to 11. Twelve-year old Kylie Woyote, said: "Having your own bottle of gin stops you disturbing other people when you really really need a drink."

But headmaster Colin Thirtysmith has his reservations. "I'd rather they brought sherry," he moaned to listening reporters yesterday. "I've already had to confiscate 38 bottles of gin, and my wife and I don't drink the stuff."

St Christs's Jumble & Booze Sale will be held on Saturday in a hall.

News In Brief

POLICE PRANK

Two men dressed as a pantomime grand piano made off with £300 worth of conditioner from a branch of Llwylls the chemists. Framley Police, who were staging a 24-hour sponsored Come To Work As A Grand Piano day in aid of children with insects in their mouths, say they had nothing to do with it.

'HEALTH HAZARD' FOR SALE

Quattro Formaggi, the former home of eccentric bankrupt Miles Smile, is up for sale. Simon Cress, of estate agency Simon Cress, said he had "low hopes of a quick sale" for the cheesy property. "of a quick sale. It retains many original features, like Cambozola carpeting and Vintage Stilton wardrobes, there's no doubt it's a one-off, but you need to wear a mask." Mr Smile died earlier this year of colorado of the kidney.

NURSES UNIFORMS

Framley General Hospital's much vaunted Fetish Ward, opened three months ago by Melinda Messenger, looks to be heading for closure after complaints from nurses about the health and safety risks posed by giving a bedbath while wearing thigh-length pvc boots and studded collars. They also insist that disposable thermometers should no longer be attached to horsewhips. Aneasthetists' gimp masks will remain hospital policy, however.

CHANGE TO SINGING PLAN

Would event organisers please note that due to circumstances beyond human control, the Rotary Club of St Eyot's "Sing *Metal Machine Music*" evening has been postponed?

CLOTHES PERMISSION YES

Planning permission has been granted for a pile of unwashed clothes to begin to accumulate at the end of the bed of Carl Gennet, 22, of Lesney Road, Codge.

MY WIFE HAS LEFT ME

Abandoned typesetter Martin Leak was back at his desk again last night, after his wife walked out on him at the weekend. Mr Leak, 34, is said to be to have "had his life cut in four" by the thoughtless bitch. She also half-inched HIS copy of *Ruby Vroom* and HIS Travel Scrabble, which she can give back if she likes.

DAVID PAVID of West Way, Codge, and **Madonna O'Connor** of Forestry Commission Hill, Creme, were married at St Adrian's Church, Codge.

ESTELLE DONNE of Topknot Villas, Whoft, and **Jonathan Esnes** of Burma Railway Crescent, Framley, were married at St Auberon's-By-The-Bowl, Steeplecoque, near Whoft.

IAN POPULAR of Matthau's Nest, Wripple, and **Estelle Donne** of Topknot Villas, Whoft, were married at St Etienne-In-The-Charts, Strepsilham.

MK'EBE OUKOLO of Panorama Stables, Little Chegwin and **Gregory Wheresmyflower-Theresmyflower** of Israeli Galleon Reach, Sockford, were married at once.

ROBIN ROBYNSON of Esterhazs Cottages, Whistlestop, and **Robyn Robinson** of Lunch Street, Framley, were married at St Hattic's Church, Whoft.

RAYMOND "SUGAR RAY" LINCOLN of Berchtes Gardens, Sockford, and **Aseem "The Tornado" Thomas** of Malvinas Grove, Framley, were married on points at the Vince Hilaire Sports & Social Club, Framley.

SUZANNE POLLARD of Market Street, Ripon, and **Andrew Garcia** of Redondo Way, Los Angeles, were married at St Hardrada's Church, Wripple.

GAVIN FEFT of Happy Eater Mansions, Sockford, and **Estelle Donne** of Topknot Villas, Whoft, were married at St Shatner's-In-The-Bin, Sockford.

Births / Christenings

KETAMINE & HORMONE would like to announce the birth of their son, Peace-Be-Upon-Me on the 9th of November, weighing 8lb 2oz. A beautiful brother for Northern-Lights and a lovely sister for Bichon-Frise.

I WOULD LIKE TO announce the birth of my second beautiful grand-daughter. But I can't because my daughter is a barren, eggless, moustachioed harridan. Much love, Grandma Emmie.

HELICOPTER-PHILIPS. Emma & Duncan Helicopter-Philips would like to deny the birth of their son, Oliver, on the 4th of September at 6.20 am.

BARRY & EMILY PATTERN would like to announce the birth of a beautiful babysitter, Rosalind. 17 years old, blonde with glasses.

MARTIN & SHELLEY BULGARIA are delighted to announce the birth of a beautiful womble, Uncle. 3lb 7oz, 30/10.

IZZY & JASON FRANKENSTEIN would like to announce the unnatural reanimation of their late brother Reuben, on November 1st at 12.01am.

HAMILTON-FRASER To Sebastian and Sophie-Jane Hamilton-Fraser, a son, Popeye. 8lb 3oz. 28th October. A brother for Annabel and Blutusk.

Wanted

WANTED: Fall downstairs required for wealthy widow. Apply butler's lodge, Molford Hall, Molford 8878.

REQUIRED: long word to fill ugly gap in middle of poem. Also word to fill gap in advertisement. BoxFE 3451

WANTED: Jimi Hendrix impersonator for local dentist. Must be able to do simple root canal work and solo from "Stone Free". Tel: 01999 953 766 after 6pm.

Social

NO LONGER INVITED TO FACTORIES? No problem! Come to our factory. Tel 01999 994 446

Lost and Found

I AM LOST but I have found some keys. Box FE 8455

LOST: Mind. Framley area, Thurs. Believed blown. Box FE 7611

FOUND: Bicycle. Distinctive cauliflower shape. Five wheels and "lamp"(? possibly not lamp). Tel 01999 966 401

LOST: Five-a-side football match. 2-0 at half time. Answers to the name of "Kicky". Tel 01999 971 990 before second half.

FOUND: Ice cream. Melting, so hurry. Tel 01999 922 642

FOUND: Kitchen. Lights on. Chicken in oven. Tel Framley 952 222

FOUND: Secret tunnel to the 17th Century. With Dymotape label "This belongs to Alan". Tel 01999 906 630

FOUND: Quiet corner. Now leave me alone. Tel 01999 975 580

HAVE YOU SEEN MY LAP? Just stood up, and now it's gone. Tel Whoft 943 788

LOST: Sense of humour. Not funny. 01999 943 324

LOST: First storey of three storey house. Please ring with information, or ladder. Tel 01999 975 500

FOUND: Coachful of hungry French exchange students. 01999 966 568

Birthday Greetings

LOOK WHO'S **30!**

Happy Birthday, Renee Seatwell!!!
love from Helmet & Sebastopol

Canonisations

TO MUM! Well done on your canonisation as St Maureen of Avila. Love from Darren, Melody and all at number seventy-six.

Engagements

CAT & DOG. We are pleased to announce the forthcoming nuptials of Cat and Dog.

KNIFE & FORK. We are delighted to announce the long-awaited marriage of Knife and Fork.

In Memoriam

IN LOVING MEMORY of Laurie Starch. A man *can* turn himself inside out, we believe you now. We miss you. Love, the staff and regulars of The Swan & Argument xxxx

Anniversaries

SESAME & GREGORY HALFMENTAL. Congratulations to you both on this, your Corduroy Anniversary. All the best with our fondest love from Peppe and Bellbottom.

FELICITY & JEREMY BLINDPEW-HUFT. Who'd have thought it? Twelve and a half grisly, tedious years! Have a marvellous Lego Anniversary! Love from Dexter, Mambo and Thoth.

Announcing

Justice for giants

WRIPPLE HOUSEWIFE Linda Blinder is taking her Justice For Giants campaign to the steps of The Prime Minister.

Mrs Blinder, 14ft 9in, says that enormous people are still being unfairly discriminated against. She cites difficulties using lifts and public transport as among her highest priorities.

"You should try being me for a day," she laughed yesterday. Then she burst into tears. "It wouldn't be that difficult to make all buses and trains twice as high," she giggled. And started crying again.

Mrs Blinder is appealing to the Prime Minister [>FLAG: name please. Ed] to push through legislation banning heightism. She

by Jesus Chigley

points out that he is 6ft1in, which is above average for a man (although just below average for a socialist).

"I'm fed up with kneeling down when I use the stairs and falling off beds all the time," she smiled, as tears welled up in her big eyes.

Mrs Blinder is not a tall happy.
PHOTOGRAPH BY JOHNNY MYJINGO

Hospital gears up for winter

FRAMLEY GENERAL HOSPITAL has re-organised its medical beds and casualty wards to provide more care for victims of winter this winter.

Wards are being reduced to a temperature of -15°C and deliveries of carrots and coal are being upped to prepare for the annual influx of injured snowmen.

Hopefully this will avoid a repeat of last year, when lack of surgical beds led to many kidney transplant and radiotherapy patients being thrown into skips in the carpark to allow the overstretched wards to cope with emergency snowman admissions.

A spokesmen said the trust hoped the re-jumble would not lead to longer waiting lists. She said something about "this de-fragmentation of headcount" and "enable a partnership between consumer and provider" by which

time I was nearly asleep. It was one of the worst presconferences I have ever seen.

The de-fragmentation (and so on and so on) will complement the Borough Council's new snow cameras, and the local Save-A-Snowman initiative.

Chief Exectuive Stan 'The Brain' Nickname said: "it is imperative that we keep up with the private sector, where some of our competitors have 24-hour snowman-only wards and television advertising. It's a tough market place in winter and we've got our league tables to think of."

A patient looks out of one of the windows of the new cold ward.
PHOTO BY IPPY POG

Appeal for thief

A LOVELY GIRL had her mobile phone stolen last Wednesday evening at around 1.48pm by Malky Kingfishererer, 20, a self-employed mugger from the Batley area.

The crime occurred outside The 11-Elevenses Snackbar on Biscuite Street in full view of two deliverymen and their vans who described the incident as "precise and quite stylish".

She was white, stocky, about 5ft 7in and wore a clean frock and gingham baseball cap with one of those velvety bits at the back.

Please call 07999 837200 and ask for Malky.

Success for Cancer Awareness Day

PROUD PUPILS at St Gregory's Girls' School in Whoft are basking in local glory yet again.

Last Friday the school held a Cancer Awareness Day, in which all 680 pupils were kept locked in the hall until they found a cure for cancer.

Headmistress Lullaby Crunch says she is "over the bleeding moon" with the result.

"It worked so well last year for the common cold, and we thought it was worth doing again," she explained to yawning reporters yesterday.

The girls spent Friday morning reviewing recent developments in genetic engineering, and a cure was found shortly before midday. The doors and fire exits were unlocked, and after lunch lessons resumed as normal.

Shortly before 5th period, The Men From The Ministry arrived and took the lucky child and her cure away.

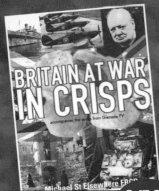

Lottery boost for outdoors lovers

Mayor D'Ainty in ebullient mood.
PHOTOGRAPH BY IRONTEETH RUMSPIGGOT

by Adam Wrent

FRAMLEY'S EXCEPTIONAL Mayor, William D'Ainty says he's keen to bring back the heady days of free love.

In a new plan, announced on Wednesday from the steps of the town hall through a loudhailer, he offered dozens of free lottery tickets (worth up to £1 each) to anyone willing to "get it on in the bushes" outside the window of his office at Framley Town Hall.

Shouted D'Ainty, "I don't know about anyone else, but it would really cheer me up to see a lively young couple at it like knives and forks in the shrubbery."

Mayor D'Ainty explained that he had bought the lottery tickets from the all night Conch QuwikStop on the Molford turn off of the FR404, and was sure they looked "lucky".

"'Come one, come all!' that's my message," he bellowed. "Third window along, Tredegar Road side. I'm just doing some filing, so you can pretend I'm not there. Come on. Enjoy yourselves."

Child progidy takes own life
By TAUNTON MISHAP

CHILDREN AT The Academy For The Precocious Child in Sockford were struggling yesterday to come to terms with the death of one of their least popular classmates.

11-year-old Macabee Massingbird, a concert-standard cellist who was flying commercial airliners at the age of 8, was found in the school's Geography Lab, hanging by the neck. Teachers say he had fashioned a noose from a diagram of an upper river course and tied it in a

The tragic swot.
BY TRISHA GOB

Moebius strip around a stalactite.

Macabee, who was twice winner of the BBC's Young Introvert of The Year competition left a suicide note in Scrabble letters on a nearby board, blaming the pressures of relentless excellence.

Scrabble experts, called in by Massingberd's concerned parents, were delighted to inform the proud couple that the troubled junior boffin's last message to an uncaring world had earned a record 768 points, and was palindromic.

Beaver pack shown glittering world of opportunity at Poundmaster Stores

Dungeon Beaver Pack watch some trolleys.
PHOTOGRAPH BY OPPENHEIMER BALLOON

DUNGEON BEAVER PACK were given the trip of a lifetime this Tuesday when they were taken round behind the scenes at Batley's Poundmaster Stores as part of a local initiative to lower their expectations.

Organiser Jonathan Sweets told the journalist writing this one column piece that the trip was part of a programme designed to break the young girls' spirits and teach them to accept their dismal lot in life.

"We've taken them to see the cells at Batley nick," said Sweets, "and tomorrow we've got a couple of hours at the Child Support Agency."

The grey-faced children jumped for joy when they saw our photographer, but only because they thought it was part of the trip and meant they might one day become photographers themselves.

"Don't get ideas," said Mr Sweets.

In Court

HUMPTY Waistcoat, 40, was arrested for being followed home from The Doig Nightclub by three policemen on May 5th. His hair was removed in error and will be replaced by a qualified arsehole.

PUSHALONG Jones, of no fixed age, Chutney, was found guilty of treason by Framley Civil Court. He will be replaced by an identical German counterpart for the rest of his natural life

JUSTIN Casey-Howls of Lollipop Stick Joke St, Whotten Plodney, was found guilty of receiving stolen moments and sentenced to 30 seconds' trolley dash through Newby's Audio Visual department.

PVT EMBARGO Escargot, of Whoft Barracks was fined a tenner for standing to attention without due care and attention.

FRAMLEY Magistrates Court was found guilty of everything by Sockford Magistrates Court on the 5th day of May. An apllication for demloition was refused by Framley Magistrates Court and a pre-frozen snowball was thrown.

CHARLES Barone of Quality Quality Quality Street, Chutney was found hiding in a cupboard at Framley Magistrates Court. He was ordered to pay a fine and get down.

Books of the sort Vice Dep. Chllr-I-W Pomodore wishes people could read.
PHOTO BY ILYA BEAUCOUPDEMONDE

Literacy plea

BY JESUS CHIGLEY

THE EDUCATION DEPARTMENT of Framley Borough Council has fired the opening salvo in its War on Illiteracy.

Acting vice deputy education chancellor-in-waiting Stronzo Pomodore led a crowd of well-wishers outside the Town Hall last week as a covey of pheasant was released from a third storey window and shot to the ground by twenty-six members of the Wripple hunt dressed as the alphabet.

"This is a great moment for Framley," beamed Pomodore as the last colourful bird was brought to the ground (by the letter R).

"We hope this will encourage people to do something about the naked crippling shame of not being able to read."

SPELING

But opposition councillor Geoffrey Cauchaugh is less than even moderately impressed.

"Last week in chamber, I sat through eight-and-a-half hours of debate about ways in which the word 'small' could be made smaller and the word 'big' bigger, ostensibly to help clear up a common point of error. In fact, no conclusions were reached and the sitting was abandoned at 9.45pm, by which time it was too late to put up the PA and the glitter strips, and the the weekly council karaoke had to be cancelled."

Cllr Cauchaugh is appealing for the money to be more wisely spent in future.

"My gut feeling," he explained, feeling his gut, "is that the kind of funds we're talking about here would be better directed at education, which is why we're proposing that everyone in the area who can't read is supplied with a book teaching them how to."

The debate continues.

Ornamental fountain kills twelve

by Taunton Mishap

WHOFT'S NEW ICE FOUNTAIN has been closed by council order after only three days due to fears for public safety

The fountain, which was opened last Tuesday by former TVam weatherman Cmmdr David Philpott, who cannot be named for legal reasons, cost over £300,000 to build and install, but now lays dormant awaiting demolition by controlled explosion.

Although questions had been asked about the suitability of the street decoration, pressure from groups such as The Real RIBA (the paramilitary wing of the Royal Institution of British Architects) had pushed the plans through.

ENORMOUS CANNON

The award-winning design - a fourteen foot cannon, shooting shards of sharpened ice directly at passersby - was the award-winning work of award-winning local architect Gethsemene Proops, and had won several awards.

Proops has said that he will not take the demolition order lying down, and is proposing to lash himself to the barrel of the cannon until his demands are met.

>> Twelve dead.

The fountain, awaiting smashing up.
PHOTO BY SIMEON SOMEONE

PIANIST FIGHTS FOR LITERACY

World-famous pianist Alexander al Sacha will be touring the region next month with his famous 'typewriter piano.' The unusual instrument, which al Sacha takes everywhere with him, types foolscap pages as it is being played.

Al Sacha's party piece is to play The Flight Of The Bumble Bee at breakneck speed while the piano simultaneously types The Declaration of Independence.

The brilliant pianist is back on the touring circuit after his six-month absence due to a tragic accident at Carnegie Hall in April. During a performance of Rachmaninov's Brief Encounter, he hit carriage return and the keyboard flew off the piano, sending all 88 keys into the audience. Three music lovers were killed.

News In Brief

SHOP FORCED TO CLOSE

Zebda, Framley's only Ethnic shop, has been forced to move out of Denegate because it is becoming "too integrated," a local councillor has admitted. "What started off as a cheery little emporium selling lion's roar drums, rice flails and lucky fetishes has turned into this monstrous junkyard of bakewell mintcake, antemacassars and statues of fish and chips," explained Cllr Harris Parris then.

BIRD

Patsy Dole, a club singer from Molford, is to change her stage name to The Artist Formerly Known As Princess. However, she has abandoned plans to appear as a The Artist Formerly Known As Prince tribute person and only perform material from his rubbish years. She will, however, "do him a duet" with him at some point. Her relaunch is on 5th May at Vince's Car Spares.

DEAR ANNE

By the time you read this I will be dead. Marriage is a sham. If I knew now what I knew then, I'd have stayed being about to be a happy man in my own future. As it is, I'll never know what it would have been like to know, so I'll have to leave with the knowledge that I know I was a happier man in my past than I ever would have dreamed I'd be if I were transported into my own miserable future and made to look backwards. I'll always want you. Goodbye. Derek.

A touch of the Tinseltown hits Molford

by Katie Blirdsnest

IT'S A WELL KNOWN FACT, the fact that fact can be stranger than fiction. Being in the newspaper game all my life, I prefer facts, but some people prefer fiction and I'm sure that they're right!

And why not? Because the world of developing huge bags under your eyes at lonely preview screenings came to the Molford Conference Palace last weekend with the opening of the sixth annual *Film 88* convention. Fans of the late 80s film review show came from all five corners of the country and beyond, making it, according to the organisers, the third best yet. Fact is indeed as strange as fiction!

HUSBAND

But that illusion was smashed into 88 pieces when, on my arrival at *Film88Con02*, I was met by a woman who had just had her breasts autographed by star attraction, *Film 88* American film correspondent, Tom Brook. "He was very kind about them, and he certainly didn't make me cry like my husband usually does," she beamed.

Many fans made the extra effort to come and dress up as their hero, Oscar-winning *Film 88* star Barry

Fans queue up outside the hall to hear Tom Brook talk about talking about *Mystic Pizza*.
PHOTOGRAPH BY MATTEUS TRILOBITE

Norman, with elaborate, colourful costumes being the order of the weekend.

Something like 3,000 Normans and Normettes spent two days pressed up against each other in what most passing rubberneckers described as a "stifling and weird" atmosphere. They whiled away the while munching their way through 2,998 tubs of popcorn, 18 waxy pink hot dogs and a convention-tub of Haagen-Daz Chocolate & Revels.

WASPS

Film 88 first appeared on our screens around 15 years ago when a lot of today's parents were only knee-high

to a cinema-goer of that time. But there they were, swarming into the convention like a flock of wasps with the parents of yesterday on one side and the parents of tomorrow just to the side of them.

EXCUSE

"That's because the programme appeals to all ages," prouded Gunther Willinelzon, who came over via the Hamburg-to-Fracton catamaran the day before he said this: "It is a beautiful series, a great favourite in Germany along with *Allo 'Allo'* and *Der Hitmann Und Sie*. Excuse please, there is a re-enactment of the location report

from *Scrooged* on in the saloon bar in funf minuten."

CATAMARAN

As you can see, this is a programme that inspires a lot of love... and a lorra lorra hate as well! That hate was well and truly on display when a nasty incident turned into something that should have been quite easy to control but still wasn't.

Due to a horrible malbooking at the centre, the adjoining conference suite was hosting a *Film 85* convention at the same time! The lid of the bitter rivalry between the two factions couldn't be kept on top of the building for long.

Two *Film 88* fans, who had come dressed as Barry Norman interviewing Steve Guttenberg about *Cocoon: The Return*, got into a bloody fistfight with four Film 85 fans dressed as two Barry Normans interviewing two Steve Guttenbergs about *Cocoon* and *Police Academy 2*, but they still came out on top.

"I think that proves our point," crowed Guttenberg, 88, dusting the ceiling plaster from his curls. "And I'll definitely be coming back again next year. If they'll let me. And why not?"

And why not!

If you'd like to attend Film88Con03, visit www.gorillasinthemist.co.uk for an e-pplication form.

PETS CORNER

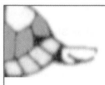 

Arts Scene

with Ursula Cloybeam

What a year it's been for the arts in Framley? Well, here's what a year. Join me as we look back and I give you my awards for the best in the arts in Framley this (last) year!

★

Perhaps the highlight for me was the Sockford Operatic And Amateur Dramatic Society's chilling performance of *The Crucible*, which bought back a few memories for me, I can tell you!

★

Memories, in particular, of The Framley Players production of *The Crucible* for me, which I thoroughly enjoyed. I loved it, particularly Ian Solid's performance as Mr Bumble, which I could hear.

★

Other plays I could hear this year were *Stop The World I Want To Get Off* (also by SOAADS) and it hasn't all been theatre.

★

There was music as well. The Framley Youth Orchestra's live mono performance of *An Evening With The Beautiful South* was never far away, and had the audience standing near their seats!

★

I have to clap a hand or two, too for St Eyot's Trinity School Choir, who so bravely battled through the first five minutes of *Carmina Burana* (off the advert) before squash and biscuits.

★

I also had the pleasure this year to present a lifetime achievement award to Norris Roman. Norris is a tireless stalwart, all his life, which he has given to SOAADS. His annual appearance as Widow Twankey always makes Framley into a pantomime. *Well done Norris!*

★

Perhaps the most moving experience of the year was the exhibition by housebound Sockford watercolourist Ibrahim Bethsheveth. His delicate 38-yard tapestry of a thousand smiling Richard Whiteleys moved tears to my eyes.

★

And on a equally tear-filled note, we said goodbye to Norris Roman this year, whose annual appearance as Widow Twankey will be sadly missing.

★

But disappointments this year were many. For instance the shoddy sets in Theatre Molford's production of *Lawrence of Arabia* were sh*t, shit, sh*t and nine-year-old 'prodigy' Oliver Date's performance of Bach's Double Violin Concerto had my teeth on their ends and was also sh*t.

Here's to next year!

Framley concert orchestra to perform Hitler's First Symphony

by Adam Wrent

FRAMLEY CIVIC Hall is to be the venue for a very special premiere this weekend - the first performance in this country of Hitler's Symphony No.1 in F Sharp.

Framley Concert Orchestra conductor Peter Werrill bought the score in August at an on-line auction of the fuhrer's artefacts and personal memorabilia last week for a record undisclosed sum.

'I've spent the last few months learning the piece,' yesterday. 'For an amateur composer - which is all Hitler could claim himself to be, it's a remarkable achievement. He has an unusually tight contrapuntal clutch. It's a photocopy.'

The symphony, which is twelve minutes long, will until then (Saturday) only have been heard as a recording of a CD by the National Orchestra of Tonga, who gave the world premiere of the piece in 1986 at

The Framley Concert Orchestra with, inset, the controversial composer.
PHOTOGRAPH BY MARTIN WRIST

the Center Vava'u in Nuku'alofa, at which 10 musicians and 29 members of the audience were killed and a further 112 injured.jured.

Among those who have refused to attend, is the Mayor and comedian Jim Davidson.

But local Jewish groups are unimpressed.

Molford Spectacular is to will be the 'best yet'

Special Report by Jesus Chigley

AUGUST IS SPECTACULAR month again in Molford, and that can only mean one thing - the Molford Spectacular. And this August is no different.

And this August there's a difference! The Framley Examiner is sponsoring its very own stage.

The 'Framley Examiner New Bands Wigwam', right slap bang at the heart of the Spectacular, will play host at some of the biggest chart-topping acts in the business today.

Barely recognisable TV chef Octopus Kedgeree (tragically disfigured last August in a riding accident) will introduce his own band, Octopus Kedgeree Au Gratin,

as well as there will be no alcohol served on the day Tight Fit, Bow Bow Wow (Bauhaus? can't read this) and Die Trip Computer Die.

Organiser Glasner Pommedeterre says this year's Molford Spectacular will be the best yet. Organiser Glasner Pommedeterre says this year's Molford Spectacular will be the most spectacular yet.

Last year's Spectacular, also in August, at which police had to act quickly when Cleo Laine's zeppelin was set on fire by drunken revellers who overturned cars and other drunken revellers.

7pm curfew. No alcohol on site.

Organiser Glasner Pommedeterre says this year's Molford Spectacular will be the last.

Menace to Society 'menace to society'

LOCAL up-and-coming rock band, Menace to Society, have been branded a 'menace to society' by a Whoft greengrocer.

Laurie Streethorse claims that the band have been upsetting his fruit since they began practicing in the basement of a Whoft greengrocer, Laurie Streethorse claims that the band have been upsetting a Whoft greengrocer Laurie Streethorse.

"It's just noise, really. No tune," he complained. "And it turns my plums."

But the band fear that without the basement practice area to practice in, they will become increasingly bad, leaving Whoft without music. :-(

NEWS

Police plans to introduce tagging

by Bunco Booth

Police in Framley and Molford are to adopt a novel new scheme for tagging prisoners, designed to stop the criminals reoffending once they leave custody.

Framley Chief Constable Rupert Bone, a regular churchgoer, explained the new plan to journalists and prison officers on Tuesday.

"The tagging starts in prison. One of my men, dressed as a police clown, will visit prisoners due for release, handing out balloons," Bone explained.

"Lags love a balloon. After years in the drab prison environment, they are fascinated by a balloon's round shape and gay colour.

"The hope is that, after returning home, the released prisoner will become attached to his balloon, taking it everywhere he goes."

The helium-filled balloon, tethered by an eighteen foot string, will bob above the rooftops, Bone explained, making the felon a great deal easier to keep tabs on, particular in a helicopter the Chief Constable hopes to get soon.

COLOURFUL TOO

To allay public fears, the balloons are to be colour coded so that more dangerous criminals attract police attention first.

White collar criminals, like credit card fraudsters and Russian spies will be given beige balloons, whilst murderers and serial rapists will be given bright orange or blue ones.

The public are being encouraged to help with the new system too.

"If victims would kindly try to remember what colour balloon their mugger or rapist was carrying, we'll be able to identify their attacker far more quickly, or, at the very least, establish what sort of crime has probably taken place," Bone said, swigging helium from the neck of a green polkadot balloon the shape of a crinkle cut chip.

"Balloons fight crime," he squeaked.

A multiple offender is released into the community yesterday.
PHOTOGRAPH BY FABULOUS BEE

Library book finally returns

by Katy Blirdsnest

AFTER AN ABSENCE of nearly thirty years, Framley's Most Haunted Library Book has been returned to its rightful home.

The hardback edition of *American Shoes,* a pulp detective thriller by Kauffer Whitman, had been missing from Framley library's shelves since 1972, when it was rendered overdue by a mysterious nun, later found to have died in 1855.

The surprising find was made by senior librarian Twerrin Speck, who reported seeing a headless monk amongst the Book Amnesty boxes in the corner. Ghoulishly enough, Mr Speck investigated and stumbled across the spook-tacular volume.

The book's whereabout had been the subject of intense speculating since it's disappearal in the year of Ford Capris, Squlchie bars and The Bay City Roller!

Readers of the clumsy thriller had

Framley library to where the book has been returned to.
PHOTOGRAPH BY PEACOCK STRUTMASTER

previously reported cold pages, the sound of footsteps coming from chapter eight and the sense of up to twelve 'presences' reading over their shoulders at any one time.

A team from Molford Polytechnic spent a night reading the book in the dark in 1968, under the gaze of infra red cameras, tap recorders and temperature monitors. Nothing unusual was recorded, although two of the investigators claim to have heard snoring.

The book is now back in storage where Mr Speck can keep it from falling off the wrong pair of hands.

In Court

IAIN EUAN JAN, of Corrosion of Conformity Street, Molford was fined £10 for driving and drinking a car at Framley Magistrates Court on November 8th.

THE LATE ERIC DOUGALSUGAR of 14, Tey Road, Whoft, was fined £1000 with £520 prosecution costs for failing to obtain air traffic control clearance to fly a light aircraft into the roof of 14, Tey Road, Whoft.

HENRIK GABERDINE of Henrik's House, Wripple, was sentenced to the middle four years of an eight year sentence for trying to leave the court without permission.

KEREN LANCET of Humbert Avenue, Whoft, received a one year conditional discharge with £55 additional costs for possessing 5.4mgs of Framley Magistrate's Court on November 3rd.

JENIFFER VAN VAN, of Nimble Road, Framley was forced to undergo one day of manilow ® for theft of a Newby's napkin. Costs of £100 were impossible.

JUSTICE CONSTANT WAXY, of Berner's Leap, Whoft, was fined £100 for building his own special little court inside the big court.

KEVERETT ENNETH, of The Canal, Molford St Gavin, was awarded five 5.9s and a 6.0 for threatening behaviour.

MRS ISSY NOHO of Mothership Lounge, Molford was fined £4 at Framley Magistrates Court for breaking the unwritten law. The jury is still far out.

MRS JUSTICE CONSTANT WAXY of Berner's Leap, Whoft, was fined £1000 with £295 costs for not having the dinner ready when I got home.

LESLEY GRANDDAD of 14,Tiger Woods, Wripple was lowered into the Well Of Sundials for driving with defective lights on October 28th.

looking
for love
(01999) 94 76 94

The Framley Examiner

PAUL COIA LOOK-ALIKE seeks companion for long walks and dining out for platonic friendship only. No sex (except anal). Box FE8656.

STRAIGHT-ACTING Wripple male seeks straight Wripple male. Box FE8755.

NORTH SOCKFORD, good-looking professional male, 34, WLTM genuinely caring lady who will not swallow my heart whole and then shit it out onto a raging bonfire of spite. Box FE8411.

MAN STANDING too near to someone seeks greater distance from same someone. Up to 15 miles. Box FE8381.

SPORTY, fit, attractive female, 28, seeks lumpy, disastrous, 'all over in two minutes' mid-life crisis sufferer for short- to mid-term relationship. Box FE8796.

BONE ZONE
chat with over 120 guys and girls
AT THE SAME TIME!
0906 900 800

FRAMLEY MAN would like to meet anybody not from FE8100.

SPOON seeks flag. This sounds odd. So does Baked Alaska. 01999 949494.

MAN CALLED FRANK seeks woman called Maisie. Must be called Maisie. Previous applicants need not reapply. Closing date April 16th. Box FE8077.

TALK TO MY HORSE
WHILE I FINISH THIS IRONING
THANKYOU
0906 784343

CLOWN, 29, GSOH, WLTM large tent full of wild animals and acrobats. Intention: circus. Box FE8734.

COCK LIKE A TELEGRAPH POLE, shoulders like an otter. Is this you? Me too! Box FE8951.

SIKH seeks Sikh. Box FE8329.

WOMAN placing advert seeks men responsive to advertisement. Box FE8308.

CONCRETE LABIA
Think you've tried it all? Wait til you try me I will scrape and hurt you You will need surgery
0906 788591
BRICK TITS
0906 788592
MECCANO ARSEHOLE
0906 788593

MATURE FEMALE seeks black acting 18yo male for discreet friendship. Box FE8773.

MAN DRESSED AS SNAIL, GSOH, likes classical music, WLTM woman dressed as patio. No smokers, yes. Box FE8761.

BEEFY, ARYAN, rugby playing ex-squaddie, female, seeks Brian Sewell-type for late night British Bulldog. Box FE8102.

CHUFFED MAN WLTM delighted woman to be pleased with size of chair. Box FE8655.

MAKE LOVE AT ME
WHILE I SHIT IN YOUR HAIR
30% SATISFACTION
I AM PROBABLY WAITING
0906 809 809

VERY HAIRY LADY seeks sensitive male for friendship, possibly romance. Newly decorated, gch, £400pcm +bills. Box FE8542.

BASQUE SEPARATIST, 24, seeks sympathetic male, 77, for cuddles and mainland car bombings, possibly more. Box FE8221.

MAN BAKED ACCIDENTALLY INTO LOAF OF BREAD seeks knife, butter and marmalade. Box FE8414.

GAS seeks available space. I will expand to fill you. Box FE8145.

JAMIE THEAKSTON impersonator WLTM Gilda Radner lookalike or surviving relative. Box FE8529.

NICE bit of cheese seeks biscuit or mouse. No bourbons. Box FE8300.

UPTIGHT SNOB seeks narrow-minded, idiotic, trigger-happy bigot for enormous offensive argument which I will win. Box FE8310.

3 OUT OF 4 men WLTM Charlie Dimmock and take him up the no-no. Box FE8254

YOU CAN'T DO THAT without my permission. Get it. Box FE8319.

TETRIS-OBSESSED accountant, 29, seeks physically robust partner for relationship and possible gravity-related tesselating sex game. Cubic area must be divisible by four. Trampoline provided. Box FE8808.

VICTORIAN SLATTERN
Fallen woman Carnal smorgasbord extrordinaire I will manipulate you to issue No hasty pudding
0906 190 000

GINGERBREAD MAN seeks gingerbread lady. Must be single, over 8" tall and made of gingerbread. Box FE8428.

120 SINGLE MEN seek at least 3 women (single) for 'swinging.' No more wooden legs, please. Box FE8513.

BUXOM, beautiful, overcharged teenager, compulsive liar, WLTM like-minded 50-year-old cripple for canasta and trips to the moon. Box FE8314.

HOUSEWIFE WAREHOUSE
PILES OF HOUSEWIVE!
PHONE THE NOISEY BITCHS!
THEY CACKLE LIKE CRONE!
THEY FILTHY LIKE YOU!
0906 477500

BROWN-EYED 28yo male Dr Who fan, WLTM female Hazel O'Connor obsessive with own biplane and MC Hammer trousers. Will collect. Box FE8110

ARE YOU A PRINCE, or are you a frock? Professional female, busy size 12. Enquires frequently. GSOS. As seen. Box FE8661

I LOOK NOTHING LIKE THE GIRL IN THIS PHOTO
I am a pig-eyed horse-frightener with an electronic part
HEAR ME SIT DOWN
0906 298646

7'6" MAN seeks 1'2" woman to shove up bum. Only possible with these lengths. Feet first, no kinky stuff. Box FE8959.

MAN SEEKS MAN. No, honestly. Has this happened before? Box FE8181.

ASIAN GODDESS SOUGHT by debonair, athletic male, 32. Hold of terror over millions of followers a must. Extra arms an advantage. Will travel. Box FE8141.

TROUSERLESS man in wardrobe seeks woman for farce. Drainpipe outside window preferred. Vicars welcome. Box FE8898.

I ONLY WATCH SKY MOVIE Max2. What do you only watch? Do you like to watch? Box FE8529

UNDERWATER HORNETTO
100% SATISFACTION
BUBBLES ! GOLDFISH ! SORT OF SNAILS !
Hold me down! I will drown! I will actually drown!
0906 809 809

EXPERIENCED fishmonger, Bones, fillets and batters. Box FE8132

SOMETIMES A BEAR seeks Always A Beehive. Box FE8227.

GENUINE, hardy, erratic former gentleman WLTM chubby, fleshy girl with a taste for the outdoors. Special Brew evenings and combing spit out of matted beards if compatible. Box FE8199

MY WIFE DOES NOT UNDERSTAND ME. I am a Romanian cretin. FE8396.

RENAULT ESPACE seeks family of 7 for holidays and good times. Box FE8442

VAST, UNGAINLY whale of a man seeks petite women 25-35 who taste of pizza. Box FE8093

FEELING GROOVY? Homeward bound? At the zoo? Scarborough Fair / Canticle? Call Mrs Robinson on 01999 854 298

MAN LIKES pavement likes man. Covered. Absolutely covered. Box FE8130

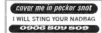

BISEXUAL UNDERAGE GRANDMOTHER
WANTS TO HEAR YOU MOAN WANTS TO MAKE YOU TEA JAM UP MY BATTENBURG
0906 756565

TALLISH, TURKISH, DARKISH, handsomish woman, would sort of like to meet. £85. Handle loose, but otherwise VGC. Box FE8947

WHO WANTS TO BE A Millionaire £64,000 winner WLTM 1985 Bob's Full House fondue set winner. (October?) Box FE8698

BLACK-EYED Wripple male seeks sensitive female with big heart and clockwork legs. Wind me up! Box FE8520

SASH-FRONTED man man WLTM understanding a woman. Box FE8713

THERE'S A LOT MORE! Female, 37, 5'7" extending to 7'2" W probably LTM creatively tall individual, for long nights in box FE8099

KNOCK! Knock! Who's there? A fuck. 01999 840 012

MIXED-RACE Pakistani / Viking seeks Graeco-Australian dwarf with NSOH. Box FE8309

SEADOG, 6 days out of Port-of-Spain. Still no sign of poon. Box FE8920

I SAW

HEADLICE Crawling with them. I ate three. Then you left, heartbreaker. Box FE8006

DRESSED IN WHITE. Lost sight of you at altar. Who were you? Box FE8424

I SAW YOU. You didn't see me. 3 weeks later, I can still see you. Call my mobile. You will hear it ring. 0945 65634

I WAS on ScreenTest. You submitted Lego film. I love you. Box FE8026

FEEL MY BIG RIPE WRISTS
and squeeze my new hands
YOU WILL NOT BE SURPRISED!
0906 454 545

I WAS IN COMBATS. You were gaffertaped to a metal chair. Who was that other guy? What were we thinking? When will we learn? Box FE8509

MET AT PAUL weller gig. I flirted. You sang and played acoustic version of "That's Entertainment" Who were you, mystery man? Box FE8799

I SCREWED you 417 times over a period of 5½ years. Who were you? Box FE8730

cover me in pecker snot
I WILL STING YOUR NADBAG
0906 809 809

WEDNESDAY 24th - Monday 29th. Number 96 bus. Bad breath. Good breath. Which one were you? I was had breath. Box FE8410

TURN YOUR "Remember that lovely night when I sat next to you at The Almeida Theatre" into crisps. Smokey Bacon or Bacon. £6 a bag.

ALL I THINK ABOUT IS IT
DO IT ON ME
LET'S DO IT
I CAN DO IT TOO
IT'S GREAT
IT
0906 48 47 46

VW PASSAT 1.8 TURBO
Alloys
ABS
Full MOT
Metallic paint
All extras
2 on 1
Pre-Op TS
0906 520 510

I CAN'T FEEL MY LEGS
WILL YOU FEEL THEM FOR ME?
YOU WILL WHEN YOU FEEL THEM!
0906 788591

'As long as they don't ram it down our throats says Framley's Mayor

FRAMLEY's Mayor gave grudging approval to the town's first Mardi Gras Festival yesterday.

Gays and lesbians from all over the planet will transform our town into a gay carnival, 'like marauding vikings', only in colourful costumes. The event is scheduled for the coming August Bank Holiday, officials warned.

"We just really felt we ought to," said Mayor William D'Ainty.

Gays will dance and kiss in the streets to the sound of higher energy music. Steps and Rod Stewart have already confirmed they will perform, while Shabba Ranks are rumoured to have also been asked.

But the most excitement amongst the gay community is being reserved for the reformed Microdisney who will be headlining both nights. "I suppose that's the sort of thing they must like," said the happily married Mayor, 52.

Community leaders have urged that young children or pets should be kept indoors, possibly due to fireworks and other 'displays'.

The colourful event will be opened by either or TV's Ainsley Herriott or TV handyman Lawrence Llewellyn-Bowen.

Local hotels and guesthouses have already claimed they are "No Vacancies" or only single rooms left.

'BEAR-' FACED CHEEK ... !!

A touch too much! Phet Loyce (in photo) delights unsuspecting fans (near him).
PHOTOGRAPH BY PHILLIPA-JANE PROBY

by Jesus Chigley

SUNDAY WAS turned to "Fun" day at the St Eyot's Police "Fun" Day last Sunday.

The first annual Funday is becoming a firm favourite with Policemen and public alike... and this year's was possibly the best yet.

Police dogs did tricks and a coconut shy. Candyfloss was very popular too.

But the hit of the day was convicted repeat sex offender Phet Loyce, who molests women while dressed as a bear. He performed for local children and groped women's breasts.

"He really put on a show," said DCI Gregan McHough, who booked the pervert for the event as part of Loyce's nine months of community service.

The deviant organised body painting competitions and invited children to pull a "surprise" from a bran tub on his lap.

"The whole day was a great success," claimed unorthodox Police FunDay psychologist, Chachampion Horsewonder, who was amongst the first to encourage the bear to attend.

Anyone wishing to book Mr Loyce for their own party or "funday" should contact St Eyot's Incident Desk who are also appealing for witnesses to come forward in complete confidence.

Radio licence

Framley's Zephyr 1375 AM has had its licence revoked. Authorities were quick to act on Tuesday when, yet again, the Breakfast News Show was interrupted by an obscene forty-eight minute musical poem about Dutch firemen.

Two cheers for hero's return

LOCAL HERO Martin Paralalalel was almost given a hero's welcome when he returned to Whoft last June.

Martin, 42, shot to attention early last year when he bravely jumped into a pond in Dumfrieshire to rescue a ball which had been kicked in.

"I just saw the ball and jumped into the pond to get it out," the unmarried IT Assistant said at the time. "I didn't think of myself, I just saw ball."

"Paralalalel, 42, was" underwhelmed "by the welcome."

"Well, I'm sure, had I got those two boys out of the pond alive, not just the ball, there would have been a lot more fuss. But I can't live in the past."

Police divers, who have spent two months searching the pond, are beginning to give up hope of finding the missing boys alive, though a further ball and three beehives have been recovered.

Exciting new proposals point to a brave new start for St Eyot's Castle

Brave new start for St Eyot's Castle

by Katy Blirdsnest

ST EYOT'S HISTORIC 14th Century castle is heading for one of the biggest shake ups in its four hundred year history!

Because the ancient building, built in 1462 to defend St Eyot's from dandy highwaymen, is to be bulldozed to the ground to make way for a new Medieval theme park - The St Eyot's Family Heritage Experience!

The new attraction is sure to have visitors flocking into the area from far and wide, because of due to the fact that it features rides, greeters dressed as the middle ages and a three-quarter scale replica of the original castle with Europe's loudest rollercoaster threaded along the battlements!

So what's it all about then? I sent myself as a roving reporter to find out exactly what it's all about then.

OUT WITH THE OLD

After a horrid journey through the traffic outside Codge, and a spot of bother turning right off the FR404 (sorry, whoever it was - I've got your wing mirror and driving gloves), I met project manager Ogilvy Grapes at the site office.

"This is a marvellous opportunity for the area to move out of the 14th Century once and for all," Grapes

Enjoying the castle grounds before they are smashed down.
PHOTOGRAPH BY MONTMORENCY BOAT

told me, indicating a model of the old castle.

"This sort of visitor attraction has a high foot-through and a proven unit satisfaction index," he explained, absentmindedly crushing the outer bailey of the model with the flat of his hand.

"Just you wait," he concluded, carelessly climbing onto the table and jumping repeatedly up and down on the tiny castle until it looked like wooden jam.

What the new castle will mean for local people in the St Eyot's area

I ASKED Developmental Project Manager Gavinder McMountain what the new castle will mean for local people in the St Eyot's area.

"Though this new development isn't a castle in the traditional sense, people have to understand that our theme park does exactly the same job as St Eyot's Castle has always done. Just as the old stone building kept people safe from marauding vikings and pillaging Hottentots, The St Eyot's Family Heritage Experience will keep people safe from boredom!

"With our interactive themed rides, spectator-centred edutainment events and nourishment concession zones, we're lowering the portcullis on the prospect of stimulation-shortfall, and raising the drawbridge on sharp-end user-non-engagement. Now get out."

Britain's first batman found in castle grounds

BY KATIE BLIRDSNEST

ARCHAEOLOGISTS, called in to have a look at St Eyot's Castle before developers bash it up, say they have found startling evidence of Britain's first batman.

Rathbone Twiddrington and Oswald Underclown say they were digging by the teashop when they unearthed an elaborate Renaissance courtier's hat and mask, sitting on the passenger seat of a horsedrawn batmobile.

Though the actual finds have been hidden under orange crates to stop magpies getting at them, the two men were more than willing to outline their theories.

Over tea and jam scones in the castle cafe, Twiddrington showed me conceptual drawings his partner had made of the so-called "ycaped crousadier".

"This batman worked under the patronage of the Wheelwright's Guild, solving crimes and foiling the wheel-hating plans of various 14th Century supervillains."

But the pair's investigations are under threat from the fact that the castle's tea shop area is due for demolition on Monday, to make way for a Third Place Coffee Lounge and Organic E-Point.

"This is a find of amazing historical significance. My partner and I must be allowed to continue our research. The site must not be disturbed."

Although the developers have insisted the archaeologists show them evidence of the finds, Twiddrington is

An artist's impression of the "Darke Knyghte".   **BY OSWALD UNDERCLOWN**

The 14th Century batman's arch-enemies (L-R) Catlady, The Renaissance Joker and Mr Fruit. The Renaissance Joker's relentless jokes about mistaken identity and allusions to cuckoldry were a particular thorn in the batman's side.

adamant that he and his friend not be moved on.

"There is nowhere else in the country that shows better evidence of Renaissance costumed vigilante activity, or serves better tea," he insisted.

"We must stay, and dig, and have another eclair."

That'll be £6284.22, please!

by Taunton Mishap

FRAMLEY mother-of-one Judith had the fright of her life just recently when she opened her latest phone bill and read the total.

Judith, 39, who works in a shop, is used to receiving phone bills of about £40 per month. She thought the phone company had made a simple mistake, fainted and had to be revived by her husband's smells.

However, when she took a closer look, she discovered that her 14-year old son had spent some 660 hours on the phone to himself in the last month.

HOW MUCH?

"I was absolutely livid," she mumbled yesterday, "I had no idea he spent that long on the phone. And he was ringing his mobile. Why he couldn't have rung himself on the land line, I can't imagine. He knew

Judith's son, with (inset) the terrifying bill that he ran up using the telephone.
PHOTOGRAPH BY BALLISTA MEMORIAL

where to find himself."

Mrs Judith's son, whose name begins with a D, was last night recovering from stab wounds in hospital. His condition was described as "stable, but dead."

Police have arrested a 39-year-old woman on suspicion.

Good times not so good

IT'S BEEN another disappointing year for Goode Stores, the oldest shop in Framley's Arnhem Centre.

In spite of rising profits in the retail sector over the last year, Goode's is still fighting low sales.

Goodman Goode, managing director of Goode Stores, complained, "People say these are the good times, but they're not that good at Goode's. Sales of Goode's luxury goods, for instance, have not been good at all. Even our brand-leader luxury good, Goodman Goode's Goodie-Goodies, isn't going particularly well."

Goodie-Goodies, Goode's famous hand-squeezed truffles with added vitamins, outsell every other Goode's luxury good. Last year's "It's a Good Time For Goodie-Goodies!" advertising campaign saw the sweets outsell Ferrari Rochers two-to-one. But the good times haven't lasted for Goodie-Goodies, or Goode's Stores or Goodman Goode.

Goode's fail to make good on good start.

"We've tried every aggressive marketing tack known to man with the Goodie-Goodies," continued Mr Goode, "and the most successful of those was our Blue Swastika week. We shifted a good 300 Goodie-Goodies that week. That was a good week, actually. But apart from maybe one good week, it's not been a good year at Goode's."

Mr Goodman is now considering a frivolous proposal to re-name Goodman Goode's Goodie-Goodies "Goodman Goode's 'Not So Good' Good Times Goodie-Goodies", and a rather less frivolous proposal to sack an unbelieveable number of staff.

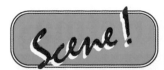

Top pub closed again and again

THE WARM ZIPPY, a Framley pub popular with young people and children, was this week closed down by police eight times in one evening, a new record for the venue.

Police repeatedly raided the Froth Street drinkerie on Tuesday night, after a series of theme nights threatened to become out of hand.

Landlord Darren Borstle told reporters, "I had organised a Quiz Night. After two hours, it was going so well I thought I'd start a Gay Night in the back bar.

"When I saw the takings were up twofold, I decided I'd get a Cowboy Night going in the snug and a Come As Your Favourite Rule Of The Highway Code Night going on the stairs. That was when the police first arrived."

Police closed the pub down, but had barely got back to the station when they were alerted that a

THE WARM ZIPPY

Talent Night, a Ketamine Night and a Warm Zippy "Unzipped" Night had broken out back at the pub.

A further eighteen theme nights, and eight closures later, the pub was finally brought under control.

This isn't the first time the controversial pub has courted controversy. In March, the headmaster of St Gahan's School For Boys found forty-six of his pupils in the upstairs pool room, sitting their GCSE Physics examinations, drunk.

"Our position in the schools league table can only suffer if my pupils are sitting their exams half cut," he was quoted at the time.

Jingle all the way to the top!

by Adam Wrent

FRAMLEY ice-cream man David Grohl is heading for the top of the pops. Or rather, his ice-cream van is heading there!

Because Dave's van has just been given a recording contract by top pop crop Pop The Planet records.

"It was a complete surprise," gasped Dave, who shares a name (though not a face) with Dave Grohl, player in the popular boy band The 100 Fighters, "it all started last year. I took the van to Glastonbury to cash in on the punter's munch, and this guy from Pop The Planet heard the van and offered it a deal on the spot. He was on drugs - stargazy teacakes, I think - at the time."

Dave's van will release its first single, *I'm Popeye The Sailor Man*, in March, under the name Dave's Van. "We're expecting great things," said Simon Shallow from Pop The Planet, the man behind such chart successes as It's A Girl Things and Judith Keppel from *Who Wants To Be A Millionaire?*, as he crouched over a dusty cistern, "although we haven't yet established what role Dave will have in the project."

Dave's Van's album's song's will

Dave's Van, soon to be Top Of The Pops. Dave (not pictured) is delighted.

PHOTOGRAPH BY REMINGTON FUZZAWAY

include *You're Popeye The Sailor Man*, rock hit *Greensleeves* and folk song *What's The Frequencies Kenneth?*. And from then on, it's work work work work for Dave and Dave's Van.

"The van's doing public appearances for the next three months," Dave, "like cd:uk, MTV Brand New and The Ministry Of Sound. It's also doing a set for Marlon Hobbs's Breezeblock. Top world DJs are in a line too like Carl Coxs, Sian Savage and DJ Mugabe have all expressed an interest in

working with her .'

Unfortunately, last week's planned public appearance at the Alderman Terrorbilly Recreation Ground had to be cancelled owing to safety concerns. A police spokespoliceman explained "that there were six thousand wide-eyed, turbo-fuelled hedonists packed into that park and there was absolutely no way that Mr Grohl would have been able to meet the unprecedented demand for ice cream. Rioting was a very real possible. Hmm? An album? Oh, I see."

Top night out

IT'S A BIG NIGHT on the cards for patrons of Earrings nightclub, Framley's hottingest nightspot.

Earrings' promotions manager Mandy Pschmoo has booked 80's legend Erroll Brown to perform a live show to mark the club's fourth anniversary.

To make the occasion extra-special, Brown has reformed 90's band The Farm, to form, for one night only, Erroll Brown and The Farm. So, Framley clubbers will be able to enjoy the hits *You Groovy Train* and *It Started With a Farm* performed by most of the original group.

Erroll, whose hits *The Full Monty* include *20 Greatest Hits* and *The Full*

Monty Soundtrack, was delighted to be renew his relationship with Farm frontman Pete Hooton.

"We've never spoken before," said the 70's star, "and I thought it was time to patch up the rift."

Liverbool-born Hooton could not be reached for comment, or to rejoin Erroll and The Farm.

Erroll Brown, upset by the snub, has also refused to appear at the event.

Pschmoo said of the evening, "I'm afraid we're going to have to cancel the show. It's a real shame. We'd sold out three times over.

"My mother's lost all her savings. There's going to be a lot of disappointed orphans."

A brief, tasteful glimpse of Val

HEADLINE-GRABBING local artist Valerie Eiglootitz will be displaying a small selection of her less-challenging work in Sockford District Library foyer between Monday and November.

The shocking artist, whose uncompromising work once made Brian Sewell hide under a chair, will be sparing the public explicit pieces

such as *Tracey Emin's Tears of a Clown*, her 1998 exhibit of her own severed legs preserved under glass and marmalade.

Art lovers will instead be treated to *Clean Sheets* (1992), and the uplifting *Scenes From A Post-Menstrual Serenghetti* (1994). The exhibition will be near the spinner with the leaflets.

possible to remove without killing one of the twins? 01999 865 428. ASAP.

WRIST MAGNETS. Set of two. Prevent unwanted clapping/waving/movement of lower arms. Fram 01999 888 946

EASTEND FOREPLAY KIT. Includes Stepney Tickle, Mile End Feathering and Bow Road Finger Insertion. Batteries included. £12.50. Call Guy on 01999 865 456

50'S SINGLES COLLECTION. All divorced/widowed/cold and confused. Some later ones missing. To complete collection or for spares. Fram 01999 821444

BICYCLE WHISK

BOX OF DELIGHTS. Push button to the left to go small, push to the right to become Poet Laureate. £19.99. Phone Mrs Hawlings on 01999 801934.

LIFT FARTS, fake gangster, some giggles. Will exchange for These Bleeds™. 01999 866 466

LIPSTICKS, assorted. Salt and vinegar, smoky bacon, soup. 9 of each. £45 the bunch. 01999 393031.

QUICK SALE. Would suit speedy Manchester. Offers. 01999 871 109

HUMMINGBEARS

QUANTUM CLOCK. Tells the time and doesn't tell the time at the same time. £20 oqo. 01999 268834.

YOUR FRONT DOOR. Get it back on 01999 835 310.

MAGIC EYE Teach Your Child To Read. Alphabets, simple stories and helpful pictures represented as 3-D images only visible when eyes are defocused. Would suit advanced 3yo that doesn't cry as much as mine. Good luck. £5. Framley 849727.

THE BLING BLING. Giving it for all the St Eyots District Domino and Billiards League Massive. Keep it safe, yeh?. 01999 832 455

FRAMLEY area phone book, complete with handwritten alphabetical index. All my own work. £450. 01999 360361.

BUZZARDS, BUZZERS & BUZZ. 3' x 8' watercolour reinterpretation of 2nd man on the moon as bespace-suited quiz show host under attack. On the moon. £500 framed. 01999 875 522

BILL & BEN, the flowerpots. Plant receptacles, red clay. Too much personality for flowerpots. Hence slightly intimidating. £12 the set. Will not be separated. 01999 800 632

BLACK & DECKER Garden Devil. Left in neighbour's garden overnight will soak oil into flowerbeds, hide sheds and turn spades inside out. It really works! All of mine moved within three months. £48. 01999 819019.

BOX SET OF BOOKS by Douglas Adams. A five part trilogy in increasingly large type. £8. Tel 01999 855 981

1974 SLOW COOKER. Far too slow. Still waiting for boiled egg. £12orwhatever. 01999 231664.

JUNIOR GRAVITY SET. Let your child experience the joy of staying on the ground. Certificate of authenticity signed by Lord Howe. No responsibility accepted. £24 01999 865 456

MONEY CAN'T BUY YOU LOVE but £2.50 will get you a cuddle. Call Vernon on or around 01999 834440.

The Framley Examiner

"I have no idea who you are or where you came from. Pour that back in the bottle and get out of my lounge."

Mrs Limoges, Sockford

LIONS AND TIGERS and bears, all mine. Fake or real, it's up to you. POA. Framley 844 644

NUMBER ONE SINGLE, Top of the Pops appearances, fan club. Will exchange for less difficult second album. 01999 844 093

GRIEF CYCLE. Denial/anger vgc, some acceptance refusals. Can't believe that I have to let this go. £16ono. 01999 849 589

A PLAYGROUND RHYME ABOUT YOU by professional 8-year old poet. Please indicate whether you have nits or fancy Kelly Vinton. 01999 850006 after 3.45pm.

POSTMAN PRAM. Keeps your postie safe and warm, rain-hood, post-Consignia design, 300 of. £750ono. 01999 831 030

OFFICIAL "ALL YOUR MEMORIES" 1982 PANINI STICKER ALBUM. Complete except for penguin falling over at London Zoo (28), that thing with Paul McDowell in it (141) and Dan & Mandy's wedding foil badge (436). £100ono. 01999 875 055

PIGGY BANK for sale. Contains roughly £38. Call Mr Hollyhock on 01999 482762 (please hang up immediately if Josie answers). £41.50

CAT LITTER. Also hamster graffiti. £6. Box FE8511

CAN YOU WAKE ME UP? I've got a train to catch. Please call 01999 872359 between 5am and 6am.

FIDDLE-STICK™. Provides evidence of child abuse by gluing offender's appendages to your kiddie. Approved by European Court of Human Rights. Box FE8009

BANG & OLUFSEN Speakers of the House of Commons. Excellent treble, Boothroyd / Martin separation exceptional. £450. Framley 802 223

WANT A NUT? I've got plenty. Selling due to protein efficiency. Must be seen. POA. 01999 866 954

READY-TO-HANG Union Jack, printed upside down, perfect for TV productions, will provoke letters of complaint to Points of View. £40. 01999 94R880.

LAVA LAMPOST, £35. Box FE8249.

BUS QUEUE in twenty foot lengths. First and third sections may contain pensioners or pushchairs. £8 per foot. 01999 845902.

REGRETS, I've had a few, but then again, too few to not sell, so call, call Gary Vest, I'm in the phone book.

GREYHOUND STABILIZERS. Once used by Romford Champion Hurdler, Miss Princess Fififi d'Bigbitch. Michelin tyres, chrome finish. Will swap for weasel mittens. Box FE8274.

CRAP. This is all crap and none of it's for sale any more. You're all such slow-witted fools. I've already bought it all. Box FE8193

TELETEXT ONLY TELEVISION. 32" widescreen FST, Dolby 5.1 Surround Sound, but ONLY teletext. £1400. Tel. 01999 824487.

INDUSTRIAL LAMINATOR. Laminates anything. I've just done my face. Can I do yours? Or your hair? Or your house? Call me now! Framley 567833.

BORING RELATIVE. Goes on and on and on. Will swap for sultana or postage stamp. Box FE8815.

WHO WILL BUY?

BISSELL "Ceiling Master" Ceiling Shampooer. Three foam rollers, stepladder and sou'wester. £55. 01999 428166.

ANTIQUE LAPTOP, 1938 Imperial, hurts lap, needs new ribbon, £101. Box FE8001.

YEAR'S SUPPLY of tampons - regular, heavy and crikey. Hysterectomy, hence quick sale, £30. 01999 610978.

BOY FOR SALE

CELL SITE, currently in children's ward of local hospital. Carcinogenic, hence controversial sale, £160. No journalists/parents. Box FE8413.

TORTOISE CRUCIFIXION KIT. 2' cross, fits neatly inside shell. Some staining. Comes with hydraulic nail-gun and crown of lettuce. Offers. Call Mr Hollyhock on 01999 482762.

CHRISTIAN paraphernalia: 'Judas Was A Sodding Catholic' t-shirts, £10 each. 'Holy Shit My Lord' mugs £3.50 each. Turin teatowels, £1 the lot. Framley Christian fellowship, 01999 231664.

OOM PA PA

HARRY BELAFONTE and The Prisoner of Azkaban. Early J.K.Rowling draft manuscript, written on the back of 500 twenty pound notes. No longer legal tender. £8. Box FE8735

BEARD, £10. Moustache, £5. Soul chip (stylish lower lip beardlet), £2. HairWare, 01999 950950.

OFFAL BALLOONS. Already full, tricky to burst, but it is possible. Great for children's parties. £4 each, raw or cooked. Call Mr Jimmy on 01999 258187.

VAGUE TAPE MEASURE. Marked "Near" at one end and "Far" at the other. £2.50. 01999 822985.

CONSTABLE'S HAYWAIN and other police pictures incl. Desk Sergeant's "Whistler's Mother" and Copper's "Bod Snap". £98 the lot or £99 the lots. Fram 01999 801010

PLANET for hire. Small, cold, barren, insufficient oxygen. Call Vince on 01999 348792.

FEATHERSTONEHAUGH'S Dyslexia Remedy. This is not a cure. Box FE8719

BITCH FLAP. Fits any door. Allows the wife to come and go. £35. 01999 352920.

TEFAL CHICKEN TOASTER. Pops up when the chicken is done. Ruined, hence £5. 01999 357553.

SPLENESMATIST

20GB C: DRIVE, full. Try to avoid My Pictures>Oh! Isn't that a really interesting thing in that folder over there?>Faeces. Offers. BoxFE8374.

100% COTTON TESTCARD, never transmitted, beautiful rarity. £250. 01999 360241.

TURN YOUR KEYPAD TONES OFF. All of you who have a mobile phone that beeps every time you touch a button, it's really fucking annoying. Sort it out, you wankers. Call 01999 871336 if you can do it without me having to punch your face off. I'll see you on the train, no doubt.

MOULINEX OrangeBigger™. Makes oranges bigger. Satsumas - 4ft, Seville - 8ft. Plus CheeseGreater™ £20. Box FE8234.

CONKER, championship-winner, Stuttgart 1983. Filled with glitter for spectacular ending. 29lb. £29. Call Friedrich on 01999 373119

BESTGLOW log effect 2kW scissors. Too hot to hold, honestly. £7. 01999 442700.

SCREAMING BLUE MURDER alarm clock. Screams really really really really loudly all the time. Stops when it's time to wake up. Everlasting batteries. £FOC. 01999 487555.

TWEED EFFECT pet igloo with two hotplates and grill. £25. 01999 258 476

GOBLIN TEASDRUNK Wake up every morning to a hot, empty cup. £15. 01999 841569.

FAST SHOW shampoo and conditioner. Rub those catchphrases into your hair and scalp for a longlasting, hilarious shine. Box of ten. £8. 01999 846466.

CARAVAN COSY. Six years of knitting. No longer required. Caravan now cosy. £8ono. 01999 895523.

TOOTH HOOVER, adult and milk. Sucks or blows. Variety of nozzles for high corners and narrow gaps. Slightly damaged root extractor (doesn't cope with wisdom very well). Divorce threatened hence £25. Box FE8363.

DOG PERISCOPE. Fits most breeds (except retrievers). Russian Navy surplus. £160. Box FE8747

MILK. Will separate. £100 Whoft 3554

KRAUT ROCK, 13 sticks. Has "A Present From Amon Duul II" written all the way through. £14. 01999 845519.

THE REAL PAULA YATES bread-bins. Inspired by the hit Channel 4 programme. Made by local carpenter, twelve designs, mostly tasteful. All £25 each, except 48 Litre "Geldof Jereboam" (£50). All proceeds to charity or CSA. 01999 899 765

ENORMOUS MINT IMPERIAL decorated with elaborate scrimshaw design of 1100 anatomically correct birds in flight. Signed by Rudolf Hess / Rolf Harris (?). £110. Framley 01999 822745.

INFLATABLE BREADBOARD. Used once. Very disappointing. £2. 01999 854488.

ZILDJIAN / PEARL 5 piece exercise kit. With cymbals, 22lb rack toms and drumbells. £200ono. Will separate, except hi-hat. Take the hi-hat. I said, "take it". Here, I'll put it in the boot of your car, just so you don't forget it. 01999 893995.

THE LIPSYL STORY

FRIGIDAIRE 'Refrigerator' - miraculous! A very cold cupboard! £4.11.6d, FRAmley 330 before 1949.

SCRABBLE CHEATING MACHINE. Over 50,000 imagined words. Accepts all new entries programmed in during games. Has some trouble with legitimate words. You will win. 01999 845354 OIRO £300.

A BONE OF YOUR OWN! I have your ribs, your ulna, your patella and part of your spine. Phone me to find out how. 01999 378858.

MIRROR THAT REFLECTS THE 1950s. See yourself as a Teddyboy or Teddybird, Daddy-O! Call Chip on 01999 849010.

MOUSE TIMPANI

HALF HOUR DELAY. Would suit busy person wishing to be late. £99 or £180 for an hour. Box FE8770.

IMITATION CHESHIRE CHEESE SOAP. I wouldn't use it, would you? OK, then, it's yours. £40 nqa 01999 841211

The Framley Examiner

Over 1300 tonnes of fried eggs are sold every day through Framley Examiner Classifieds.

UNWANTED CHRISTMAS GIFT. Given by unwanted aunt. Will swap. £20 Fram 01999 867955

ASSORTED MEXICAN Jumping Men in low ceilinged container. Some concussion. A quid. Fram 01999 857743

BLUE PULLOVER full of kittens. Kids love it. Kittens don't. Don't do it. £30 Fram Evenings Only 01999 822256

BORSTAL BAILEY annuals 1942-78. Private sale, best not to shout about this one. £50 ono. BoxFE8599.

BRIAN GLOVER GLOVES and Brian Jacks Jacket. I wore both and looked like neither, neither will you. Or will you? No you won't. £800. Fram 01999 865545

GIANT CHILDREN'S PLAY CRANE. Suitable for small home improvements. Vertiginous fun for the giant child in your house. Fram 01999 899566

COLLECTION OF Shredded Wheat pencil case stickers circa 1980. inc. "I saw Sir on Top of the Pops", "Sums are Gay", "Sir's crack pipe stinks", "My Smart Desk", "I'm A Two Tone Tyrant". Offers. Fram 01999 956666

MIKE NESMITH'S HAT

WHAT'S IT ALL ABOUT? This is what. I'm placing an advert for a lovely chair. It's yours if you can tell me why I'm selling it, but be quick, it's on fire! Fram 01999 844566

COCONUT MATT. Likeness of Matthew Perry made entirely from coconuts. Makes sound of galloping horses when operated. Chewing mechanism disabled for child safety. Fram 01999 856111

STETHOSCOPE TELESCOPE. See the stars and hear them thump at the same time. £15. Box FE8433.

CHILD'S CHARLIE CHAPLIN RUG. Teaches children how to tie and eat their shoelaces. Fram 01999 845221

BABY GROW. Results in minutes. As recommended on TV's Big Brother programme. Fram 822113

ALL-IN-ONE COOKER/FREEZER. Hot on outside, cold on inside. Difficult to open due to heat. May still contain all my food. Buyer to collect. Whoft 5879

LUCKY PREGNANCY TEST KIT. Used once. Negative. Sealed bids to BoxFE8284.

VERRAY PARFIT Fyn Coverchiefs Golde, alle clene and faire and nat too olde. 10 quid the lotte. Fram 889 765 after 6pm.

TUESDAY AFTERNOON AT WORK. Really boring. Would swap for Friday, 3pm with prospect of drink afterwards. £5. Whoft 8888

PAT COOMBS SEX doll. Polyvinyl, asexual, rat-voiced supporting cast-member fetish action. Will deliver and watch. £30 flat or £40 inflated. 01999 893 300

ADULT POPCORN MAKER. Popcorn's never sounded or looked so much like adults. Tastes of Rum Punch. Fram 856556

FLUFFY DICE, 18-sided, crate of. Would suit Advanced D&D fan with haulage firm? £200 01999 800007.

DREAMBOAT, 'The I Can Fly Can't I?', luxury, 60'. Toffee galley with infinite fridge, cloudy beds and priest wearing all the lifejackets at once. Nightmare dinghy, full of burning glass. £6,571. Call Dr Glacier on 01999 864177.

PLAYSTATION 6. Quick. They're after me. £offers. 01999 877 653

BIG PRIZE CROSSWORD COMPETITION
SOLUTION

M	I	A	N	M	A	C	G	A	S	K	I	L	L
I		B	I				B			L			
C	O	D		V	O	L	V	O	B		L		W
H		N	E		O		A	I	M		M	I	
E		B	A	N	T	A	M		N	O	G	U	N
A	N	A	L		T		O	L	A		A		C
E		12		B	R	E	A	D	R	O	L	L	E
L		E		R	R		R	F	L	Y			Y
F		G	R	A	V	Y	B	O	A	T		O	W
I		B		T		C			A	N	T	I	
S	I	S	Q	O		I	C	K	E	T	S		L
H	B		M	Y	A		E		I	S			L
	S		B	S	H	R	U	G		E	E	L	S
P	A		B				E	O				I	
M	I	C	H	E	A	E	L	B	U	R	K	E	S

Solution to Big Prize Crossword Number 1161

Quick Quiz

1. If the answer is half of two, what is the question?
2. Tiny Tim is finishing his Christmas Turkey with Scrooge. He is asked what he wants for dessert, but politely refuses. What is the name of his 1968 top ten hit single?
3. Complete the following sequence:
   NAME'S, BOND, JAMES, _____.
4. Solve the following picture conundrum:

 **BIG**  **small**

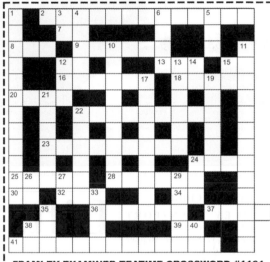

ALL BIDS CLOCKWISE are parried. Held cards are frantic, except **spades** and **deuces**, which count double. **Baggage**, and **paired "wet" cards**, pass to dealer's left, unless declared by a player holding either *The Hanged Man* or *Secret Tunnel Discovered In Chapel.*

WE JOIN the game just after the first round of secondary bidding has left all the court cards **open**. Though this gave East a possible folded-trick advantage, West has opted to freeze the table at **twelve (12)**, and the face card on the discards (the **2 of balls**) is now the boundary suit, unless the bid is **raised**. You have won second prize in a beauty competition!

North to move first and win in four months, before food runs out.

ACROSTIC
This week's alchemical acrostic is:

S A T O R
A R E P O
T E N E T
O P E R A
R O T A S

Last week's winner, who cracked the puzzle and revealed the Enochian language of the angels, was Mr Hugh Passiter from Molford St Malcolm, who can now turn base metals into gold and converse directly with God.

Well done, Hugh.

BIG PRIZE CROSSWORD
Set by "Invictus"

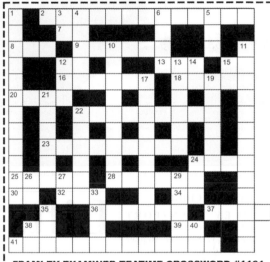

Number 1161 Here's your chance to win one of hundreds of Framley Examiner t-shirts or a brand new Saab 9000 Turbo in the **Framley Examiner Coffeetime Big Prize Crossword**. (We regret this competition is no longer open to employees of The Framley Examiner or "Invictus")

FRAMLEY EXAMINER TEATIME CROSSWORD #1161

Name _____

Address _____

_____ Framley   Postcode FM _____

Preferred prize: T-Shirt ☐ S ☐ M ☐ L ☐ XL ☐ Saab 9000
(please tick)

DOWN CLUES

1 TV weatherman (8,4)
3 Half of French & Saunders (2)
4 David _____, actor and inventor of hand cream (5)
5 "___ break every bone in your body." (3)
6 Eurovision winning Swedish group whose hits include *Waterloo Sunset* and *Come Dancing Queen* (4)
10D & 28A You've got to buy it to be in it to win it! (plural) (7,7)
11 TV weatherman (6,7)
12 Not Bloody Likely! (acron.) (3)
13 Now, where did I put that old box of shoes? (2,4)
14 First name of politician Mo Mowlam (2)
15 Cow / cat noise (2)
17 ___s against ___s, Brighton, 1963 (9)
19 Standard measure of Angel Delight (6)
21 A dozen (1,12,4)
22 TV superhero (3,3)
24 The first three letters of "assembly", perhaps? (3)
26 Bi (anag) (2)
27 James Bond's bosses (1,1)
29 "_____, tyger, burning bright" (Kipling?) (5)
33 Swedish group who won Eurovision with *Dedicated Follower of Fa-Fa-Fashion* (4)
35 Ballbag (3)
38 Two (3.14159)
40 "Can you put the cat out?" "____" (2)

ACROSS CLUES

2 TV Weatherman (3,10)
3 lb (anag) (2)
8 English national dish; fish and ____ (3)
9 Eurovision winning Swedish car whose hits include *A Winner Takes It All* and 6 Down (5)
12 Geographical area of Britain containing Manchester (2)
13 "On your marks, get set, _____" (3)
15 "_____, a drop of golden rain" (Sound of Music) (2)
16 Cock (6)
18 Basic error leads to lost duel (2,3)
20 "And all because the lady loves _____" (4)
22 "I'll have a nice ____ _____, please, Mr baker" (5,4)
23 Gravy vessel (5,4)
24 "Able was ant, ___ ___ saw Elba" (3,1)
25 San Fran ____ (5)
28 see 10 Down
30 The company that makes pencils (2)
31 Regiment of Bennies, we hear? (11,6,3)
32 "Look at ____ _unt!" (2,1)
34 More than one 'I ' (2)
36 SH + ~~DR~~ UGS (5)
37 A long, snakelike fish (4)
38 "Look at me, _____! Top of the world!" (Cagney & Lacey) (2)
39 "Old MacDonald had a farm, ___ E-I-O!" (2)
41 TV weatherman (8,5)

SIMON CADELL'S WEEKEND IN DORSET WITH A LIME
#37754   By Rollo

Mayor's actions show he has finally lost all respect for town

STONES

by Challenger Putney

THE FUTURE of the famous Framley Stones, Britain's oldest earthwork, has been plunged into uncertainty yet again.

The famous Stones, a 3rd century circle of 'standing stones' (or menhirs) - presumed a place of worship - and Britain's oldest earthwork, were under threat of construction from the borough's proposed Outer Ring Road Project (ORRP).

The Stones became the subject of a compulsory purchase order by the council, prompting local architectural historian Sir Cocoa Wufflemere to claim that Billiam D'Ainty, Framley's colourful mayor, has "lost all respect for the town."

Wufflemere, who has done three books about Framley, made his startling allegation after a ten-minute meeting with the mayor in his plush office last week.

"I asked him about the future of the Framley Stones, and he told me not to worry, they were being preserved," gasped Wufflemere.

HERE'S THE MAYOR

Mayor D'Ainty, long since the

A proposed map of the project.

ILLUSTRATION ARCHIE BUBBLES

ORRP's noisiest approbator, had already signed compulsory purchase orders for a 14th-century mansion house, the village of Whoft and the world's largest penny farthing. At an Extraordinary Meeting last week, D'Ainty told councillors that the future of the Stones was "under my review."

"I asked him where his review was

at," warmed Cocoa, "and that's when he told me that the Stones were going to be included as a feature on a roundabout on the road.

"Then he whispered that actually, the road scheme wouldn't be going ahead, but that he was going to build a roundabout around the stones anyway. And he blew a fart at me.

"I just lost it. I flew at him and

punched him on the nose," went Sir.

POLICE TOLD ABOUT

Mayor D'Ainty has told policemen and people dressed as policemen that he plans to press charges of common assault against Wufflemere. He has also brushed off claims that the Stones are as old as everybody thinks, claiming the earliest photograph of it dates from the 1920s.

"I'm on the side of proof," spat the Mayor as he gripped his blood-drenched handkerchief to his gushing nostrils as he passed me as he left his office where I was on the spot.

ENTER THE HIPPIES

A pride of hippies has arrived at the site of the Framley Circle, claiming they will "make love to the stones right up til the bulldozers get it together," says a red-faced farmer from St Eyot's.

"They've arrived in their Volkswagen Caravans, covered in beads, and they're sicking up joints all over my farm," he boiled last night.

Edwin Nimby, 42, jokingly threatened to "go on a hippy-peppering spree with a couple of friends from the National Front."

All In A FLap!

FRAMLEY BOROUGH COUNCIL today warned of further chaos as industrial action by the local owl community entered its fourth fortnight.

The dish-eyed birds, who are demanding their own parliament, have been working to rule for 8 weeks, doing only the bare miminum required by the terms of their contracts

The majority of Framley's owl population will now only move their heads 90 degrees in either direction when looking for mice, while one breakaway wolery is operating a "fly slow", moving through the air at less than 4cm an hour, crashing slowly into pedestrians' heads and obscuring lines of sight for drivers and lollipop people.

One teenager boy was last night being councilled by his family after

by Katie Blirdsnest

he froze with fear because of the fact that an owl flew at a constant 30cm from his face for two and half hours last week.

Tawny owls, who are refusing to follow the co-operative's hardline "one whit, one whoo" policy, have been crossing picket lines and manning a skeleton owl service, but this is proving nowhere near enough to cope with demand for owls in Framley, which was at an all-time high until this.

A spokesmen for the Department of the Environment, Traffic and the Regions (DEFRA) has invited the nocturnal birds to arbitration in Athens.

There is a species of owl called the New Zealand laughing owl.

An owl, refusing to budge
PHOTO BY BURGER BOY

MOTÖRHEAD

with Oliver Singultus-Hiccup

Sockford comes up trumps with new car

SOCKFORD MOTORWORKS hasn't produced a new model in over 150 years, so I was more than excited to be asked to road-test their latest prototype, the Sockford Narwhal R150.

On first impressions, I was impressed by the car's roomy, warm interior, with its impressive array of climate controls and 8" temperature gauge, situated unexpectedly in the centre of the windscreen. Right, Oliver, I said to myself, let's you and me see what this baby can do.

With a throaty roar, I pulled out into traffic, licking my lips and mopping my brow. With engine response like this, I thought, things might get too hot to handle!

At 60mph, the windows shut automatically, and my glasses

began to really steam up. Quite a ride!

My fingers started to sizzle and pop on the steering wheel, and I thought it best to prick them with the dashboard fork provided. Just outside Whoft, I reached for the gearstick, and slammed the car into Gas Mark Six. Soon the skin began to blister and lift from the bridge of my nose. Excellent.

Partway up the F420 to St Eyots, there was a loud ping and I knew that I had been done to perfection. All that remained was to get home and find that cranberry sauce!

With this thrilling new model, Sockford should find themselves back at the top of a tree. But, if you, like us, can't wait to get your hands on one, you'll have to wait. Pending investigation of a few undisclosed teething problems, Narwhal production has been suspended indefinitely.

If you want details of this or any of Oliver's previous recipes, call us on 01999 877 7777 ext 467.

It's never toi-late to go to the toilet!

The queue for the award winning toilet that many are calling "the most exciting thing ever to happen in Framley"
PHOTOGRAPH BY MATTEUS TRILOBITE

by Damiun Clavalier

By Damium Clavalier

FLUFF STREET conveniences have been voted the best in Framley, only a year after they were voted the worst in Framley.

Gus Wetherlady, the conveniences' sole attendant was present at the presentation at Framley Hall. "I'm going to put the award on the wall under last years'", he announced to the gathered, "Clean toilets are more fun. And the extra cash helped."

And indeed he's right! More than £150,000 was ploughed into the project, most of which was targeted at two serious blockages that had troubled visitors for years.

These weren't the only improvements that were noted by the judges. All areas of the conveniences are now accessible to wheelchair users, including the famous pitched roof and store cupboard. There's even a coffee shop, lift and museum celebrating 100 years of effluent.

Q

If you'd like to use the facilities, however, you'd better cross your legs. On a good day last week, the queue for the cubicles stretched back past the war memorial a mile away, with many more people joining the line 'just in case'.

"I didn't need to use them when I first joined the queue," I quoted someone as saying, "but I'm grateful to be here now, I am telling you."

The regulars seem happy as well. After inspecting the facilities, one of the judges locked himself in a cubicle and refused to leave. Staff have since fitted a glass window in the door so you can see him smiling and enjoying his visit.

Archaeoaelogists find evidence of the past

THE NEWS is just in for golfists - if you want to score a golf-in-one, you'll have to steer clear of Molford Golf Course for the next few weeks. The greens have been cordoned off by a pair of local archaeologists who have declared the course a "site of ludicrous historical significance".

Rathbone Twiddrington and Oswald Underclown of the Framley Archaeological Survey have been digging in the bunkers of Molford Golf Course since the beginning of last month, and they have already unearthed a veritable corn-on-the-copia of treasure troves.

So far, they've uncovered a viking longball, a woad club dating back to the 3rd century and a fossilized dinosaur carrying a golf bag.

One of the finds.
(OSWALD UNDERCLOWN)

RIDICULOUS

"This is a site of ridiculous importance," Twiddrington said yesterday from the bottom of an eight foot trench in the fairway. "Every day we're learning more and more about the evolution of the game of golf. If these early finds are anything to go by, I wouldn't be surprised if, before long, we find evidence of the fabled 'Missing Links', a prehistoric golf course built by sabre-toothed tigers."

Senior clubmembers at Molford Golf Club however are annoyed at this disruption to their game, and insist that the archaeologists are "making it all up".

PENFOLD HEARTS

"The course has only been in use since 1982," one told me. "So the discovery of these artefacts is extremely unlikely. What's more, neither of these so-called archaeologists has shown us any real evidence, just shapes under a tarpaulin most of the time."

Another clubmember was concerned that the few 'finds' he had seen were obviously shoddy fabrications. "That viking longball was just a Slazenger No7 with a beard drawn on it. If you ask me, they're just inventing stuff so they've got a reason to stay"

Twiddrington pooh-poohs the clubmembers' concerns.

"Of course we like it here, and I won't deny that the bar is excellent, but this is a sensitive and serious piece of scientific field research. Look at all the stuff we've found. Only this morning, I dug up a golf cart with the skeleton of Henry VIII in it. It's over there, under that blanket. Anyone fancy a snifter?"

Mayor Mash

by Challenger Putney

MAYOR D'AINTY faced a formidable sight when he arrived for his weekly Council briefing this Monday evening, at 6 for 6.30pm, on floor two of the Town Hall (please avoid using the lift.)

As he attempted to enter the conferencarium, the mayor's path was blocked by a dollop of dinner ladies from The Teapop School, Sockford, all throwing mash and calling him a bender.

From their colourful placards, it was clear that the disher-uppers were peeved at The mayor's plans to withdraw free school dinners from local school pupils.

Chairs were overturned and a glass statue of a clown was thrown, missing the mayor by only a few minutes.

RATED

The "D'Ainty Dinner Plan", that made them so very, very cross will phase out the school's traditional menu of free chips and cheese pizza in favour of an à la carte selection from Framley's Michelin rated Belgian restaurant, Alimentaria.

"Children love posh food," Mayor D'Ainty told reporters at the launch of the plan last March, "and the proposed winelist is first class."

Controversially, the children will be billed at the restaurant's usual rate, with Visa, Diners Club and Newbycard all accepted.

Alimentaria owner Jacques Shit, who bankrolled the Mayor's winning election campaign in 1974, was delighted with the plan.

"No discount for groups," he chuckled, rubbing all his hands together.

The old dinner scheme cost the council to the tune of £2.750,000m a year, the new one will cost nought.

"The children will finally pay for their own lunches at last, saving us money, and teaching them valuable restaurant skills that will help them in future lives," said D'Ainty, climbing into bed, "Goodnight, dear."

DEMI-BOUTEILLE

But the daily cost to pupils (starting from £20, based on three courses and a demi-bouteille of Chardonnay) has upset school meal staff. No, they are not happy one bit, turning up in mass on Monday to make their protesting felt.

"A lot of our pupils have learning difficulties. They're bound to have trouble calculating the 12.5% service charge," whinged a spokesdinnerperson. "And none of them like mussels anyway."

But the mayor dismissed their protests.

"Mussels are delicious and nutritious. I have them all the time. These people are talking rubbish," scoffed Mayor D'Ainty, speaking of the incident at a presconference. "If there's one thing I know, it's how much children like mussels. Popeye eats them."

Mayor is so chuffed with new railwa7

by Challenger Putney

FRAMLEY'S CHARISMATIC Mayor, William D'Ainty announced a mayor new building project for the Framley district at a presconference on Tuesday.

"I have drawn up blueprints for a new underground railway system, which will drag Framley into the 20th century, once and for all. I am glad to announce that building work will start right away," he said.

The Mayor insisted that the creation of this vital rail network will bring hundreds of construction workers to the region from all over the country, and probably boost the economy or something.

LIKE

The tube system, which will have two stations and almost four hundred yards of tunnels, is sure to be the envy of neighbouring tubeless boroughs, like Bellaire and Prince's Freshborough.

The Mayor's desk, with the exciting new blueprint on it that he drew himself.
PHOTOGRAPH BY SUE PUTNEY

"I have designed a new municipal crest with a train on it too, and smoke coming out," the Mayor insisted. "Within a couple of years I'll be confident Framley will be known as the pivot of a brave new railway world."

Defending the cost of the enterprise, Mayor D'Ainty pointed to the £2.750,000m surplus that had recently appeared in the Council budget. "That'll be plenty," he beamed.

Troublemakers have already started asking questions about the proposed route of the Framley tube, but it's "the usual bloody suspects and they're talking rubbish."

Trains will run every six minutes between the mayor's house and the Framley golf course. An express service will also run at 10.45am and 11.30pm, with a fully licensed buffet bar.

Mayor D'Ainty stressed what good news this was for the people of the area as he left for work.

PARTICULARLY

"These two stations are essential for the smooth running of daily life in the borough. Commuters will be able to make this journey in half the time it would take by car. This will reduce traffic congestion along the FR404 between my house and the golf course, and there's a slim chance it could attract tourists and discourage foxes."

"And, as an added bonus, the tube line will prove very useful for me. I have always said how important it is that the mayor keep in touch with the citizens of Framley, and this will enable me to forge a close personal bond with local people, particularly those who live in and around Golf Station. Or my house."

Framley

Final competition

FRAMLEY CAMERA CLUB. - The club's final competition had the theme of "Framley - or something else" and was judged by guest Little Willy Spanish, picture editor of Magazine! magazine. The following gained the highest awards. **Prints** - Beginners - Colour: Prize, Marlon Wild, *Foot*; Merit, Bernardo Wild, *Feet*. **Advanced Monochrome:** Prize, Cmdr David Philpott, *Hamster Enjoying 'Ground Force'*; Merit, Duncan Dunkerque, *Hoverjew*. **Advanced Colour** - Prize, Wendy Bendy, *Where Children Shouldn't Really Play*; Merit, St Dave Yates, *Peacock & Thumb*.

The club met every Tuesday at 8pm on a rotating basis. Guests were never welcome.

Crack morning

THOSE BLOODY METHODISTS AGAIN. - There will be a crack morning tomorrow (Saturday) from 10am to midnight in aid of Doug 'The Destroyer' Pettygrew, currently doing a 14-stretch in HMP Chutney. There will be refreshments, a cake stall, bring and buy, and chill-out room.

Tudor Life

AFTERNOON WI. - At their fortnightly meeting, members welcomed three new members, Mrs Robinson, Mrs Robinson and Mrs Robinson. They also welcomed three visitors to their afternoon meeting, Mrs Robinson, Mrs Robinson and Mrs Robinson. Mrs Robinson proposed a toast to Mrs Robinson, who was celebrating her 85th birthday and supplied cakes for fellow Mrs Robinsons to enjoy. The speaker was Mrs Robinson, who took on the guise of 'Mrs Robinson,' a tudor Mrs Robinson at Robinson Hall. Any members who accidentally returned to

the wrong lives after the meeting are urged to call Mrs Robinson on 01999 418010.

Family film

ETHEL DUNNING CLUB. - On April 2nd, members of the club enjoyed a special BBC1 screening of popular film, The Wizard of Oz. In her vote of thanks Ethel Dunning said it had been a wonderful afternoon's entertainment and that it had reminded her of when she was a little girl. During tea, Ethel announced next week's visit to the supermarket to herself and that she also missed her late husband. With no more business, members had a soda biscuit and an early night.

Sockford

Organ recital

MOTHER'S UNION. - Sockford MU members were treated to a special organ recital from world-renowned organ reciter, Leo Hopkirk. Leo recited a list of all of the notes played by all of the keys on all of the three keyboards of the Sockford church organ. At last, he finally encored with a lengthy sequence of noises that each of the stops make when the organ is actually in use. Secretary Mrs Beryl Mothers noted the members' disappointment that Mr Hopkirk had failed to mention the third octave F# but that they all went home humming the sound of the 8' diapason.

A Busy Week

SOCKFORD WORKHOUSE. - A week in Sockford Workhouse was organised by Framley Conservatives. Members were made to scrub flagstone floors with lye, sleep in draughty cellars overridden with rodents, and were forced to subsist on a diet of gruel and heavy beatings. At the end of the week, several members asked for more, but were

NEW SIGNS MEAN SAFETY

NEW SIGNS have been erected outisde the village of Gartside Green in response to a series of near misses. In the three years since the first "Gartside Green: Please drive carefully" sign was erected, over four hundred vehicles have struck the sign, killing almost a thousand people. The new signs read "Please drive carefully" to warn drivers of the presence of the sign, then, twelve yards later "Thankyou for driving carefully" to signal that the emergency is over. The signs have been worded by a local poet and cost over a quarter of a million pounds.

PHOTO BY EDWARD IAN FURNITURE

denied this by club beadle Gavin Bumble MP.

Guest Speaker

SOCKFORD WI. - The speaker at the monthly meeting was Oliver Benz. Under the title 'It Could Have Happened To You,' Oliver described growing up in a hessian potato sack, and how he had been taught to swim by a man dressed as a man doing a handstand, and of how unhappy he was working as a quality control officer in a jazz quintet. Oliver displayed a large selection of maracas, air fresheners, boxing gloves and loft insulation. The floor was opened to questions and members unanimously asked Oliver to explain any of what he had been saying in the previous two and a half hours.

Chutney

REFITTED UNARMED CHURCH. - At 10.45am on Sunday, the service was led by guest preacher Mr Clem Froust, with Mr Basil Bedouin in the organ. The subject of the sermon was "Why Are The Poor So Annoying?". Mr Froust took as his text a 160 character message from his mate Bob about that bloke who lies around on the ground near the cash machines in the Arnhem Centre. The serivice

concluded with a game of Bingo, using the new font balls. Attendees exchanged the peace and snogged. After the congregation had left, Mr Bedouin was teased out from the organ with a saucer of milk and humanely destroyed. Next service will probably be on Sunday too, led by the minister, the Rev Jonathan Bang. Tickets limited to three per caller. Book early to avoid disappointment.

Molford

Delicious apple

LADIES' GUILD. - The weekly meeting of the Molford District Ladies' Guild was held on Monday, 3rd at 3pm. A record attendance welcomed Mrs Sarah Convoy who brought a delicious apple for everyone to look at. This proved a popular theme for meeting, which was a great success and adjourned at four in the morning. Those members who were unable to attend and so missed the delicious apple will be glad to hear that Mrs Convoy has promised to come back next week with either a pear or a glove. Crowds expected.

Magnificent Illness

MOLFORD CONSERVATIVE CLUB. - The first meeting of

the new bimester was held on Friday, 28th, in the Treasurer's Hall. Chairman Peter Unguent was absent, citing his recent acquisition of a majestic dose of clap. His place at the head of the meeting was taken by his five year old daughter Hannah, who led an entertaining round of "If You're Happy And You Know It Clap Your Hands" and drew a rabbit. The drawing was passed unanimously round the table. Meeting adjourned.

Molford St Gavin

Fascinating Talk

MOLFORD LITERARY CIRCLE. - The third anniversary meeting of the Molford Literary Circle was held on Thursday and a great success. Mrs Honeydew Melton, acting chair, welcomed newcomers and old members and others and introduced Mrs Aggeline Fant, who spoke about the world of Jane Austen. Aggie illustrated her talk with slides and was born in 1775, lived her early days as the youngest of seven children, Northanger Abbey. She illustrated her talk with slides of places Jane Austen had visited and was buried in Winchester Cathedral.

Meeting Cancelled

ANY OTHER BUSINESS. - The February meeting of the Molford St Gavin Any Other Business Club was cancelled due to the over-running of the January and December meetings.

Molford St Malcolm

Gentle exercises

ROYAL BRITISH LEGION WOMEN'S SECTION. -The chairman, Mrs Etta Pulse, welcomed those members who had turned out on such a frosty night. Apologies for absence were received from Mrs Luge, Mrs Front and Mrs LeTroux, all of whom had perished in the snow on the way there. Mrs Euridice, who had become stuck fast with cold to the latch of the church hall was chipped free by a vote of 8 to 6.

CORRESPONDENTS PLEASE NOTE:

WOULD village correspondents <u>wherever possible</u> please e-mail their copy to the following address:

damiunclavalier@framleyexaminer.com

Please title your e-mail "my tiny little life" and indicate which village it is that you're on about. Oh, and send your village news piece as plain text, not an 8MB Bitmap scan of your bloody minutes, and yes, I *am* talking to you, Robert.

The Framley Examiner

Framley's Traditional Favourite since 1978

PRICE 45p

STYLE

The latest beards

WIN!

Two months in bed

PROPERTY

It's a full house!

De'spite Queen's past snub's to town, its Golden Jubilee fever!

LEFT: Scenes of spontaneous celebration were arranged to mark Her Majesty The Queen's fifty years since wearing the crown. **ABOVE:** the local man who celebrated.

PHOTOGRAPHS BY NESQUIK RUBETTE

FRAMLEY CITIZEN CELEBRATES 50 GLORIOUS YEARS

by Taunton Mishap

TWO-HUNDRED THOUSAND half-grapefruit hedgehogs, bearing over a million portions of cheese and pineapple on sticks went uneaten as Framley celebrated HM the Queen's glorious 50th jubilee last weekend.

The event, which had been dubbed "the party of the century" by organiser Glasner Pommedeterre, marked the glorious 25th Anniversary of the Queen's glorious Silver Jubilee in 1977, with street parties, souvenir mugs and cake, just like in the historic summer of The Stranglers and *Kramer Vs Kramer*.

Though the Queen is still widely resented in the area for having taken away Framley's prized Seaside Status - following a disappointing holiday to the landlocked town in 1954 - the scars of the past were soon forgotten in a riot of iced gems and Onion Jacks.

Everywhere I went, people were in the party mood.

"I'm going to watch the football," said Graham Unch, 78, an unemployed candyfloss vendor from Framley's now derelict promenade district. "What party? Is there a free bar?"

And from behind the smoky doors of the Sailor's Wave pub in Harbour Way, I could hear the sound of a game of Jubilee snooker, and the occasional hearty cry of "you're barred" as a Jubilee dart hit the Jubilee board.

Back at the scene of the street party the next day, organisers were clearing away the pickle-smeared plate and cup. Mr Pommedeterre mopped a tear and congratulated the unnamed Framley man who had helped make the party go with such a bang.

"I'd like to thank you," he said yesterday, "whoever you are. Please contact me to collect your commemorative coin.

"Actually, you can have a couple if you like."

MORE JUBILEE NEWS AND PICTURES IN OUR HALF PAGE PULLOUT - SEE PAGE 26, COLUMN 2

Rain forecast

By PHARAOH CLUTCHSTRAW

EXPERTS predict that a light shower, heading for the Framley area and due to arrive in the early hours of Wednesday morning, may last some years.

The shower, of the genus *fluctus in simpulo*, will be enough to ruin drying washing, says John Never of the St Eyot's Meteorological Society. However, he insists, it will not send people rushing for cover, and drivers will not need to use the fast setting on their windscreen wipers.

The last time it rained for several years in Framley was several years ago.

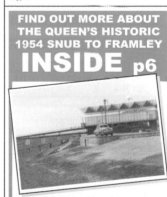

FRAMLEY'S grass pier, 1961, just prior to its tragic, unnecessary closure.

Judge rules that man, suffering from multiple fractures and self-inflicted chin injuries after allegedly attempting to climb over 40ft 'impenetrable' wall of iron into leisure centre's new outdoor swimming complex, should be held in custody until police responsible for the arrest come forward and give irrefutable evidence that it was him and not them who had broken into the building, slid up the water flume backwards and caused more than £250,000 of damage to the new facilites

by Challenger Putney

The police are searching for a receipt which shows they were at the cinema on the evening in question.

Raisin' Arizona

A LUCKY FRACTON schoolboy is set to jet off to the Americas after drawing a dried fruit.

7-year-old Egbert Nosh beat off five other hopefuls to come first in a PlumpBoy Raisin™ competition to design a 'New Raisin For the Millennium'

As well as having the kind folks at PlumpBoy put his raisin into mass production, Egbert is also set to fly to Arizona as part of the prize, where he will get to wear the costume of Grapegomery, the PlumpBoy mascot.

PlumpBoy spokesperson Tina Intricate said, "This is a once in a lifetime opportunity for Egbert to spend 4 weeks in a sweltering factory in Tucson dressed as a grape. He'll get to see first hand how raisins are made."

"The transition is more effective without water", she said as his plane departed, "The sacrifice of the Shrivelled Child will appease the god of our vineyards."

Key to town found in large jacket

43 YEARS AFTER its mysterious disappearance, the key to the town of Framley has turned up... in the pocket of a huge jacket in the Town Hall!

The jacket was discovered hanging up in a disused wardrobe by cleaners, who were turning over the mayor's office looking for dust.

In the years since the town key's disappearance a huge cardboard key has been used as a replacement for special occasions and presentation ceremonies. This key was destroyed in 1972 after it was found to fit the vault door at the Framley Safe Deposit. Since then Framley has been officially keyless.

Council officials are currently discussing plans to fit a huge, flashing fob to the key to avoid the possibility of it going missing in future.

News In Brief

MAN JAILED FOR LIFE

Due to a judicial error, a man who had been found guilty of murdering four children, was jailed by Justice Headley for the "length of my natural life". Justice Headley who has terminal bowel cancer is not expected to see next spring. The man, who is still a danger to the public, will be released, almost certainly, within the next six months.

RUB-A-DUB SHUT

The Golden Ticket public house in Ocksted has been closed to the public while pest controllers deal with an infestation of Pearly Kings. Verminists found a twenty foot Pearly Queen's nest under the floorboards of the saloon bar where up to 1,200 drone Kings, would service the Queen, bringing her cockles and mussels. The nest was neutralised on Sunday by PC Officers who eventually managed to roll out the Queen in a barrel. T h e pub remains closed while experts check the site for loose shiny buttons that may attract the Kings back.

AND FINALLY...

Framley residents are reminded that they are strongly recommended to evacuate the town on Saturday 13th in order for essential crop spraying experiments to take place. Failure to do so will, in all cases, result in paralysis, mental vomiting, dry saliva, mix-ups, and may also cause some pleasant hallucinogenic effects.

TRIATHLON WINNERS CELEBRATE IN STYLE

Stan and Edie toast their victory shortly before Edie tried to put her tongue in my ear.
PHOTOGRAPH BY ALISON HANDSOMEBOYMODELLLINGSCHOOL

IT WAS ADVOCAAT snowballs all round as Molford's all-conquering triathletes celebrated their historic win last Thursday.

Stan Rimshot (76) and his wife Edie (71) walked away with the Framley District Athletic Association Special Achievement Cup after a stunning victory in the Modern Triathlon - a newly introduced event consisting of Bowls, Knitting and BMX Freestyle.

Though the pair won through with ease, Stan told me that the event hadn't been plain sailing.

"My wife and I have been keen bowls enthusiasts for years, and we both enjoy knitting, but I have to admit, the BMX was a surprise. We hadn't really trained for it. But once I was up on the halfpipe, I found it surprisingly easy.

"I suppose riding a bike is like riding a bike. You never forget," he chuckled.

Edie then made another round of snowballs for the assembled journalists while Stan visited the smallest room and was sick down his shirt.

Sockford fisherman wins a personal best

ANGLING
Framley Municipal Park Open

SOCKFORD HERO, ATLANTIS GREENE, beat the regional records tumbling when he landed a superb personal best of nearly catching a fish at the Ned's Atomic Dustbin-sponsored Framley Municipal Park Open.

Greeen was overcome with emotions after landing the severed torso of the late Robert Shaw, using alternate maggot and caster baits.

The paddling pond was teeming with salmon, perch and a bream flown in especially for the competition - which was donated by famous fish farm, Keith Moon.

Second place went to Boz 'Alfie' Scaggs who tempted a 27lb mirror carp with a lot of skill and a Milkybar all covered in Marmite, winning himself a holding net full of two damp £5 notes.

JUNIOR WINNER

The title of Junior Angler of a Year was claimed by Minogue Hoffman,

12, whose resounding victory was never in doubt after scoring an eighth for 16lb50 off of Big Mick at the poolside hot dog stand. Proud parents, Anastacia and Valerie Helpmann were said to be very pleased with Minogue's catch and immediately offered to double his stash.

The victorious Minogue
PHOTO BY STAN MOOD

The first annual third annual angling contest was deemed a huge success by spectators, organizers and fish alike and there is expected to be fierce bidding for the television coverage rights of next year's second annual third annual angling contest from rival channels Sky Fishing 12 and Sky Fishing 139.

SPORTS extra

The football action is never far from away

SOCCER
Framley Veterans Cup

IT TOOK EXTRA TIME, penalties and a quarter-pound bag of aniseed balls to split **Whoft Moonies** and **Batley Spinner**. The match ended 0-0 with goals from Cyd Shariff (Whoft) and Basil Jet (Whoft) early in the second half. Batley finally edged the shoot-out 8-0. The replay will be next Wednesday.

●

FRAMLEY POLICE called on their excellent home form to claim a 124-6 victory over **Molford St Gavin** after nine of the visiting side were arrested under the Prevention of Terrorism Act (1973) shortly before kick-off. MSG keeper, Richmond Nettle, was stretchered off within two minutes after a nasty clash of head and truncheons, leaving brave centre-half Andy Vlap to put up a spirited 88-minute performance against the eleven burly coppers. Surely it won't be long before the County Intermediate League comes knocking as Vlap never looked out of his depth despite being forced to score 91 own goals.

●

IN AN EXCRUCIATING game at Wripple Celtic Park, the away side **Framley Caledonian** Thistle lost out by the odd goal in two to **Wripple Glasgow Celtic** whilst **Benjamin Disraeli Town** beat **Bad Seagull** absolutely bloody hollow.

By Pigshit Nelson

NEWBY'S OF MOLFORD CITY ran riot at home with just over half of the team on the scoresheet and just over two-thirds of the team tipping the **Framley Pagoda** team bus over after having set fire to the visiting players.

●

FRAMLEY NORTH-EAST CONSERVATIVES new signing, Westcott Malaise, scored a dubious offside on his debut against **Wripple Old Nonagenarians**. FNEC ball/manager, Marcus Help!, was delighted with and by Malaise's contribution to the team's performance which was marred only by the necessity to substitute local MP and wing-back, Ianbeale Steeplecocque, five minutes before the end of the match and, again, five minutes before the beginning of the match.

●

THE SEMI-FINAL line up was completed with a convincing display from **The Sockford Reverends** whose absent opponents **Tuesday Wednesday**'s chutzpah was rewarded with a bye into the final. Wednesday's coach, The Marty Marty, revealed at a local presconference that there was no point in them turning up for the game as they would definitely have tonked the in-form Vicars 5-0 anyway.

SPORTS ROUNDUP

BRITISH BULLDOG
After a series of grazed knee injuries, Leanne Pelvis has been forced to pull out of next Monday's British Bulldog Championships. According to her coach, Mrs Maureen Pelvis, she's had a bit too much blue pop and she's just tired and overexcited. Concerns that there would be tears before bedtime were also a factor in Pelvis' withdrawal from the competition.

NEW SIGNING
Molford Descriptive FC have signed a new bass player. Juice Oblong, 19, will make his debut next Saturday.

SEMI-FINAL CLASH
The semi-finals of the Sockford Intermediate League Basketboxing championships will take place on Tuesday. Leroy "Wildtrack" Ingle will face The Fracton Windmills. Winner to be decided by two slamdunks or a knockout.

Our food critic visits Framley's newest restaurant and finds it lives up to his high expectations

Ladies first

EATING OUT
with Vernon Palliard

IT TAKES SOMEONE of particular vision to bring their own particular vision to the world of top-end dining, but if there's one thing you can depend on, it's that that someone is going to be local gourmet and restauranteur Cameron Stad.

Stad's unconventional sense of design first caught my eye when I visited *Chez Cap'n*, his fishfinger restaurant in old Framley harbour in 1996. With its distinctive cod-shaped dining area and cutlery anchors, this was a whole new experience for the jaded food critic, but I'm pleased to announce that the ever restless restauranteur's arresting new restaurant outstrips it.

Called simply *Ladies*, Stad's new eatery stands in the centre of Van Dyke Park, at the bottom of a flight of steps, its exclusivity guaranteed by an 8 foot railing, which my dining partner, Django, and I negotiated with some difficulty.

DINING STALLS

Access to the dining area is via a skylight and there's a lengthy drop onto broken glass for all guests. The Maitre d' seated us in adjacent "dining stalls", and pointed us towards the menu, which had been cleverly printed onto a long roll and mounted on the cubicle wall.

Most of the dishes on offer were cold. Gazpacho, green salad, or nice 'n' spicy Nik Naks for starters; biscuits and cheese for main course. As Cameron explained to me from his facing stall, the kitchens at *Ladies* are not equipped with anything as vulgar as an oven - a kitchen utensil which Stad regards as "a distraction from the real business of washing and arranging food on the plate".

And I had to agree that my food was clean as a whistle. My Nik Naks had been washed thoroughly, removing all the gaudy flavouring, and bringing out a pale, pure, beige colour I had never anticipated.

Cameron shows us round the facilities at *Ladies*, his new premium dining experience. **CLOCKWISE FROM TOP:** the welcoming sign; the kitchens; one of the dining stalls; entering the restaurant.   **PHOTOGRAPHY BY ARRIFLEX WELLING**

In a similarly imaginative touch, Django's simple glass of tap water was frosted with a pink, soapy substance that acted as a marvellous palate cleaner. As bubbles floated above his stall divider, my appetite was truly whetted. I couldn't wait for my main course to arrive.

BISCUIT

And what a main course! A fan of spotlessly clean Sports Biscuits, topped with a single Emmenthal Baby Bel.

My partner opted for a pyramid of Krackawheat, washed in their own juice. I was delighted to note that the chef had decorated each cracker with a smiley of Primula cheese spread, a straight-from-the-tube flourish that is typical of Stad's diligent approach to *la cuisine moderne*.

Fully sated, we skipped dessert and went straight to the delicious bill and mints. Still reeling from the heady flavours, we congratulated the *patron* and clambered back out into the night air by shinning up the cistern by the skylight. I was in love.

VERDICT: This is a truly exceptional restaurant, and well worth a visit. ★★★★

LADIES, Van Dyke Park, Framley. 01999 644 379. Typical cost £45 per head with bottle of house water. No dogs. No toilets.

Local National

have vacancies for bus passengers. Full training for suitable applicants, life insurance, paid holidays, free uniform, free travel, employee share scheme.

If the idea of combining being a passenger with meeting bus drivers appeals, call
01999 877 677

Local National

Hamster monitor

£65K p/a.

Suit ambitious 8-year old, good team player, with interest in pets and summer holiday free.

St Icklebrick's Primary School
"Excellence in Education"

01999 985 005

£50,000 P.A. OTE

Yes! I have been here 12 months and have made £12,000 already! Halfway there! You could be halfway there too!
- 01999 688 754 -

BEE REQUIRED

by trainee beekeeper

Call Simon Eminem on
01999 963 023

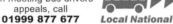

FRAMLEY DOG RESCUE

Framley Dog Rescue have vacancies for butchers, sous-chefs and experienced waiting staff.

Framley Dog Rescue also require unwanted pets for use in promotional film. We're sorry, we can't return any of your pets, but there is a prize for all those shown.

Call Isadorabella on 01999 600 610

VEGETARIAN BINGO CALLER

Must have own complete set of 1-100 cherry bingo tomatoes.
£5 per hour p/h

PODIUM BINGO
01999 677 865

St Gahan's School for Boys

are looking for a
BAD LANGUAGE ASSISTANT

3 years min experience as sailor, dockworker or squaddie preferred. Salary negotiable depending on salary.
01999 470 872

MILKMEN AND WOMEN

The Onion Milk Company Ltd require milk men and women to turn around sales figures on our new range of Onion Milks. Previous deserters need not reapply.

01999 744 743

THE ONION MILK COMPANY
So misunderstood...

PART-TIME EVENING CLEANER

required to partially clean office.

£4.50 / hr. 7pm-9pm. Don't touch that drawer.

01999 939 018

RAIN MAN WANTED

to act as human spreadsheet for Framley technophobe.

Must not be taller than Tom Cruz, and preferably be able to sing theme from *"Goodnight Cowboy"*.

OIRO £1200 pcm.
01999 851 711

TEMPORARY BAR STAFF / ASTRONAUTS

needed for Sockford wine bar. Previous bar experience preferred.

5 days p/wk
(4 days bar work /
1 day suborbital satellite maintenance)

Some on-the-job training given.

Mandy 01999 850 080

DESIGNER
required

to design this advertisement

successful applicants will already have this job

WHOFT HOSPICE
STAFF WANTED

Do you think hospices are places of doom and gloom? Not all of our patients come here to die. But they all do. In the end.

We're looking for a sensitive, caring individual with their own spade and a strong back, who understands that life can be short as well as long, and wants to join us in this fast-moving, high-turnover business.

For job details, call Amylase or Saliva on 01999 842 842

BUILDER'S MATES

Builder's mates required.

I've just woken up in a skip. Where is everybody?

Mike? Dave? Jimbo? Come on, a joke's a joke.

07999 908 651

CAN YOU COOK?*

The Horse and Further Horse pub / restaurant needs you tomorrow*!

Are you prepared to work hard*, be part of a team*, deliver top quality service*?

Morning, lunchtime and evening work available*. Good pay*. Excellent scope for promotion*.

*Tuesday 16th April only.

Applications by 3pm today at the latest.

The Horse & Further Horse, Adrian Mill, Wripple, Nr Framley FM5 6RE

SOCKFORD HAPPINESS CAMP

has vacancies for a delighter, a pleasurer and a laughterist. Apply to the chief conjuror on
01999 620 105

MOLFORD EMPLOYER

seeks
FULL TIME PERSON

Must be a person ALL THE TIME. Must not sometimes be a pot plant or an octopus or a cloud.

Previous applicants may reapply if they are now a full-time person.

01999 855 902

WEB DESIGNER

wanted for crap spider

01999 833 901

WINE DEMONSTRATOR

We have a vacancy for a wine demonstrator at our busy Molford Retail Park outlet.

You will be between 40 and 60 years of age and covered in dribble.

Slumping, sleeping, swearing, stealing packets of jelly and sicking up wine will be just part of your job, which will also include some urinating against the back wall.

Good interpersonal skills a must. £48K starting salary. Uniform provided.

Call Cathy or Spagger on 01999 932 022 or send CV and beard sample to
CORKER'S WINE
Unit 48b, Molford Retail Park, FM7 6TT

We have 20 vacancies for
SALESPEOPLE

to sell double glazing in Whoft to Mr Jack Bicknacre of Basement Flat, 38a, Woollen Grove. You will join a committed existing team, working long hours on this project. £38K pa. 58h p/wk (+OT)

Call Stevhen, Marhie or Colhin at
THE JACK BICKNACRE WINDOW DEVELOPMENT SALES FORCE
Units 12-19, Cormorant Industrial Estate, Whoft FM3
01999 854 711 / 712 / 713 / 714 / 715 / 716

FRAMLEY POLICE

WE HAVE A VACANCIES FOR A

BENT COPPER

Must be disliked. We're looking for someone who doesn't do things by the book. You will preferably be motivated by greed, power and money and be an excellent team traitor.
Apply Det Ch Insp Barry Judas, Vice (Ref 7754)

BURGLAR

Traditional burglar required. Striped jersey, bag marked "Swag" and Fred Flintstone Five O'Clock shadow. Easily spotted melodramatic tiptoeing motion if possible. For training new officers. Previous inexperience inconsequential.
Apply Supt. I. Triangle, Training Dept (Ref 7710)

MURDERER OF JOANNE PEST

You'll be a socially awkward loner, 5'8" - 5'10" with a loping walk, goatee beard and distinctive blue shoes. This is a permanent position and the successful applicant must be prepared to do long hours (30 years minimum).
Apply Det Sgt Ulan-Bator, Framley CID (Ref 7710)

For full details of all these vacancies, call Framley Police on 999

DESPATCH CLERK

required by retired Sockford businessman to send A3 envelopes full of hot gravel to everyone who's ever annoyed me.

Des on 01999 710 940

We have a
POSSIBLE VACANCY

for an invisible receptionist. This post may already have been filled. We're not sure.

Phone the front desk on
01999 622 192
and see if anyone answers.

Calls cost £8.75 per minute.

Framley Community College
FINE ART DEPARTMENT

Require a

TRANSFORMER

to teach sculpture and ceramics.

You will be over 8 feet tall and able to turn into a lorry.

16K, 36h p/wk 01999 954 968

Time running out for tiny farm

THE FOUR WEEK SIEGE at Wripple's Rappapoort Farm has entered its third week. The owner of the smallholding, Mr David Futumsch, has barricaded himself in and is refusing to leave the farm, which has been in his family since the age of Robin Hood. The authorities, who have surrounded the farm with little tanks, insist it is still too tiny. PHOTOGRAPH BY RANDALL OMEN

Vandals attack statue

"SHITKICKING THUGS" are being blamed for damage valued at £4,000 caused to a statue in Van Dyke Park at the weekend.

The statue, Venus Tumescing by Dame Olga Cello, depicts womankind as a orgasm-shaped baby holding a frying pan full of ironing, and has been a favourite with locals since its unveiling in 1969.

"It's a pornographic disgrace that this slur on the mysteries of womanhood is brazenly and publicly on display," said one enthusiast recently, "and I love it."

Even Sid, the notoriously poker-faced park-eeper, loves it!

"What, the climbing frame?" he

Van Dyke Park
PHOTO: DOMINO RUIN

told me as we went through the dog bins for change.

The vandals wrote "PIF PIF PIF" all over the frying pan and drew treble clefs on the baby.

Ne'er-do-wells from the nearby Dungeon estate are being blamed, largely because they're easy targets but also because most of them can't read.

Record shop raided

by Adam Wrent

THE OWNER of Bob's Records, Sockford's only independent record shop, has been imprisoned for fraud.

Bob Eliteonemodellingagency, who has run the shop for over twenty years, was found guilty of conspiracy to deceive the record-buying public, and sentenced to four years sitting in a prison cell.

The court heard how the 47-year old shopkeeper, finding it hard to afford new stock, had taken to recording the albums himself and passing them off as the work of the original artists - pop stars like Celine Dion, The Crazy World of Arthur Brown and Autechre.

EDS OF SCREAMING F

Although Bob's actions were apparently against some law or other, the vast majority of his customers were horrified by his arrest, with hundreds of screaming fans turning up outside the court to stand behind him.

"Bob's version of the Zero 7 album pisses on the original," said one. "The artwork was better as well."

Similarly, Bob's version of Sir Georg Solti conducting the Berlin Sinfonietta doing Mahler's Third had critics raving ("The best music ever made" - *Boston Globe*). The record, which came with a bonus CD of rarities and a signed poster, is now changing hands amongst collectors for over £200.

BONUS TRACKS

Though they were aware of Eliteonemodellingagency's deception, police didn't act until the 47-year old shopkeeper began to get carried away, inserting his own extra tracks

Bob's record shop, Bob''s Records, with (inset) the fraudulent owner.
PHOTOGRAPH BY IMMAC NOSTRIL

into the middle of well known records.

Det Insp Jerutha Damaja of Sockford CID told reporters, "*Sgt Pepper* never had a track called *Uncle Albert's Handlebar Moustache* on it. That was the giveaway. We had to move in. It may be one of my favourite songs on the album, but I'm afraid it's still fraud."

SIM TIMENON

A benefit concert in aid of the 47-year old shopkeeper is being organised by Bomb The Bass singer Tim Simenon and Peter Gabriel (from that video with all the fruit). Stars such as Celine Dion and The Crazy World of Autechre will be performing their versions of some of Bob's greatest hits.

Bob's daughter Stephanie says she will be running the shop in his absence. She is described as having a pleasing descant quality to her voice and a good ear for countermelody.

Man waits two weeks to be served in restaurant

By JESUS CHIGLEY

WHEN JEAKE PERKIN ordered a plate of grilled cod with asparagus and lime jus at Squaffables Restaurant, he didn't expect to be quite so hungry by the time it arrived at his table.

"I only came in for a light lunch after a business meeting in the area," he told a reporter yesterday. "I ordered the cod and a glass of Pinot Grigio, and waited. I was still waiting when the restaurant closed that night, but I thought there might have been a mistake."

HIS LIFE IS RUINED

Three days later, Mr Perkin told the waitress he was still waiting. A day later, he asked again. But, despite his two protestations, it would be a further ten days before the hot fish sat between his cutlery.

The restaurant, which was not asked for its opinion, refused to comment.

"It's ruined my life," sobbed a blubbing Perkin, 41, "I've lost my job, my wife thinks I'm Martin Guerre and, to be honest, I'm still hungry.

"How could they treat me like this? I mean, what were they doing in there? Growing the sea?"

the Framley Examiner

Thursday March 16th 1978 7½p if sold

Framley's traditional favourite since March

BOFFINS SAY "THE COMPUTER IS HERE!"

by Jesus Chigley

FRAMLEY POLYTECHNIC has brought the pride of the computer age to town!

After two years of fundraising, the college has finally been able to pay a record £7,350 for a brand-new Quickticus Wolf III, one of the most powerful computers in the world. Roger Lemon, head of engineering at the poly, is beyond delight.

"This is a marvellous acquisition," he explained through his beard. "The Wolf is a giant of technology: it has six screens, five banks of valves and a breathtaking 400-bite magnetic storage and retrieval system."

The state-of-the-art machine has left the engineering department stunned.

"We'd never even seen a computer this big before The Wolf arrived. We're actually at a loss to make full use of it, so infinite is its power," continued Prof Lemon.

COMPUTER CHIPS

But one bright spark has found a cheeky use for the futuristic beast. Physics student Daniel Tidd is writing a programme that will produce dozens of computerised school dinners.

"I've tested it," admitted Mr Tidd, "and so far it can do 22lbs of potatoes in two hours. With that kind of power, it should be able to manage a staggered system of complete lunches for up to eleven hours at a time. Look out, dinner ladies!"

Meanwhile, back on the serious side of the story, Prof Lemon has high hopes for the future.

INTO THE FUTURE

"If this kind of technology continues to be developed at this pace and on this scale," I think he said, "we could see computers the size of entire office blocks by the mid-1980s. And imagine what a machine that crikey big could do."

"I feel invincible," he added.

The polytechnic professors plan to spend the next 18 months writing a programme that can add two numbers together without overheating.

This new mechanical brain challenging the way we live.
PHOTOGRAPH BY TARTAN CARBLANKET

Foreign Secretary coming

The Foreign Secretary, Dr David Oven, is visiting Little Godley next week, to try to repair relations with the genteel village after it declared itself a hostile state by resident renegade Haris Paris.

Councillor Paris, 41, orchestrated the coup de village in December, after somebody threw a snowball at his wife's legs.

Chamber of Commerce welcomes drop in inflation

FRAMLEY's Chamber of Commerce has welcomed the drop in inflation, and predicted that it will start to reverse the decline of manufacturing in the town.

The monthly rate has dropped to 99% - the first time it has been below 100% since 1973.

New newspaper

FRAMLEY woke up to a bright new day on its doormat this morning with the arrival of the area's first COLOUR newspaper!

It's called the Framley Exanimer, and it's packed full of all your favourite local news, but told in a new COLOURful way!

The newspaper will mark a new era for local news. The Franley Examiner will be the first to inform you of all the breaking stories, from bus timetable changes to new BBC radio frequencies *as they happen*.

In these fast-changing times, you can be sure of one thing - The Framley examiner will be he

He's got the whole world in his photograph!

by Adam Wrent

FRAMLEY EXAMINER PHOTOGRAPHER Matteus Trilobite is going for the big one! On July 18th, the snapper, who specialises in group shots, is going to try and get over 3 billion people into a single photograph.

Trilobite is one of the newspaper's trustiest snapsmen, and reprints of his photos are amongst the best-selling pictures in the Framley Examiner's archive.

His wide angle view of seventeen local rotary clubs all fighting to give big cheques to a man from Unicef was very popular amongst members of local rotary clubs, and his pin-sharp sports pictures regular sell to every single spectator in the ground.

8 x 10 PRINT

"People love to have a picture of themselves making the news, and at £9.99 for an 8x10 print, these group shots are very lucrative for myself and the paper," he told co-workers who wrote down what he said and put it in this story.

"I used to specialise in portrait shots, but that barely pays for

Smile! What the earth might look like from space..
PHOTOGRAPH BY NATHANIEL AERONAUTICSANDSPACEADMINISTRATION

chemicals," he explained yesterday. "For every couple of yards I step back, I get four more people in the shot. Big money."

For his next photo, accompanying an under-tens' chess report, Trilobite is planning his most populated picture yet.

"This job is a dream come true," he told us. "I am going to cover the story from space."

CHESSBOARD

Using a special handmade rocket, Trilobite will travel outside the earth's atmosphere. He then proposes to take the picture from geostationary orbit, 600km above the chessboard, hopefully getting every man, woman and child in the Northern Hemisphere into the frame.

Local inventor Babbage Wilson-Wilson, who is building Matteus' rocket, is convinced the mission will be a success.

"I'll certainly be buying a copy. I'm not much interested in junior chess, but I will be waving from my garden, and the photo will make a lovely present for my grandchildren."

If you're going to be in the Northern Hemisphere on July 18th, and would like to pre-order a copy of Matteus' photograph, send £9.99 to the usual Framley Examiner address.

40% of drivers would fail test says top copper

40% OF DRIVERS would fail a new blood test, according to PC Damascus Bitesize of St Eyot's Police.

The new test, introduced last week by the same policeman, tests for purity and flavour and is reportedly the hardest yet.

"I'm the only one who's passed so far," said PC Bitesize, picking a clot from between his teeth.

Drivers' groups are not yet impressed.

News In Brief

BUBBLE TROUBLE

Rapscallions and guttersnipes who spit their bubble gum onto the pavement will in future be publicly named and shamed, Framley Borough Council has decided. From next January, anyone caught expectorating masticatable rubber paste products onto a public foot surface will be forced to spend an entire day walking around the town centre blindfold wearing a suit made of tomatoes.

MORE TROUBLE

Fighter pilots at nearby RAF Harmonium are threatening a work-to-rule if conditions aboard aircraft carrier HMS Who Wants To Be A Millionaire are not improved. Talk of industrial action follows complaints from serving officers in The Sea's Own 32nd Regiment Mounted Marines about the treatment of horses. "They keep slipping over when they gallop around the walkways. We lost 14 in the steeplechase," said one anonymous floating soldier.

CCTV TROUBLE

CCTV closed circuit television cameras are to be installed in the control room of the town's CCTV monitoring system after a series of thefts which led to the hi-tech office's 22 staff being stolen and all 58,000 hours of videotape being replaced with copies of *The World's Craziest CCTV Footage*. Police will investigate when they can work out where to start.

(NO) TROUBLE AT T'MILL

Plans to convert the decrepit Framley Fluff Works into a museum and crafts centre are to go before the council next month. The famous Fluff Works were the area's biggest industrial resource for nearly a century, milling and bundling fluff, and later, supplying power to an area of 50 square miles from its unique fluff-powered turbines. The building was decommissioned in 1963 when I was two.

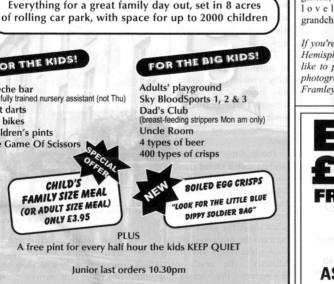

Sadly Missed

Albert "Chalky" Snowdon

Gored in Spain, 20th February, aged 91.

Dearly loved father of Jesus and Concepcion and the finest matador Framley ever produced.

In Loving Memory

Gordon Clive Sinclair

"The boy stood on the burning deck,
His legs were all a-quiver,
He gave a cough,
His leg fell off
And floated down the river."

Thanks to the Framley River Police and the staff of Ward 3J for all their efforts.

"United again in heaven"

Mum and Dad xxx

Your advert here could be reaching over 14,000 readers!

The Framley Examiner
Framley's Traditional Funerals Since 1978

Acknowledgement

Dandy Hummingbyrd

Humbert wishes to THANK all relatives and friends for their kindness and support following his recent loss, but it's not going to bring her back. It was a great comfort to see so many other funerals taking place at the crematorium. Please accept this as my most sincere acknowledgement, and if you've got any lonely female friends, why not give me a bell?

Michael Bettenden

accidentally during mining disaster at Bee Gees concert, Framley Pagoda, 11th March

In our thoughts.

Carol, Stephanie, Robin, Maurice and Andy

In Loving Memory

Jim Cleuworth

"Dad, we miss you in our lives,
In our hearts you live forever.
But where did you put the car keys?"

Miriam, Lance & Hansel

In Memoriam

William Selway

Lost at sea.

No flowers, but donations can be made to The Alzheimer's Society and RNLI.

In Memoriam

Maureen Sprent

Mother to Alan, Grandmother to David and Great Grandfather to Diane

February 19th. Peacefully, in our sleep.

Fucking Hell & Sons
Funeral Directors

"When you see our logo on the hearse, you know it's a Fucking Hell funeral..."

01999 875 908

Bertle "Fred" Bassett

of 35, Leslie Rise, St Eyots, died, as he had lived, noisily in his sleep.

"The snoring may have stopped, but you will be with us whenever we are awoken by a dustcart or a man with a jackhammer."

all at number 33 xxx

Eirich Chapnelle

suddenly in hospital, March 2nd.

Confused as to why he was suddenly in hospital, he passed away, immediately, of surprise.

We missed you. J & F.

Carol Bettenden

accidentally during mining disaster at Bee Gees concert, Molford Odelisk, 12th March

Your spirit lives on.

Stephanie, Robin, Maurice and Andy

Missing you...

Ian David D'Avid

"I'd swap everything I have for one more day with you. Or a speedboat."

Leanne xxx

Stephanie Bettenden

during mining disaster at Bee Gees concert, Sockford Plantaganet Centre, 16th March

Stayin' Alive in our hearts,

Robin, Maurice and Andy

Irene "Lispy" Scissorssenhurst

Thanks to all the staff of Ward B6 who kept Irene on a gurney in a corridor with a sheet thrown over her whilst we finished our cruise.

Cheers!
Jeremy and Charlotte

New Arrivals

WILLIAMS

DeForest and Rococo (née Roxanne). Congratulations on the birth of your beautiful chinchilla Doughnutz, born on 1st February, a welcome daughter for Loopie and a fellow pet for Fleas, Fangs, Sgt Mincemeat and The Comptroller. With love from Rain.

IT'S ANOTHER BLOODY GIRL

James and Tessa Herringhamham announce the birth of Emma, on Feb 22nd. A sister for Chloe, Hermione, Cassandara, Siobhan, Jane, Emma, Emma and Emma.

HAPPENSTANCE

Janet and Mark Happenstance are delighted to announce the arrival of their new son, Daryl, born 7.20pm, Feb 17th, and would like to thank all those who may have taken part in his conception.

IT'S A ABORTION!

Karen and Robert Misterman are delighted to announce that their daughter Sharelle will no longer be having the baby of Gary Skag.

FEATHERSTONEHAUGH

Nigel and Robyn Featherstone would like to announce the birth of a beautiful baby person, D. An excellent additional challenge to the nanny's job managing A, B and C. She's from Gstaad, you know. Very pretty girl.

IT'S A GIRL

Martin and Lesley Wiltham are delighted to announce the birth of a beautiful, 32-year-old daughter, Miss Regina Divine (né Tony Wiltham)

IT'S A GIRLFRIEND!

The parents of Richard Jeremy Paynting, 39, are pleased to announce the arrival of Donna, a 5'6", 37-year-old County Records Office filing assistant with sufficiently low standards.

Property, page 86, Richard!

BLIMEY!

Ciaran and Daine **Meltis-Fruit** are surprised to announce the birth of a beautiful Aunt Sally, "Aunt Sally", 175lbs. Feb 27th, 5am.

SIXTIES

Terry and Julie Sixties are proud to announce the arrival of a daughter, Ringo. A beautiful sister for John, Paul and Georgeharrison.

IT'S STILL A GIRL

Leah and Andrew Slippers are pleased to announce the continuing birth of their daughter, Alice, 11lb 4oz, 14' 6" and still apparently plenty more to come

---

NEW ARRIVAL!

Arreta Trains are delighted to announce the late arrival of the 8.32 from Winchhandle Junction. This was due to driver action.

NEW BABY

To Jennie Dowell-Bishop and Ian Walden-Sutherland, a strapping son, Jack. Congratulations my darling girl, Jen. For God's sake don't give him all your surnames. Love Mum.

Occasions

Happy 18th birthday

CHUNDERTHWAITE Kelly. To Smelly Kelly with the big ears and the national health glasses and the bad breath and these days, frankly, raging thrush. Dad. xxx

---

NOT LONG NOW, ELSIE!

J & L xxx

............FRAMLEY EXAMINER SPECIAL REPORT............

Why don't you eat it all up now, won't you?

By Beaky Coxwain

THE YOUTH OF FRAMLEY ARE ALL going to die if they carry on like this.

Children as young as yours are eating all the wrong things like we never used to and they're running the risk of planting a cancer or heart disease time bomb in their arteries because they should eat up their vegetables.

A recent poll into the eating practices of kids throughout the county rang warning shots when it produced alarming evidence that no child in Framley has eaten any fruit or vegetables since November 1978.

It also revealed that whilst families living in the Framley area eat more fast food than almost anywhere else in the country, it was still only a quarter of the Government's recommended amount.

So with this at the back of my mind I invited myself to lunch at St Icklebrick's Primary School to see what teachers really eat these days.

AND A MINT VISCOUNT

Headmister Dr St John St Peter held his gut in and put his arms around my shoulder as he showed me what a well-oiled army of primary schoolchildren really eat these days.

School dinners have certainly come a long way since my last one was finished! No longer the mountains of rotting brown cabbage, stale plastic mash and pork substitute of my miserable schooldays - the choice on offer was simply more than my poor stomach could understand so I made my excuses and left. But it looked lovely.

NEW BALLS, PLEASE

Out in the playground it was a different story. Boys and girls alike showed that packed lunches and huzzing tennis balls at each other can mix. Looking inside their boxes I found that sandwiches were made with maybe a yoghurt or even cheese and meat as well as the traditionally compulsory bag of crisps.

Wendell Theefff, spokesresearch scientist for The Healthy Eating Disorder Researching Campaign, told me on their website that the risks are high.

"We all know how difficult it is to encourage people to eat more green. But what we don't know yet is whether this will lead on to problems later in life. There may be all sorts of stuff that they won't be able to be encouraged to do when they get older. It's very scientific."

Although bread is good for children, this boy's diet could cause rickets or scurvy.
PICTURE BY ARAPAHO CENTRIFUGE

European Weather View

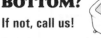
>> Christ alone knows what this is all about. Give it to Wendy, she's usually got sod all to do on a Tuesday. xxxxxxxxxxxxxxxxxxxxxxxxxxxxxxxxxxxxxxxxxxxxxxxxxxxxxxxxxxx

NEWS

Statue honours Framley mayor

by Challenger Putney

THE PEOPLE OF FRAMLEY received a special surprise this week from its friends across the Atlantic - a statue of its elegant mayor!

The statue, which arrived by skip together with forty-eight lengths of broken plywood and a binbag full of grass clippings, was sent as a gift by the citizens of Framley's twin town, Baden Schleissgarten.

CEMENT

Cllr. Geoffrey Cauchaugh greeted the statue with open arms, saying, "That we should be blessed with this beautiful statue shows the unique relationship we have forged with our German neighbours."

Framley was twinned with Baden Schleissgarten in September 1943, a controversial move now recognised by the Guinness Book Of Records as Britain's last attempt at appeasement with the then Third Reich.

The statue, which is nearly four feet tall and made of cement, with a removable plastic bucket inside, has been erected at the southern edge of the swan pond in Philpott Park.

Although the opening ceremony attracted many local dignitaries and some swans, the statue has, so far, elicited only a guarded reaction from its subject, Mayor William D'Ainty.

"Go away, Challenger, I'm trying to watch *Never Mind The Buzzcocks*," he told journalists at a presconference yesterday. "When's dinner ready?"

A handwritten message taped to the skip read simply "Dein Stadt nicht richtig geschmeckt. Claus xxx", a sentiment which the Framley Community College German department has so far been unable to translate.

CAPTAIN

Local primary school pupils, excited by the gift, are currently designing a statue to send to Germany in return. Initial leaked blueprints indicate a 28' tall animatronic gold-plated octopus, called Captain Fishfingers, that shoots rays from its beak and solves underwater crime. It will bear the face of Baden Schleissgarten's Mayor, Claus Freneddt and cost over £280,000, plus postage.

The cement statue will be a symbol of the close relationship between Mayor D'Ainty (inset) and Mayor Frennedt (not pictured).
PHOTOGRAPH BY RANKIN, STYLING BY MIRABELLE

Headline here

A MAN WHO WAS REFUSED PERMISSION for a an extension to his bathroom has taken his protest to the roads.

Gilliam Sensible, 42, of High Hopes, Whoft, has been having a "whopping Crippen of a row" with Framly Borough Council since they refused him permission for an extension to his bathroom in 1990.

"I've started this fight, and I don't intend to continue it without finishing it," he explained to passing reporters yesterday.

"The council have treated me like fluff," he went further.

UNCOVERED

Mr Sensible's latest protest was UNCOVERED by policemen who pulled him over on the FR404 for travelling at 4mph. However, when they knocked on the window of his Ford Turnip, he was in the shower.

On further investigation, they discovered that the glovebox had been converted into a soapdish and that one of the rear seats was a toilet. Mr Sensible was banned from driving for 18 months.

"I've got to wash somewhere," explained a soapy Gilliam from his passenger seat yesterday.

ROAD REPORT

with Oliver Singultus-Hiccup

A MAJOR ROAD REDESIGNATION is planned for this weekend in Codge. Little Passage, between Killiard's Pet Shop and The Bride and Best Man pub is being reclassified from a one-way street to a three-way street. Motorists are advised to negotiate the three-way system using a new virtual roundabout that has been erected at www.littlepassageroadworks.gov.uk. Double click your mouse when you wish to leave the roundabout and leave plenty of time for your journey.

TEMPORARY TRAFFIC LIGHTS are in operation every four feet along the FR303 to slow speeding traffic during the Vetiver's Bachanaal at Molford County Showground. So, that's a road to avoid this week, unless you really like traffic lights.

MAJOR STRUCTURAL ENGINEERING WORK is taking place on the pedestrian bridge by Sockford Fire Station. The work, to raise the footbridge over 40 feet, will allow the passage of the fire engine's ladder at full perpendicular stretch, and seemed a good idea at the time.

Boy robbed

A TERRIFIED 8-YEAR OLD was attacked at rulerpoint and locked in a horrid toilet during a partly armed robbery in Chutney.

School Counsellor Tricky Dixon of Chutney Junior School told reporters how it happened.

"It was the last day of term," he said, "and, like her classmates, the little girl had brought a toy into school. Everything was fine until a robber, tempted by the look of the girl's toy, jumped on her in the bogs.

The suspect smacked his victim in the chops, calling her a 'stink' and a 'frutter,' before making off with her favourite toy - a million pounds.

He then came back, tied her hands to her face with rubber bands, stuffed stuff up her nose and locked her in a toilet that had not been flushed for several days.

The girl, Sarah Pepperkite, who cannot be named for the usual reasons, cried for "ages and ages and ages and ages," said a spokesfriend

Police are baffled by the attack. "Why would anyone want to steal a million pounds?" asked Sgt Stig Bluff of Chutney Constambulary.

Her attacker is described as white, 4ft tall and about eight. He wore grey and blue trainers and school uniform, and smelled of cheese and onion crisps.

Anyone with information should contact Molford Police on or Crimestoppers on 0800 555111.

'Tis the season to be missing!

by Katy Blirdsnest

A POPULAR MP screamed non-stop for seventeen hours this week when he realised what kind of a world he was living in!

For it was he - Ianbeale Steeplecocque, a popular MP for Framley NE - who first noticed that Codge, where he lives, hasn't had an Autumn since 1998!

According to the time-watching MP, the blame for the missing season lies with calendar manufacturers. Since 1997, a persistent printing error has caused the W.I. charity calendar (used by most of Codge's residents) to be printed with the Autumn months missing. Knowing no better, for four years, the village has gone straight from Summer to Winter overnight. It is only now, Steeplecocque told me, that the cost of three years' worth of missing September's, October's and December's are starting to count their own cost.

DEAD HEDGEHOGS

Steeplecocque first noticed that something wasn't quite alright when he found "a load of dead field-mice,

Mr Thubnall's aeroplane lies in the wreckage it caused with its crash.
PHOTOGRAPH BY JEMMA SVENGALLIGAN

tortoises and hedgehogs" literally around his back garden. The sudden change in climate from very hot to not hot at all must of happened far too quickly for them to be able to collect any nuts or warmth, I'd expect, and he agrees.

"After I'd cleared up their sweet little corpses with my favourite Newby's rake I realised that this was the first time that I'd used it for several", whimpered Steeplecocque, "years.

BAD FRUIT

"Then, staring at my fruit trees, I realised that not a single leaf had fallen from them since the birth of my son, Peterbeale, in 1999."

Steeplecocque

"The trunks had buckled, branches were creaking at me and there were thousands upon thousands of grotesquely impacted apples and strawberries still hanging from their swollen stalks."

And it's not just MPs! Local scientists had until recently been baffled as to why darkness tended to fall just as they took their elevenses. Apparently it's just something to do with clocks.

"I only hope we've caught this problem in time," fretted Steeplecocque.

SHAVEN

It may not be that easy, though. The ladies of Codge Women's Institute have warned calendar users that they have already prepared themselves for next year's *Shaven W.I.* and it will now be too much bother for them to find three more volunteers who are willing to participate in any way at allsoever.

So it looks like Spring, Summer, Winter for the village of Codge for a while to come!

AIR CRASH HORROR

Squirrels find themselves frozen before they have time to buy nuts for the winter.
PHOTOGRAPH BY SIMON ROAST

RESIDENTS of St Eyot's have been restaging the terrifying moment when a light aircraft hit overhead power cables and crashed into their homes.

The pilot of the Cessna single-engine aircraft, Terry Thubnall, was trapped in the cockpit for ten minutes after it hit the 440,000 volt power line and plummeted pilot-first into innocent villagers' lives a month ago.

Mr Thubnall, 46, of Copcobmanbury, was shown to Framley General hospital, but later pronounced dodo.

HUGE

Sindy Doyle, of Kidney Lane, St Eyot's, said she was outside cleaning the lawn when she saw a "huge" flash and heard a "huge" bang. She later called the emergency services with a phone.

Ms Doyle was among 250 villagers involved in the restaging of the incident last Thursday, which included a perfect replica of the Cessna and a Mr Thubnall lookalike.

"I did my bit - I went out and cleaned the lawn again and waited for the huge bang," wizened Ms Doyle yesterday, "but I didn't really enjoy it. Especially the huge flash and the huge bang. They were a bit too huge - not really in keeping with the spirit of the original crash."

However, one villager who wasn't taking part is Tim and Sally Shoppington, whose daughter Flax was being born during the explosion.

"We couldn't really commit to it, what with the baby," explained busty stunner Sally yesterday, "but we might join in next month."

"Queen 'will never die' say voices" says man

A DOCTOR from Whoft claims to have heard voices telling him that Her Majesty The Queen will never die.

Overweight GP Colyn Graveyard, 62, said yesterday, "I regularly receives testimony concerning the monarch's immortality.

Her Majesty will probably live forever I believe everything they say. Would you like a gypsy cream?"

One neighbour described Graveyard as a "old queen with a whopping barbiturate habit" who asked to remain anonymous.

Police say they do not understand.

CAN DO!

by Taunton Mishap

A WRIPPLE SCHOOLBOY who raised £4200 for a TV charity, has received the highest award ever given by long-running children's programme *Flagship*.

14-year-old Kerin Fitzperrin collected over 16,000 empty aluminium cans to send to *Flagship*'s annual charity appeal - more than any other viewer - entitling him to a Gold Flagship Badge with real fur and moving eyes.

The producer of the show, Baxterby Parnell, recognised Kerin's achievement at a special ceremony, held in Fitzperrin's absence at the Marbleborough Hotel, Sockford.

"Thanks to Kerin's amazing effort, we have enough aluminium to buy a whole herd of caribou for Eritrean blind children. We'd like to wish Kerin a speedy recovery. His was truly an amazing effort," Parnell told.

Kerin, most of whose cans had previously contained lager, India Pale Ale and stout, took a month off

Kerin toasts our photographer shortly before his hospitalisation.
PHOTOGRAPH BY EMELINE AWARDWINNER

school to prepare and recover from his charity project. Doctors at Framley Intensive Care Ward estimate that this is the most beer a human being has ever put in their body.

The award was given in Kerin's absence to *Flagship*'s second-best fundraiser, an 11-year-old girl, who had sent the programme 7 catfood tins and a box of spoons.

"I am not an emergency," screams Framley man, 42

THE ROLE of the emergency services in Framley is to be re-examined after a string of embarrassing incidents.

Martin Sister, an unemployed venerealogist from Whoft, claims he has become the victim of victimisation by police officers, firefighters and ambulances.

Three months ago, Mr Sister snagged a fingernail while opening a carton of milk in his kitchen. Within ten minutes, three separate crews of paramedics had arrived at his home and were fighting each other to perform cardiopulminary resuscitation (CRP) and inject Mr Sister with naloxone and adrenalin.

A few days later, Mr Sister was hosed with water cannon from six fire engines when he lit a cigarette in a pub. And, he claims, two lifeboats arrived when his bath was too hot.

A spokesman for Framley Fire Service apologised to Mr Sister, but claimed "we genuinely thought it was a genuine emergency."

Mr Sister, however, has yet to receive either an apology or compensation from the police, who arrested and charged him with GBH for clapping at a football match.

An emergency vehicle of the sort that won't leave Mr Sister alone.
PHOTOGRAPH BY PINNY SOUSE

An unrepentant Chief Constable Rupert Bone yesterday woofed, "It seemed very clear to my officers that his right hand was trying to maim, or at least kill, his left hand - and they acted accordingly."

Ch Con Bone later went to bed.

Nit suitable for the children !

PARENTS are being warned not to let their children buy copies of a new hit film over the internet - because it has nits.

Skip Butane, Mall Jockey was the biggest grossing movie amongst US filmgoers aged 4-18 last summer, and youngsters on this side of the American Ocean are quite literally bursting with anticipation at the thought of seeing it before its official UK release date of 2012.

Many keen teens are resorting to ordering copies of the film over the net direct from the US, but doctors are warning that the American edition of the film may pose a health risk.

"We feel we must warn parents," said a representative of the World Health Organisation, "that the vast majority of copies of this film have nits."

But internet traders and film fans have tried to calm fears.

"It's not a problem," one told me. "These are Region 1 nits. They won't work on British children, who are coded for Region 2."

"There's nothing to worry about unless your child has been chipped."

Twenty-one piece rap collective return as duo

The two remaining members of the group.
PHOTOSHOP BY STEPHANIE SCHLATER

Something familiar, something amusing, something for everyone, there's some comedy this week

Frankie, a well known Framley face, is hoping to tickle your funny bone "good and hard."
PHOTOSHOP BY RYAN STUBBLEFIELD

 by Ursula Cloybeam

THE LAUGHING BULLET, Whoft's only comedy club will finally be reopened this Friday night after a protracted legal battle with Framley Borough Council Trading Standards ended in the horrific death of the main complainant.

And Frankie "Oh dear, are we crying now?" Hayes, the club's owner and compère, persuaded me in no uncertain terms that there's seven shades of fun to be kicked out of an evening at his new *Go On, Make Me A Laughter I Can't Refuse* show every Saturday night, and I'm certainly agreeing to write about it every week.

THREATENING NUTTER

"We're very excited about our opening night, aren't we, Ursula? Are you writing all of this down?" pointed out Frankie. "We've got a true star, Barrie Lyle, appearing on the main stage with what he's promised on his young son's life will be the best performance of his entire career."

Lyle opened for Jackie Mason during his Broadway run last year and whilst he received several Hollywood movie offers apparently he still

needed to be reminded that he owed Frankie more than a few favours!

"Without me, Ursula, he'd be absolutely funning nowhere and if he ever treats me with that sort of disrespect again he'll certainly know which side his coffin is buttered on," he continued to scare me.

EIGHTEEN STITCHES

But don't be put off just because Lyle may be visibly shaking on the night. Frankie says that the *Puppetry of the Groin* section of Barrie's act will always go down a storm. From what Frankie told me, when Barrie asks for a couple of helpers from the audience, you should be prepared for some eye opening tricks with two safety pins and an elastic band.

And don't forget, if you're thinking of coming along on Friday that, by Frankie's popular demand, the Heckler's Gibbet will be operational from the moment the doors open.

And the moment that the doors open at the Gammon Way venue is 8pm. Tickets are priced at £10 or £8 for your dear old mum and can be booked in advance although woe betide you if you then fail to turn up.

cc this to Frankie for approval, would you, Stephanie?

by Adam Wrent

UP AND COMING local 21-piece rap collective The Christian Cross have relaunched themselves as a duo.

Leading lights of the self-promclaimed Soolin Liquid Beatz Bruthahood, The Christian Cross are Whoft's most popular crew, drawing crowds to their old-skool barn-parties and, in their words of one of their own songs, "keepin' it real from Whoft to the boundaries of St Eyot's churchyard."

The group's distinctive look, with clothes worn back-to-front and two days running, has sparked a craze amongst their fans, and forced several local launderettes to the brink of bankruptcy.

"It's all about unity and pulling together," said K-Rabbit, one of only two members to survive the brutal infighting that has decimated the group in the two weeks since their formation.

His partner, Mixmaster Timothy Bennett agreed. "Though many of our brothers have died in the course

of recording our demo, the message of our music is still 'Peace'."

The factional divisions within the group led to a clear "Eastside" and "Westside" split that had always threatened to erupt into murder. A series of tit-for-tat driveby poisonings in the past week was only the cherry on the cake of the violence that has driven the group to become smaller.

"Two members / is the way it's gonna be / goin' back to our roots / like Peters and Lee," rapped K-Rabbit to me, before looking suitably embarrassed.

The Christian Cross' first demo *Help Tha Police (With Their Enquiries)* is available by sending a cheque or postal order for £1.99 (made out to Mrs Bennett) to The SLBB, 27a Browning Crescent, Whoft, FM4 6PP.

Lorem ipsum dolor sit amet

LOREM IPSUM dolor sit amet, consetetur sadipscing elitr, sed diam nonumy eirmod tempor invidunt ut labore et dolore magna aliquyam erat, sed diam voluptua.

At vero eos et accusam et justo duo dolores et ea rebum. Stet clita kasd gubergren, no sea takimata sanctus est Lorem ipsum dolor sit amet.

Lorem ipsum dolor sit amet, consetetur sadipscing elitr, sed diam nonumy eirmod tempor invidunt ut labore et dolore magna aliquyam erat, sed diam voluptua. At vero eos et accusam et justo duo dolores et ea rebum.

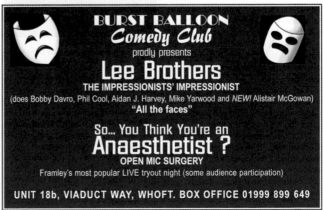

dredged the lake for four solid hours but only one of the trolley wheels and a bobble hat was recovered. A vote was unanimously passed that safety measures be reviewed before the next race.

Smashing

Interesting guest

GARDENING CLUB. - The speaker for the February meeting was the gardening correspondent of the *Whoft Sentinel*, The Amazing Dantini. The Amazing Dantini talked at length about the history of conjuring, showed overhead projector drawings of master magicians like Harry Houdini and David Nixon, and pulled a tulip bulb from behind the chairman's ear. Questions from the floor about gardening were dismissed, but some rings were made to link and unlink at will. As the appreciative members passed a unanimous vote of thanks, The Amazing Dantini had a bit of a cry.

Fracton

Just desserts

WOMEN'S INSTITUTE. - The meeting opened at 11.20am, and attendance records were taken. All were welcomed and a birthday kicking was administered to Mrs Jowett, Mrs Franklyn and Mrs Overboard. A plea of "mercy" was passed by 3 to 1. Next meeting on the 19th.

Litter discussed

FRACTON AND AREA LITTER WARDENS ASSOCIATION. - A meeting was held on Tuesday 4th at Lismond House under the chairman Leonard Flintlock. The following is a brief resume of what took place, although a full account of the minutes would blow your mind. Increased litter levels in Oscarwinninganimatornick Park were noted by the committee. The new bags were given out, with all members expressing their delight at the new logo. A vote was taken regarding the choice of refreshment for the next meeting, with Bacardi Breezers and Nik Naks being passed by 183 votes to 171. The secretary, Mrs Josephine LaPatapap, in her report, outlined the activities of the society during the year, highlighting those of special interest, such as the informative weekend spent trapped behind the curtains in August. The issue of hiring bands of alien mercenaries to help with the wardens' work was again brought up by committee member Mr Voules, but gained little support.

St Eyot's

The waste of a time

ST EYOT'S FRIENDS OF A GREEN. - Invited speaker, Frank Boseunit, gave an insightful presentation by explaining, in particularly graphic detail, how he recycled all of his own waste. After several members made their excuses and fainted, he went on to produce even more of his award-winning mucus. In retaliation, the committee

voted unanimously to present the speaker with an ice cream cone stuffed with handfuls of members' loose pubic hair. Mr Boseunit was finally forced to play his trump card - setting fire to his toenails. The evening was adjudged a huge success as Boseunit ran screaming towards the boating lake with great purpose.

Semi-skimmed

THE BROTHERHOOD OF CHRISTIAN MILKMEN. - The St Eyot's Dairy BOCM met at their monthly meeting in the monthly meeting hall of St Eyot's Dairy. The meeting was opened by chairmilkman Br Nicholas "Creamy" Simpson, and the minutes of the previous meeting were read. The power of the Lord was felt moving the table to discuss gold top orders in Welling Street, and prayers were taken for an increased natural yoghurt uptake in the northern districts. Br Galadriel Float witnessed to the love of Christ through his gift of the Dairylea Cheese Triangle, and showed slides. Truly, the assembled members were told, the Lord moves in a mysterious way, gently, at about six miles an hour under electric power, with a slight rattling sound, quite early in the morning, his wonders to perform. Prayers and milkshakes.

Codge

Well Adjusted

WELL GREEN RENOVATION GROUP. - The Well Green renovation has been attractively completed, but within a matter of days, despite the raising of the perimeter wall to 11 inches,

the new benching had been struck by a pigeon lime and the inverted cross was back. A motion proposing the addition of a twelfth inch was passed by 13 to 1, and it was suggested that a protective copper dome be constructed just under the sky, where pigeons live. A vote of 13 to 1 passed the motion that the inverted cross be removed by the Green Warden.

Bellaire

Appalling Acts

UNITED FELLOWHOOD CHURCH. - Members welcomed the Rev Timothy Lipschitz, from Christ's Church UFC in Framley, to lead their service. Timothy opened with the words, "The Lord is all I have, so I put my hope in him" and the hymn *And Did Those Feet In Ancient Times Walk Upon England's Mountains Green And Was The Holy Lamb Of God*. In his talk, Timothy said that he needed a ladder to see over such things as the World Trade Center, and was promptly arrested by police under the Prevention of Terrorism Act. As he struggled with armed officers and was bundled into the back of a car, he was shouting about the ladder in the dream of Jacob as described in the book of Genesis.

Slide Show

RENDEZVOUS. - On Wednesday, members and their wives were given a slide show entitled 'The Land of Chalk Drawings' presented by Rendezvous member David Frigg. He explained how he remembered visiting the land in the 1970s quite clearly, although he admitted it might just have been on the television.

Sponsored Bollocks

BELLAIRE PENSIONERS. - Bellaire's elderly residents took part in a Sponsored Bollocks this month. Entrants' specialist subjects ranged from 'Why We'll Never Join The Common Market' and 'Here, Don't Tell Your Dad' to 'Even Doing Nothing Costs Too Bloody Much' and 'This New-fangled Running Water.' The event raised £380 towards new DJ decks at the Retired Persons Tea Dance.

Prince's Freshborough

A party

GRANDPARENTS, PARENTS AND TODDLERS FEDERATION. - The Grandparents, Parents and Toddlers Federation recognises that up to 100% of grandparents, parents and toddlers spend time with each other. Many grandparents care for their grandchildren while parents care for their parents (the grandparents) and their children (the grandchildren). The Grandparents, Parents and Toddlers Federation has funding to set up Grandparents, Parents and Toddlers Federations throughout the district, and is linking with the Toddlers, Tinkers, Tots and Pre-Tots Group that meets every year in the home of the Grandparents, Parents and Toddlers Federation, Grandparents, Parents and Toddlers Federation House in Molford. A party will be held on September 5th to try to decide the joint federations' purpose and a new name, as it is now unanimously agreed that The Grandparents, Parents, Toddlers, Tinkers, Tots and Pre-Tots Group Federation was too expensive to put on stationery. The party will also give everyone a chance to offer help to absolutely everyone else

Slovenly

Namesake

ROTARY CLUB. - The Slovenly Rotarians were treated to an evening's entertaining anecdotes by guest speaker Stanley Lebor. In his delightful and lively address, 'Not THE Stanley Lebor!' he described some of the hilarious pitfalls of having the same name as a famous celebrity, the actor Stanley Lebor, who played Howard Hughes in the BBC TV Series *Ever Decreasing Circles*.

The big one

SLOVENLY SURVIVALISTS. - Mr Norris led an interesting discussion on tinned food and showed members his Armalite

What's on

MONDAY	**WEDNESDAY**	**FRIDAY**
The South Molford Players present 'An Evening in Wripple' by Adrain Showler, The Social Club, Molford St. Darren, 7.45pm. Tickets £5, concessions £3.50. Residents of Wripple are advised that they will find some scenes distasteful and consequently are asked not to attend.	**Lunchtime Recital** with Malcolm Breach, violin, and Martin Ridgewell, Playstation2. Selections from Bruch, Fifa 2002 and Rodgers & Hammerstein 2002. St. Darren's Church, Molford, 1pm to 2.30pm, admission free but there is a savings-linked exit charge.	**'From Explosive Anger to Inner Peace for a short time and then right back to Full-Blown Rage'**, Troy Griffiths shares 20 years of intermittently successful research into controlling his temper around the wife & kids. Sockford Mill, Sockford Green, 7.30pm, wear loose clothing.
TUESDAY	**Story & Song Time**, Adult Literature section, Framley County Library, 10am to 12pm. Hosted by Suzi DD, an occasion for all the family men, strictly no audience participation.	**Charity coffee morning** in aid of Robert Mugabe's election fund, the grounds of Wensleydate Manor, 11am to 1pm. Bring your own damn coffee.
Barn Dance with Grand Funk Railroad, The Dressingham Memorial Hall, 7.30pm to 11pm. Tickets £7 including ploughman's breakfast and raffle entry (top prize - white label copy of the Rollo remix of GFR's *Time Machine*).		**SATURDAY**
	THURSDAY	**Fundraising sale**, Framley Wildlife Reserve Visitor Centre, 10am-4pm, Thu. Many rare birds eggs, otter teeth, commemorative stuffed and mounted endangered species from our own wetlands.
Keep-Fit for Good-Looking Frustrated Mature Ladies, The Hightower Rooms, Sockford, 3.30pm to 4.30pm. For further details contact Vince on 01999 480 086	**Quiz Night**, teams of up to 2-82 people. Entry fee £3 per person, answers available beforehand at £5 each, £2 on the day after. The Naked Landlord, Big Godley, tel 01999 722693.	

FOCUS ON... BATLEY

with Katie Blirdsnest

This week in our weekly A-X of Framley District Councils, we reach B, and that's for Batley!

Batley is one of Framley's most deprived neighbourhoods, and home to the notorious Dungeon sink estate, but that doesn't seem to get the locals down!

We sent our roving reporters to bring us the skinny on the Framley district with the fastest growing population in the Northern Hemisphere! And that must be something to SHOUT about, probably!

FOCUS ON FACTS
Dungeon

In Dungeon, you're never more than 30 feet from a social worker.

The number of pupils shot in the head by staff at Dungeon Infant School has fallen for 2 out of the previous 3 years.

Due to repeated incidents, local pub The Drink & Drive has had all glass removed "by police request". Window panes have been put into storage and beer is poured straight into customers' cupped hands.

Dungeon was built on an ancient Indian burial ground.

The estate was opened by Enoch Powell in 1964 and made the headlines in 1987 when Princess Diana visited the new Community Centre and was not attacked.

Every single home in Dungeon is broken into every single night, often, police believe, by the same man; a burglar dressed as a different burglar.

Dungeon has more single fathers than there are grains of sand in the mighty desert.

Residents of neighbouring estates have complained about the level of noise on the Dungeon Estate caused by Dungeon residents complaining about the level of noise on the estate.

A CRY FOR THE HELP

THE TREE, which Batley Council installed two weeks ago in an attempt to brighten up the Dungeon Estate, committed suicide on Tuesday by felling itself. Stump psychologists believe the felling to have been a cry for help. The Council is next proposing to erect a CoffeeStop on the site, where residents will be able to enjoy a wide range of executive business breakfast options and a shiatsu sausage.

PHOTOGRAPH BY JEREMY OW

Whores' plumbing "all messed up"

THERE WERE FRESH calls

TREEHOUSE INTERIORS
WENDY HOUSE JOINERY & DESIGN
**GOLDEN SHOWERS, SUB DOM
PRE-OP TRANSEXUAL
CITY & GUILDS CDT
18 YEAR OLD NEW IN AREA**
call SHELLEY on 09
competitive rates

One of the popular calling cards, swapped with a child by our reporter.

yesterday for the authorities to act to introduce legislation to attempt to begin to encourage moves to start to curb the activities of prostitutes operating on the Dungeon Estate, writes one of our writers.

The Framley District Plumbers guild, who are the main movers behind the new demands, are up in arms, citing the level and number of services being offered by enterprising streetmadams.

"No-one minds the ladies of the night earning an honest crust, but there are some things they are simply not qualified to do, like bleed radiators or service a boiler," said Grand Plumber Christopher Testquardc. "We want to stress to the public that, should you find a build up of waste matter in your outflow pipe, please call a certified plumber, not a tart."

But local residents think the prostitutes are merely plugging a gap in the markets.

"I waited four months for a registered plumbist to fix my storage tank," said one smiling local homeowner, "but a quick call to a number I found in a phone box got me a whore with an adjustable spanner, who not only did an excellent job in under an hour, but took it in the gob. And swallowed too."

And it's not just plumbing! According to delirious residents, the women of easy virtue are doing everything from babysitting to satellite television installation, all alongside their usual excellent work up trap two. Plumbers are furious.

"We could try and claw back some of the ground we've lost, but there are some things my members just won't do," shrugged Mr Testquardc, and hung up. Click!

If you require a prostitute, call our 24 hr helpdesk on 01999 854 766.

Joyrider bother

YOUNG HOOLIGANS from the Dungeon estate, some as old as fourteen, have been crying havoc and letting slip the dogs of joyriding!

Car theft has always been a problem on the estate, but gangs of teenages have now begun welding the stolen vehicles together to make one big car, which they then race around the streets, keeping residents awake at all hours of the day and all of the night.

Annoyed residents have told police of a car the size of a cross-channel ferry looming out of the fog at them, shattering windows with a single blast on its massive horn, then vanishing into the night as quickly as it appeared. The car, which is crewed by up to eighty joyriders, rips up pavements and eats postboxes as if they were Shredded Wheat Bitesize. Although officers have searched several lockup garages for the enormous car, they have only found a skateboard and some old paint with a stick in it.

"They'll soon get bored of it, they always do," said community liaison officer PC Mary Pleistocene. "Last year all we had were complaints about the kids stealing lampposts to play 'Street Snooker', now there's this big car. Until a third person is killed, it won't be high on our list of priorities."

Playground vandaled

A PENSIONERS' playground on the Dungeon estate has been vandalised by rioting children, who sprayed the word "bum" on the side of the slide then set it all on fire with their tiny children's torches.

The children had rioted after their last remaining play area was eaten by Wolves.

Former midfield dynamo and England international the late Billy Wright was unavailable for comment yesterday, though chairman Sir Jack Hayward has issued a formal apology.

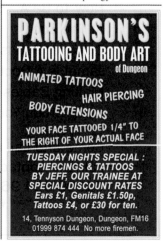

Zoo arrival nerves

by Pharaoh Clutchstraw

STAFF AT FRAMLEY ZOO are keeping their fingers crossed for a historic new arrival this spring. For the fifth year in succession, veterinary experts are trying to persuade two zookeepers to breed successfully in captivity.

Zookeepers *(bestiarius vulgaris)* are an endangered species, their numbers in the wild having dwingled to around 1000 globally, with perhaps another approximate 110 in possible captivity maybe.

"They're notoriously shy creatures," explained Breeding Committee chief Danny Vemble in his broad Australian brogue, "and although they're not without charisma, they do prefer to sit around eating for twelve hours a day, which isn't very horny."

Zookeepers mate between March and May, and predicting the female's fertile period remains a frustratingly elusive challenge.

"We test for raised levels of oestrus in the female zookeeper," explained Vemble, "but the mating period only lasts three days, so we have to be as accurate as someone trying to land a cut-glass jumbo jet on a grain of rice.

IT GETS WORSE

"And the real danger is if we

Look at the penguin.

PHOTOGRAPH BY INSERAT BONT

introduce the female to the male too early, because they end up fighting over the bamboo buffet or kicking the daylights out of the staff toilets."

The pair, Xiao Lin and Bun Hat, were first introduced to each other six years ago. Xiao Lin is on long term loan from Ueno Zoo in Szechuan, and Bun Hat was one of three cubs born to a pair of zookeepers from San Diego Zoo in

1972.

There were concerns at the time that, because the father of Bun Hat was The Man From The Elephant House, their birth-line may have been weakened, but he has since sired three other offspring, one in the wild, so the team from Framley have little doubt about the fertility of their prize specimen.

THEN

Mr Vemble showed me pictures of Bun Hat's visible arousal, which were fascinating, if uncomfortable, and explained how zookeepers communicate by scent released from glands under their peaked caps. He then showed me further pictures of genitalia, and commented on the similarities between the "undercarriage" of a male Red Zookeeper and the "Sunday lunch" of a Giant Zookeeper.

"We'll know if we've been successful by July," concluded Mr Vemble. "Look at the Xmas stocking on that one!"

Woman shrugs and drives off after being killed

A woman shrugged her shoulders and drove off after being killed as she attempted to reverse her car into her kitchen, a court was told.

Pamomile Kilter, 41, of Kidney Bean Passage, Whoft, posthumously admitted driving without much care and attention and failing to submit to a breath test after the crash at a car park in Wripple. Kilter was fined £200 with £55 costs and had her licence endorsed with points.

Hunt for right bugger

Police are looking for a man who broke into Stapney's Nudist Supplies in Codge on Tuesday. The man, described as a "right bugger", stole a marble statue of a bear and four copies of *Exchange and Mart*.

The public are being warned not to approach the man, who is also wanted in connection with the theft of a matelot's costume from Pegg's The Chemist and the removal of the colour violet from the Sockford Reservoir rainbow.

Murder amnesty

Feb 14th has a special significance this year - it's being declared a controversial Murder Amnesty day, when murderers can freely declare themselves to anyone who likes being murdered. What have I got to do to get sacked? Love, Damiun.

Man, 78, sees own reflection for first time

ALBERTON BEASTMASTER, a retired monogamist from St Eyot's, had the shock of his life last Wednesday when he caught sight of his reflection for the very first time in his life.

"I'd just left the chemists, having bought a lollipop and some Bonjela. There was a noise behind me - I later discovered it was a moth - so I turned round, and, bless my soul, there was another me, still inside the shop."

Rev Beastmaster

Mr Beastmaster attempted to leave the shop again, but "it turned out to be impossible. I couldn't work out what was going on."

"It was like I had an identical twin, mocking my every move - but an identical twin who looked nothing like me."

Alberton, whose only previous encounter with his appearance was through a photograph of himself taken in 1951, is having a great deal of trouble coming to terms with the collapse of his face over the last fifty years.

"I didn't know it was me at first. I mean, I never had this stupid haircut before, and loads more teeth, and I was on a donkey. What in God's name is going on?"

Vernon Tutbury, senior lecturer in Physics at Framley Community College said Mr Beastmaster's reflection wasn't likely to be a one off.

"Everyone has a reflection, it just depends what you're standing in front of. You will see your reflection quite clearly in the highly polished surface of my silver shoes, for example, while your reflection in a brick wall is very dim indeed."

Mr Beastmaster says he will be staying indoors from now on, near some cloth.

NEWS

VANDAL ATTACK ON 'OLD PERCY'

By BUNCO BOOTH

MINDLESS vandal no-do-wells have added a saucy 30-metre tall figure around Chutney Hill's famous ancient chalk phallus.

The original Anglo Saxon cock, the only one of its kind in the whole wide world, is generally thought to have been discovered in 1952 by a passing lawnmower.

The addition to the turf penis, or 'Old Percy' as locals have been known to call it, was executed in white paint late on Saturday evening.

Local archeologists believe that the jubilatory gentleman may have been added by beer lags as part of an ancient booze ritual.

Robert Hilfiger of Whoft Archaeological Society, who's an expert on these things, appeared horrified by the addition.

"The sick individuals responsible for this are the scum of the earth. They're not fit to lick the shoes off my feet"

The vandals' work and the original figure (inset)
PHOTOGRAPH BY WILMINGTON LONGMAN

A local parent is also worried. Worried about the effect that the hill figure could have on her children.

"Everyone loved 'Old Percy', but this is pure filth.", said she. "It leaves nothing to the imagination. Imagine if one of my own saw it and tried to copy it?"

Not everyone is annoyed at the recent appearance of the paint man, however. Trevor St Saint, an upstanding member of Chutney parish seemed pleased by its presence.

"It's fantastic", he said gesturing at me using fingers thick with white paint, "It was only a matter of time before someone revealed the joyous owner of this god-like nob"

Mr St. Saint went on to suggest that in a matter of weeks, hundreds of chalk offspring could appear on surrounding hills, bowling greens and perhaps even on the walls of municipal buildings.

"Now that Old Percy has been given arms, legs and the wherewithal to walk, it's entirely possible that he may attempt to make congress with the prehistoric chalk vagina on the other side of the hill."

Drugs star in rock charge

by CHALLENGER PUTNEY

Local celebrity Leon Orbit, former rock guitarist with the former rock group Deaf Horse, is spending some time in the company of the police after a raid at his home in Wripple.

Following an anonymous tip-off from a local magistrate, a search warrant was issued and fourteen uniform officers arrived at Shangri-La-De-Da, Orbit's luxury 9-bedroom bungalow, in the early hours of Saturday afternoon.

They seized an extremely large quantity of illegal substances including canasta, purple parliaments, methamphethamphethameths, hundreds and thousands, and several bottles of barbarbarans.

They also took away scales, mirrors, rolling pins, bungs, exhaust pipes, children's socks, birthday cards, needles, thread, two boxes of non-safety matches, a Ladyshave and a copy of the Reader's Digest Book of Herbs. Oh, and they rolled up his lawn and took it away for analysis.

Mr Orbit denies absolutely anything.

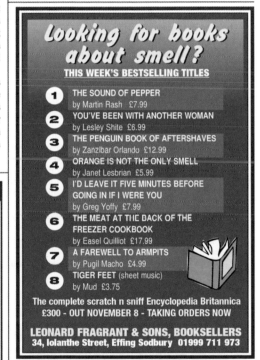

Codge vicar suspended

A VICAR from Codge has been suspended after an investigation into his activities revealed he ought to be suspended, a conclusion reached after an investigation proved this to be the case.

The Reverend Easy-Peasy Carlton, 61, has been stripped of his dog collar and ordered to "become an ironmonger or something" by the General Synod of the Church of England, the standard punsihment for clerical misdemeanour.

Although details of the activities that led to his suspension are hazy, parishioners suspect his practice of "riding" the bells during Sunday services may have been a factor.

"He'd clamber onto the 12-3-21 Tenor bell, over the bearing, and across the gudgeon, onto the headstock, wrap his legs around the sound bow, and read his sermon from there, swinging back and forth," said one churchgoer confusing me completely with too much information about bells.

The Right Reverend Gussard Prime, Bishop of Framley, was "horrified" by tales of Rev Carlton's activities.

"This is the sort of behaviour that would have God turning in his grave," the Bishop said.

I come to bury school production not to praise it

Julius Caesar
St Gahan's School, Framley

by Ursula Cloybeam

NO WORDS OF MINE can adequately describe the shambles masquerading as a production of *Julius Caesar*, that was presented to an audience of about a hundred snoring people at St Gahan's School last Saturday evening. But I'm going to try to try to convey it as best as I can.

This was supposed to be the swansong of retiring Head of Drama, Colin Frilly, and certainly bore comparison with what he apparently considers the fine work that he has been produced at the school over the years.

UNMITIGATED BALLS

As in so many school productions, cast members were practically inaudible and mumbled their speeches - in sharp contrast to this reviewer, whose excellently projected criticisms were s h o u t e d a t t h e s t a g e w i t h considerable vigour and clarity.

The cast and scenery included Martin Ffooulkess in the lead role,

whom was considered a controversial choice by this reviewer as he was significantly too young and too short and too ginger to play someone less like a schoolboy than Julius Caesar than could be imagined by this reviewer.

I understand that Mr Ffooulkkess harbours some desire to become a professional actor one day. On this showing, I would advise him to pay a swift visit to his careers Advisor for extra car park attendant lessons, and believe me if there's anything I know about, I know about acting! And music was composed and performed by (mosaic teacher?) David Daddy.

HOPELESS CRETINS

Also appearing were Barry de Lemon as an immature Brutus, Denny Bin as an underage Cassius, Martin Ffooulkess doubling up as an underdeveloped ginger man in a dress called Calphurnia, and Mark Anthony in an unimpressive debut as Nathan Haircut.

The audience were little help at all and refused to join in either my rousing chants of "Ceasar, he's behind you!" or "the director's a wanker", both of which are usually consideried a highlight of any Frilly show.

BRILLIANT AEROPLANE

However, things improved after I made a paper aeroplane from my programme to repeatedly throw at the actors. The little dance I did every time I went up to retrieve it certainly livened things up onstage, and I was beset by parents during the

interval eager to speak to me about it. (Does anyone know how to get orange squash and biscuit stains out of a cream polyester blouse?)

Then the second bit of the play got underway and I had to start humming again to keep from falling asleep.

STUPID COLIN

There were tears aplenty after the final curtain as Mr Frilly was called upon to give a farewell speech to the strangely upset cast. As they consoled each other, it fell to the many former

Barry de Lemon as Brutus confronts Elizabeth Nounce as Fagin in this unengaging production.
PHOTOGRAPH BY JEREMY FONZ

pupils, who had foolishly attended the final night of Colin's godawful final production, to escort me from the hall into the waiting police van.

After what has to be described as a wasted evening for all concerned, I can only repeat what I said to the arresting officer, and hope that new head of drama, Burton Touche, has considerably more joy than stupid Colin did with the empty pool of talent that St Gahan's School has to offer! Stupid Colin!

● ● ● ● ● ● ● ● ● ● ● ● ● ● ● ● ● ● ● ●●●
URSULA'S VERDICT: Shit
● ● ● ● ● ● ● ● ● ● ● ● ● ● ● ● ● ● ● ●●●

I just hit paydirt

**By our Blues Correspondent,
GEECHIE WRYLY**

DADDY BEAT me as a kiddy. Daddy used to beat me. Got myself a brand new rifle. Gonna draw a bead on him.

Oh Lord won't you help me save my Daddy's farm? Oh Lord won't you send me one last kind word? My sister got sick and I'm stinging from the weals. Got a tin of a tobacco and a blade to hawk.

My bones is dry. Them horses is whinnying.

I'm going up to the red barn with a ax. I just hit paydirt.

Next week: Where's my Jesus now?

Reader annoyed about something

MISS, -- Regarding the alleged 'Wishing Well' on Sockford Green.

I have been using this 'well' regularly for over eleven years, and yet I still haven't sprouted wings, or had an everlasting dinner with Lorraine Kelly.

How much is that to ask?

MRS RENARDIE GRALEFRIT
Wishing Well Cottage
Sockford Green
Sockford

Sponsored event raises £470

MISS, -- On behalf of Batley Safehouse, I'd like to thank the clear majority who supported our Sponsored Spend last month.

After twelve long hours in The Arnhem Centre, we had raised well over £469, and managed to spend a magnificent total of £33,000. Although this was sadly short of our intended target of £50,000, we feel the whole event was still a roaring success nonethenevertheless.

Well done, everyone!

Our next event will be the auctioning of the 26,000 loaves of bread and 1052 shirts we now have blocking our hall.

TANSAD PARIAH
Batley Safehouse,
255 cummings Dungeon
Dungeon Estate, Batley FM6

Everyone's rubbish

MISS, -- People say things always come in threes, but I'd be hard pushed to agree. What on earth can they be talking about?

Since Framley Council contracted out refuse collection to Pegasus Disposal at the end of November, my front lounge has been full of bins.

Apparently my home was reclassified from a 'collection point' to a 'delivery point' in the administrative changeover.

I have written to Mayor D'Ainty on several occasions, but he insists that nothing can be done until I provide over 15,000 photos of the dustmen responsible.

So can I have a Framley Examiner mug (Botham)?

RON OSCALATOR
Duncannorvellin', St Eyot's

What about my children?

MISS, -- I was distressed to hear that they intend to close the Gypsy House at Framley Zoo, apparently because of "human rights concerns".

I have to ask, if the Gypsy House closes, where will my children ever see Gypsies in their natural habitat, dancing and playing their caravans? Through the television?

It's political correctness gone mad!

TIMOTHY RUHR
Monk's Hoover,
Whoft

Gives her side of the story

MISS, -- I wish to complain about the tone of your coverage of my visit to the chemist's last Wednesday ("How Many Plasters Does She Need?" FE1709).

Usually your standards of journalism are of the highest. Your story about my reversing into a parking space on Denegate was a model of clarity and restraint, and the supplement on my new trousers was not only well-designed but informative and fun.

But in the case of the chemist visit story, you let yourselves down badly. I did not put my hands on my hips at the War Memorial, and the Zovirax was not £2.99, but £3.45.

JOAN TWEED
Lissop Cottage, Creme

For the latest on Joan Tweed, see main feature page 7, and 'Comment' on page 42.

Sad news isn't it about hog

MISS, -- Your readers may be sad to hear of the death of Lazenby, Framley's Biggest Hedgehog.

He had been ill for some time with prickleworm, but was making a recovery, until the unfortunate incident at St Eyot's Steam Fair on Sunday.

His tireless work for charity will not be forgotten, and a special children's ward will bear his name in memory of the many ill children he made happy and itch

He is survived by a wife, Eleanor, and 76 hoglets.

MARGARET HELFPUL
Millbury Mollymandeigh

This is madness

MISS, -- I am absolutely furious.

In 1959, after happily using my address for many years, I was informed that it needed to be extended, by the addition of a 'postcode' (FM4 6TY) at the bottom, just below where I live.

Naturally, I protested, setting fire to the Post Office counter at the Spar on forty-six separate occasions, until the police intervened and I was finally forced to accept this ludicrous situation.

Little did I imagine that, shortly after moving house in 1999, and having had new stationery printed at great expense, I would be told that we were back at square one - my postcode had been *changed* - to FM9 1RE, of all things.

What the hell is going on? There was nothing wrong with the old one, and it had served me well for 40 years. Apparently, the powers that be had given *my* postcode to someone else!

How much red tape have I got to eat in this day and age?

I'm sure many of your listeners will feel the same way, and would love to join my campaign to bring back my postcode.

COLONEL JACK "HAPPY" ISTAMBUL, DFSC (Ret)
The FM4 6TY Campaign
96, Chocolate Spiral
Fracton
FM9 1RE (née FM4 6TY)

She must of known

MISS, -- It's been said before, but I of to agree with your front page last week.

She must of known.

DR ALCOCK BROWN
Roy Newby Villas
Molford

Help me find my old pals!

MISS, -- I wonder if you can help me track down some old chums?

I was in the Whoft Blackshirts from 1935-7, and wish to get in contact with any old boys.

If enough people get in touch, I'd love to organise a traditional cockney open-air barbecue, so we could celebrate my release after 65 years of internment. It'd be great to meet up with the lads, and, who knows, maybe re-enact some old memories.

SPODELEY ARTHRITICLE
196 Tazo Collection Terrace
Massingborough Boxjunction
Whoft
FM3 6TT

Quotes of the Week

"Young people love very old people and we're giving them all a chance to see how it's done."

"We have no recollection of Mr Nugent's letter and won't be doing anything about the sky."

"This is a fantastic opportunity for the people of Framley to see my new bike."

"I know it sounds unbelievable but every single dinner lady is outside."

"That's not my bike."

"Just one feather from this bird can take your arm clean off, so we're closing the park."

"Have you done the Quotes of the Week yet, Trish?"

"The boy's definitely got a future at this club, if he can just stop scoring so many goals."

"We are interested in talking to anyone else who may have been inside the barrel at the time."

C
Y
M
K

Letters should be kept as brief as possible, and preferably be about something. Please include a name, an age, an address, your daytime phone number, and preferred size of Framley Examiner mug (regular, medium, standard or Botham). No correspondence will be entered into, and the judge's decision is final. In the event of a tie, the winner will need two clear legs advantage. Letters should be sent as quickly as possible. No cash. Why not send us letters to THE FRAMLEY EXAMINER, Unit 149b, East Cosset Industrial Park, Parkfields Bypass, Framley FR1 6LH ?

EMERGENCY SERVICES

CHEMISTS
The following chemists are opened on Sundays and in the middles of nights.

BILL'S PILLS 14, The Runs, Molford
WRIPPLE VETIVERS herbal apothecary (elixirs and balms to soothe and succour) The Old Lodge, Gibbet Lane, Wripple
SQUIRE PUFF'S OPIUM DEN Gentleman's club. Finest snuff in Christendom, D--- you! By invitation.
MIKE (07999 965544) outside The Warm Zippy. Crack, speed and speed II.
JACK TAR'S SAILOR'S REMEDY ground cuttlefish, soluble seahorse, wifestoppers and everlasting gumplops. Shed 8, Fracton docks.
WHOFT HOSPICE RADIO AMBULANCE Call Tenby or The Colonel on 01999 866566
BARON SAMEDI'S HAITIIAN CHEMIST for love, for money. Wripple churchyard.
LIBRARIAN WITH HEADACHE CHEMIST librarians with headaches ONLY. Unit 18a, Sockford Smelting Works, Sockford.
DUNGEON PHARMACY only armed chemists in Framley, twin 18mm tills in cupola, barbed wire Lemsip display. Passports must be shown and customers MUST be accompanied by a policeman. 6 Tennyson Dungeon, Batley
FAT TRISTRAM'S The Best Deal In Town. This joint's always jumpin'. Lock-in Fridays. Upstairs nightly at the County Records Office.

DENTIST
In event of dental emergency after 9pm, an emergency drill and mouthwash are kept behind the saloon bar of The Coach & Woody Boyd public house, Wripple.

FIREMEN
The Framley Fire Service is available on 01999 827 1947 (during office hours, except religious holidays).

POLICE
The relief police force covering this Wednesday and Thursday evening will be The Sockford Aeromodelling Society.

OFF-LICENCES
The following off-licences are open illegally in the tiny hours to serve the extremely thirsty.
ST TRUDE-IN-THE-FIELDS CHURCH Chest
NCP CARPARK KIOSK 8 Meaker St, Molford
THRASHER'S Arnhem Centre, Framley

M*A*S*H UNITS
The following M*A*S*H units are operating all night: **4077th** and **853rd**. That is all.

RECORDER LESSONS
ADRIENNE WOODGATE Please, genuine emergencies only. 07999 977754.

PUPPETS
Late night puppets on duty between 11pm and 6am are Alan Tracy and Edd The Duck

RELIGIOUS SERVICES

Kick off at 3 o'clock unless otherwise stated.

PENGUIN CAFE BAPTISTS Worshipping Simon Jeffes through parping and beeping since 1997. Whoft.

MOLFORD FREE CHURCH rejecting the papist conspiracy and regular jumble sales. Whoft.

ST MOSSAD'S REFORMED CHURCH counter espionage, light weapon training, carols. Whoft.

NEWBY'S PENTECOSTAL (State) Be baptised and enjoy attractive discounts on sausages, ornamental swans and Vim. Molford.

POPEYE ECUMENICAL CHURCH Setsk sail every weeksk at four pm Sunday. Well, waddya know? Whoft.

CHAPEL OF OUR LADY OLIVE OYL Closed for refurbishment. Reopening October as Swee'Pea's Late Nite Chemises. Whoft.

FOURTH BROTHERHOOD OF SLACKERS Meeting probably Thursdays. Whoft.

THE BOWLER HATS Vesperal brotherhood. Matins 10am. Postmortems 2pm. Matinees Saturdays onlies. Whoft.

FELAFEL FELLOWSHIP now incorporating Kebabs For Christ and Bibleburgers. Whoft.

ST JUDAS IN THE MANGER Unconventional bible study. Whoft.

DOVETAIL PENTECOSTAL CHURCH symmetrical worship, shampoo and set. Whoft.

MAGIC CHRISTIAN FELLOWSHIP cutting a choirboy in half, linking Ringos etc. Whoft.

SECOND AND SEVENTH DAY ADVENTISTS Wednesdays and Thursdays good for anyone? Whoft.

ST PETER & THE WOLF Pastor D. Bowie on bassoon (as the narrator). Whoft.

SCHINDLER'S MOSQUE Whose idea was this? Whoft.

ST WHIPPY'S ICE CREAM VAN AND CHURCH Mind That Jesus! Whoft & environs.

PETER WEIR'S WITNESSES HALL Whoft.

THE WORSHIPFUL COMPANY OF ENTHUSIASTS YOUTH CLUB squash and snogs. Biscuit mornings Tuesday. Whoft.

ST MAUREEN OF AVILA *NEW!* Whoft.

AUSTRALIAN ORTHODOX CHURCH Fancy dress Thursdays. Whoft.

● *A.A. Gill is on holiday.*

TAKING YET ANOTHER TRIP DOWN MEMORY DRIVE

Class of 1932

with Arcady Belvedere
Framley's premiere historian

I WAS BORN IN 1909 - but I'm only as young as I feel! So, of course, I can remember the 1930s as if they were the 1970s.

Although I should rather say that I can remember some of it, not all. And I bet that you weren't even born at the time! I didn't live in Framley either.

But I do know what I like, and what I like is reading about the ancient people from history from the Framley district from the books in Framley District Library.

Just before the library closed last Thursday evening I stumbled across a very interesting piece of fact concerning the first Framley resident ever to appear on a television, which, in those days, we still called "the variety box".

NINETEEN THIRTY-2

I can't know if you remember a success-full quiz show of the time, called *The Early-Evening Frolic,* or any of the panellists that used to feature on it? Well, it ran from 1932 to 1932 and one of the regular guests was Sir Edward Elgar, then still one of this country's most respected and popular knights of the realm.

Sir Elgar was well-known for his irascible composing and grand old English temper and they combined to add a certain frisson to his numerous appearances which, of course, was why we all loved the old goat, bless him.

On the show, a panel of celebrities would have to guess the social class of a sequence of people from all over Britain, the answers to which were only revealed after much offence had been taken.

One of the contestants - Mrs Ethel Notton, a former debutante - was a Wripple resident of many years standing and that's why I'm writing this. On the night in questions, after Mrs Notton had completed round one by reciting the show's famous tongue-twister with a whelk in her mouth, Edward Elgar turned to Wallis Simpson, seated directly to his left, and, in that endearingly blunt way of his, described Mrs Notton as a "fat cow".

SYMPHONY

How the audience laughed but Sir Edward, realising that he had metaphorically stepped over an invisible line, offered Mrs Notton an immediate apology - by composing his second symphony on the spot and dedicating it to her.

Mrs Notton, 1932

It was a memorable night for Framley folk, and even though poor Ethel failed to beat the panel and win the submarine, she received the usual consolation prize: a "Plastic Bertram" - the show's smiling mascot.

Her evening later ended in tragedy when lightning struck her eight times on the way home, the tin hat on the booby prize attracting lightning after lightning to the dashboard of her brand new open-topped car. She finally succumbed to her own death during the penultimate strike.

What a year!

50 years ago today

From the St Eyot's Flugel, 14th March 1952

ON THE ROUTE OF THE MARCH OF THE PROGRESS!

The denizens of St Eyot's and Whoft looked on agape as the Electric Age finally arrived this week.

Not that there was much to see, mind. A simple brick construction, technically termed a 'sub-station', was commissioned on Tuesday by local councillors.

"Looks like nothing so much as a windowless shed," observed one spectator, Mr Juff.

"Bully beef," quipped another.

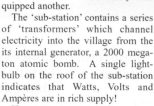

How electricity works

The 'sub-station' contains a series of 'transformers' which channel electricity into the village from the its internal generator, a 2000 mega-ton atomic bomb. A single light-bulb on the roof of the sub-station indicates that Watts, Volts and Ampères are in rich supply!

However, representatives from Standard Telephones & Power say that demand for the new, clean energy source has so far been sluggish.

"It's early days yet," said Mr Greenhalgh for ST&P, "in fact, so far, this marvellous device is only powering the light-bulb atop the building. But we expect more interest once the hairdryer has been invented."

Traditionally, St Eyot's and Whoft have been lighted and heated by dung, although some local gentry employ hot, shiny peasants.

100 years from today

ITALY CAVES IN AT LAST

Italy has finally made assisted suicide finally legal.

The so-called AS law was first adopted by Britain in 2035, the same year that Sir Steve Coogan was assassinated, the Liberal Government made hanging illegal for the second time and Wimbledon was finally abandoned due to the country's heavy summer snow.

Italy has only agreed to pass the law, though, after decades of obstinance. Only last August street riots wrecked what was left of Venice before it all fell into the sea. In addition, the Italian Congress insists the AS law is "on a renewable short-term contract" and that only people who are already dead will have the right to be helped to a peaceful end.

Italy is the last Catholic stronghold in Europe. Latin is still a compulsory second language there, although the European Federation plans to challenge this, along with other accused "atrocities" (like Clapping Prayers - *Sciccicciccicini* - and the continuing ban on marshmallows).

Elsewhere: where now for snooker?

FIRST BANANA

St Eyot's has finally seen its first real banana since before the war. The banana, which arrived in the village with great flourish on a velveted dray, is the purchase of local fruiterer Giles Molquhoun.

Molquhoun paid the princessly sum of £3 4s 6d for the yellow wonder from a contact at the Brazilian Embassy in London, which was later eaten.

Mr Molquhoun pronounced the banana "ba-na-na".

FULL-SIZE MB "Mouse Trap" game. Bowling ball missing. Man on diving board in really bad mood. £30ono. Box FE8100

3" MARCONI TV. Buyer to collect. It's in my lounge somewhere. Find it, it's yours. Tel Framley 855 501

GROWN UPS

MAMAS & PAPAS pushchair. Cyan. With vomiting Michelle Phillips doll. Converts to pram. £15. 01999 855 411

6-BERTH FLOATING dollshouse. Elaborate gypsy pontoons, tiny kitchen, Edwardian-effect bannistering. £325ono. 01999 965 422

245,000 Tiger Tokens. Enough to get six wine glasses or 3/8 of a tiger. Offers. Whoft 8651

HUFTY

"HUFTY" SLIPPERS, from TV's "The Word". Unwanted gift. £5. 01999 894 765

EGBERT NOSH

SNOOKER TABLE / Diving board, with conversion clamps and switch. £80. Box FE8711

"SPIN ME" toilet seat. Rotate while you defecate. Really quite pleasant. £12. 01999 822 2021

OVER twelve hundred farts in screwtop jars. Some labelled 1978-81. Some vegetarian. £2 each, or offers for full collection. 01999 953 3001

BREVILLE Sandwich Chimney. Flue blocked with cheese, hence quick sale. £10. Box FE8016

TELEPHONE conversation with ex-wife. Includes row and phone number. £5. Box FE8083

CORBY Christmas Tree Press. Flattens and de-tinsels. Ruins Christmas. £45. Tel 01999 807 762

SOUP TOILET. Hot flush and simmer-tight lid. 14 Bloo crouton blocks. Some Mulligatawny staining under rim, hence £90. Framley 823 649

FOR SALE: Man's black dinner jacket. As new. Would suit me, hence no longer for sale. No offers. £115. Do not tel 01999 819 997

TREE BUNGALOW. High, and yet also low at the same time. "A building, a paradox, a delight" Solihull Evening Echo. 01999 877 742

GIRL'S WORLD "Man's World" adapter set. Moustache comb, lipstick, ball ribbons. £8. Framley 801 1818

TUPPERWARE SCABS. Airtight. Never heal, hence £2. 01999 821 209

BATMAN KETTLE. With remote control and Cesar Romero kneepads. Makes occasionally delicious boiling water. £4. Tel Wripple 9054

REMINGTON Babycase. Vinyl carrying case with brass clasps. Ages 2-4. Some scratching inside. £16. 01999 854 421

SOFA SHOES. Size 10. Seat six, or eight standing. £26 the pair. 01999 872 232

NEON "Alan Titchmarsh" sign. No longer required. £40. Tel Fram 986543

TWENTY-THREE minute video of my sister taking one off the thumb. £10. 01999 851 111

SODASTREAM. With several flavouring bottles: Brocolli™, Hollandaise, All-New Marmite, Hundreds & Thousands, Jalfrezi, Milk, Vaseline, and Plain. £15. Box FE8191

CHILD'S Cot Parrot. With "No-Nonsense™" peck. £9. Box FE8033

GREENHOUSE CARAVAN. Ideal for holiday tomatoes. £1800. Tel 01999 888 942

MAGPIE extractor fan. Removes them cleanly. Never used. Never bought. £28. Tel 01999 890 913

CORNWALL, Duchy of. £28million. Mine to sell. 01999 853 310

SUNBED. Clouded over, hence £4. 01999 866 456

GROCER. Retired. 5'8". Ideal garden ornament. 01999 965 764 before 4am.

FOLDING bath and bathroom. £245ono. 01999 832 320

MATCHING bridesmaids' chickens. With lace-up wings and "Something Borrowed" beaks. £36 the pair. Will not split. 01999 894 462

12-PIECE Spain. Velour bulls. No Barcelona. £18. Tel Whoft 6543

COMPUTER SOFTWARE. Microsoft Trampoline 95. £20. Adobe Shoeshop 6.0, with "Laces" CD. £25. Tel 01999 810 007

FISHER PRICE "My First Period" set. £12. 01999 866 309

OVER 150 Hitler salutes. 4' / 6' / 2' / 1'6". Fire damaged, but moustache gesture intact. Offers. Box FE8042

TWO DOZEN loose hymns. Jumbled. Some all chorus, Some all verse. Chords hideous. £50. Previous applicants welcome. 01999 894 492

NEST of bunkbeds. Sleeps 18 progressively smaller people. £190. Box FE8795.

SHARI LEWIS and Lambchop Vietnam-era memorabilia sought to augment peacetime collection. Will trade for Watergate-hearings Charlie Horse toys. Good prices paid. Call 01999 894 475

DINING / snooker / fishing table. £110. Tel 01999 871 523

MAGIC PORRIDGE POT. Lovely mauve glow. And they pulled, and they pulled, and they pulled. £210. Molford 7854

BUDGERIGAR with Mike Reid's sideburns and attitude. Laughs like a tug. £35. 01999 842 825

INFLATABLE war memorial. Adaptable for Boer / Great / Cod. £170ono. Box FE8740

CHILD'S Formula One chassis. "You'll think she's a car!". £25. Tel 01999 895 501

FREEZER full of individually wrapped eyebrows. Mainly ginger. £180. Fram 976 641

BLACK & DECKER fire drill. With detachable muster points and head count. £28. Fram 988 818

200,000 housebricks with Roni Size's face embossed on side. Would suit really big Roni Size fan planning to build extension. £150 the lot. 01999 876 653

FIVE out of ten. Would half suit perfectionist. £50. Call 01999 854 754

ALREADY SOLD

GRANDFATHER clock, with real hands and human face. Optional second (third) hand. £200. Tel 01999 854 413

EARLY LEARNING CENTRE "Too Many Crayons" Set. Not too many crayons, hence quick sale. £6. Sockford 98541

INCREDIBLY BEAUTIFUL woman, £45. Only joking. Pig. £44. Box FE8976

WARMLITE humane gas blanket. With instruction video and scoresheets. £30. 01999 822 209

GIANT white teddy, holding heart-shaped cushion; "I'm dying". £5. Fram 809 943

INSENSITIVE carer. Racially intolerant. Poor listener. Methadone habit and some spitting. £16/hr. 01999 830 083

STAR WARS "Minnellium Falcon" skis, with "Saucy Yoda" design. £12. 01999 854 987 NC.

WICKER BODYSOCK. Very itchy. No longer a good idea. £11. Tel Whoft 9654

GLASS fish tank, with thirteen glass shebunkin and a perspex carp. £40. Fram 800 907

NINTENDO 16 games console with games. "Simon In The Land Of Chalk Drawings", "Naughty Triangle", "Maverick Milkman" and "SpyPuncher". £20. Tel 01999 895 950

RED HOT Dutch Spirograph. Beautiful curves. Leaves nothing to the imagination. £14ono. Tel 01999 809986 after 6pm.

COW AND GATE. Cow kicks. Gate doesn't. Will separate. £15 each. 01999 803 336

PISSFLAPS. Set of five. £9. Box FE 8321

GIRAFFE PELLETS. Ideal for gardeners. Kill anything smaller than a giraffe. £16 per 10 gallon drum. 01999 850 613

PARKER KNOLL chair. £45. Lady Penelope Knoll sofa. £115. Fram 874 986

CHAD Valley "Skinheads On A Raft" beans-on-toast playset. 01999 947 657

TATTOO of Lady Olga Maitland. Unwanted gift. Slight scarring. £12. Tel 01999 852 212

TRIVIAL PURSUIT, Russian Roulette Edition. Kills one in six. £5. Tel 01999 899 437

WASTED youth. Hardly used. £22. Box FE8054

JEREMY Bowen's moustache alarm clock. £10. 01999 853 021

PRINTS of Whales. £3 each. 01999 873 322

MESS YOURSELF

UPTIGHT freezer / frigidaire. Will only open when drunk. Guilty meals inevitable. £145ono NC. Whoft 65297

LIMITED EDITION, framed Brian Jacks squat-thrust, from TV's "SuperStars". £150ono. Tel 01999 822 097

ALL MY BLOOD. Delivered in 1 pint instalments over a period of whens. Will swap for all your bone marrow, or Black & Decker DinnerMate. 01999 820 940

ACTUAL SIZE statue of elephant made of billiard balls. Ears red, rest yellow. A lifetime's work. £45. Box FE8654.

FRIMPTIMPTIMPIMP

FRANCIS MONKMAN doll. Plays Where Opposites Meet Pt.1, vgc, £12. Adapter for Tristan Fry doll, £6. Box FE8744.

BARBIE Hospice. All dolls dead or dying. £25ono. Fram 821 96

TALIBAN "Egg" game. Requires 146 AA batteries. £6. Fram 811 732

COCKNEY Lord Of The Rings action figures, with Pearly Frodo. £16 the set. Framley 873900

A PICTURE of you and your partner as conjoined twins. The Ultimate Gift of Love. Joined at head, heart or hair. Chang & Eng Industries, Unit 149a East Cossett Ind. Park.

THE BIG YELLOW Fawlty Towers. Slide slightly broken. £8. 01999 644 343

SOLO FROM SONG. Not sure which song. Fast. £10. Box FE8110.

A POUND. Get yourself something nice. Don't tell your mother. Phone Grandma 01999 977494 after 5am.

IF YOU DON'T USE A TALENT GIVEN TO YOU, God takes it away. Pay attention. Box FE8140.

PADDY MUSICAL

CAPITAL H. Fell off my nerve. Phone arry 01999 894091.

SLEEP WITH YOUR HAND DOWN YOUR TROUSERS. I can teach you how. Box FE8417.

FOR SALE Metallic blue 1992 Ford Mondeo ono. Box FE8696.

PHILLIPS BabyShave. £52, or £1 a week for a year. 01999 894 921

MICHAEL RODD

NEVER MIND. Perhaps next time you'll listen to me when I spend half my life screaming my head off. Goodbye Julie. Box FE8742.

BREED WITH ME. There are only a few of us left and we MUST multiply. Box FE8181.

1980s MIRROR covered in 1980s stickers. 'That's Patrick Bossert!' 'Chew A Chunk Of Cheese,' 'I Am 1982,' 'Say Yes To Chess,' 'Owl Club,' 'Angels On The Head Of Shitty Little Pin' and far too many more. £5. Box FE8693.

MADE OF SNOW? I am made of snow. Box FE8168.

GUITAR STRINGS £4.50 per pack. Guitar, £400. Guitar case, £15. Lawnmowing incident, regrettable sale. Also gloves. 01999 900542. No well-wishers.

MOBILE HAIRDRESSING. I will cut your hair while you sit on my handlebars. Box FE8621.

HOLE, empty, used once, £15. Box FE8273.

PHONE US FIRST if you wish to speak to my wife and I before someone else. 01999 752970.

BAG HATRED

ANYTHING done (within reason) £1/hour. Box FE8888.

TELL ME SOMETHING I DON'T KNOW. I have run out of things to say. Box FE8294.

MY FRIENDS ARE BORING ME. Phone me now. 01999 331 044.

SIMPLE TEETH. So simple a child could use them. £40 a set. Box FE8613.

1000 TAP DANCING 8 YEAR OLDS needed for private occasion. Apply Framley Police (Vehicles Division)

WELCOME!

MIDDLE OF NOWHERE for sale. Sought after location. Box FE8297.

TRAVEL TWISTER, dangerous gift, unsuitable for driver, £30. Box FE8324.

OWL WIG, £5. Also vole hanky and robin glasses. 01999 704277.

CHASE THE BAD THOUGHTS FROM YOUR HEAD with new eyes. Modern, interesting surgery in louche surroundings. Free car parking. Box FE8302.

ASSORTED LADIES, size 22-28 plus, nearly new ladies, mostly Evans. Box FE8946.

SPOT THE DOG! Prizes prizes prizes! Can you spot the dog? Can you? Box F8728.

I'M COMING. Call me. 01999

FOCUS on
Robbie Nougat

Robbie stands prodly in front of the new £2.75m Blend AM transmitter.

PHOTOGRAPH BY CRAZYHORSE REDGRAVE

He's king of the air!

by Beaky Coxwain

YOU'D HAVE TO GET UP pretty early in the morning not to have heard of Framley's very own radio superstar Robbie Nougat.

The controversial DJ, who was sacked from local station Zephyr AM after a series of zany stunts and record-breaking absences certainly does things his own way, and his new dream project is no exception!

Because Robbie's started his very own station - Blend AM - and it's taking the airwaves by storm.

CARCINOGENIC MAST

Broadcasting from a 400 foot tall supertransmitter that cost Robbie every penny of his life's savings, Blend AM beams pure Nougat all over the Framley area, blocking out the Zephyr AM signal for a 60 mile radius and interfering with some emergency services too!

The transmitter - which is recognised by the United Nations as an offensive weapon - is sited in the playground of a local school and has been vital to the Blend AM success story - a story that has seen the new station become Framley's third most listened to sound (next to traffic and the boiler filling up).

50s, 70s, 80s, 90 & 92

Blend AM plays all your favourite tunes, promising its listeners "the very best of the 50s, 70s, 80s, 90 and 92". Robbie himself presents the top-rated "Breakfast Drivetime" programme every day from 4am-11am. The show is broadcast in the inimitable Nougat style from the driver's seat of Robbie's Mercedes SL55 on the hands-free set.

What's more, Robbie chooses the playlist himself, with most of the songs coming from his own personal collection of tapes in the boot.

So what better way to celebrate Framley's newest radio sensation than to take a look behind the scenes at the man who made it all probable, Robbie Nougat!

All about Robbie

ROBBIE NOUGAT'S career has always been dogged with cuntroversy. Although often in conflict with his bosses, his crazy stunts and no-nonsense style have made him one of the area's best-loved radio faces.

Robbie's shows are always shows with a difference. Whether it's boiling 13 eggs in a row, or sorting through his wallet live on air, you never know what he's going to do next.

This year, he famously took 7 months off after the death of John Thaw "out of respect" for the smooth-haired, silver-tongued actor-turned-hardman - a period which he now claims to have spent in Thailand taping the Bangkok Open Snooker Championships over his mother's collection of *Inspector Morse* videos.

But Robbie doesn't come cheap. His astronomical wage demands have made him the highest paid DJ in the country, and the fourth richest man in Europe.

Robbie relaxes at home.
PHOTO BY CAPULET HOOB

Where it began...

ROBBIE got his first start initially as the breakfast DJ on Framley's previously top-rated Zephyr AM - home of the legendary "Teatime Twosome", Tenby and The Colonel, and Britain's forty-sixth most popular medium wave station.

Zephyr AM has existed in one form or another since the late 14th Century, and the breakfast presenter's job is a hereditary title. Usually it is passed to the first born son on the death of the father, however in a break with tradition, Robbie inherited the role while his father, Richard Coeur de Nougat was away fighting in the crusades.

His abdication from the position caused a constitutional crisis at the station, only resolved when Tenby and The Colonel stepped in to the breach, adopting the titles of breakfast presenter and breakfast presenter consort.

HERE'S HOW TO ERECT YOUR ROBBIE NOUGAT FACT PYRAMID!

GLUE

AGE: 36

NUMBER OF YEARS IN THE BIZ: 3

FAVOURITE COLOUR ON A BEE: Yellow?

SHOE SIZE: 12

SHOE SIZE: 1

FLUFF MISERY

Families use a "boat" to row for shelter as an unusual amount of fluff begins to start filling the streets of Whoft.

PHOTOGRAPH BY LYSANDER FITZMARMITE

by Challenger Putney

FRAMLEY Fire and Rescue dealt with more than 400 calls as fluff returned to the area with a vengeance at the weekend.

Dozens of Whoft and St Eyot's residents were yesterday involved in a huge sweep-up operation, and the army was called in in Sockford to help with the business of cleaning.

"This was a one in 150 years event," said a spokescouncillor for Framley Borough, "although I may have to check the books, as this is the third time since 1993."

Roads and schools were closed as the fluff took hold on Thursday morning. By 1pm, St Eyot's Green was six inches deep, and by the evening the village was up to its letterboxes in fluff.

An Environment Agency press statement confirmed that "we are aware of the problem, sweetcakes, and will look right into it real soon."

FLUFF

But as usual this isn't enough for some people.

"Fluff has ruined our home twice since we moved here," screamed blue-faced churchwarden Mo Watmough, known locally, who said the weekend had been more than she could stand. "You have to understand, it's about time somebody took a stand."

"My cat choked," added juggler Apple 'Mac' McIntosh, "and my dog only got out alive because she was up high when the fluff started to overwhelm."

Estimates put the weekend's damage at up to and including £60,000. Fluff insurance experts are

predicting a huge rise in premiums, which they advise people to pay.

One resident left counting the profit was shrewd local grandmother Mrs Elise Elsinore, 82, who, eight years ago, placed an each-way bet on it being a fluffy August. Billy Turps, of Billy Turps Bookmakers, Whoft, was left counting the estimated £73,000 cost alone.

and some roads are not expected to be liberated until the end of the week.

Residents now have the difficult task of deciding what preparations should be prepared for any further unseasonal build-ups of fluff. The Parish Council has already advocated a series of velcro fences along the main routes into the village, but the Borough Council thinks its pilot scheme of static-electric-milkfloats will work better.

News In Brief

UNIVITED GUEST

A 140-year old woman with a wooden toe answered the door to a man who attempted to stain her. The woman, who lives near Cottonpicker Row, said a man overwhelmed her at 3.30pm on September 24th and rumblaged through her stuff. The man who is left handed left empty handed.

KEY FRAUD WASN'T

A man was found not guilty of forgery after it was revealed that he had copies of the house keys to 315 addresses in the Framley area. Mr Justice Trufflingly Cockleboiling ruled that Eric Pointy, 55, had little more than a "fascinating hobby." Mr Pointy has run the Heel N Key Bar at Framley Station since 1972.

PRISON OPEN DAY

Last Friday's open day at HM Prison Chutney ended in chaos when all the computers were stolen and 76 inmates escaped. Prison Governor Christopher Trace-Singleton issued a statement declaring the day "a shameful out-and-out failure from start to finish," and considering his position.

WINS A CAR

Dad of three Heston Shrimproy is celebrating after kissing his way to a £16,000 Mercedes A Class. He was among five contestants who puckered up to five police dogs in a bathroom showroom last week. Dad of three Heston managed to kiss the dog for 58 hours.

RING A MING BING

Local Bing Crosby impersonator Bingo Crosbier beat off sixteen other interested parties for a 575-year old Ming vase at an auction last week. He bid by phone .

BEE BAN

Bees are to be banned from local flowers from next July, after Framley Borough Council passed a bye-law to this effect. According to council officials, the bees were "in the way". Local apiarist Roger Mixture, long opposed to the thing, blubbed, "it's a wanton act of enviromental porn-terrorism - they'll be banning the birds from the trees next." [Annie: check apiriast.]

SOCKER SOCK BLOCK-KNOCK ROCKER SHOCK

Framley Zabadak's new signing, defender Cerrutti Iglesias, was sent off in the six-pointer against Leeds last Wednesday for trying to kill the referee with a sock. He was previously sent off for attacking the linesman with a swan.

VOICE OF DEVIL HEARD

The voice of the Devil has again been heard in Sockford. Police last year received more than 350 incidents of Satan's cruel whispering. The latest victim was Rev Carteblanche Laissez-Faire, whom the devil told to get his hair cut and clean his stupid shoes.

In Court

NATWEST Ovenglove, 28, of Magulliger Bottom, Framley, was bound over for ever and received a Chinese burn for punching a motorbike in the face outside The Warm Zippy public house on May 13.

JIGSAW Giant, 18, of Hitlerdale, Chutney, received a suspended burning at the stake for drinking while under the influence of alcohol on February 29.

MR JUSTICE Bitmap Johnson, QC, was fined a million gazillion pounds by a jury of eight year olds who didn't appear to understand the legal process at all, at St Cardigan's CofE Primary School last Wednesday last Thursday.

SEBASTIAN Finger, 35, of Beauty Parade, Molford, was jailed for seven weekends and denied access to his television remote control for driving with undue care and attention on April 3.

RATTIGAN Disney, 39, of Original Glade, Whoft, received 120 seconds community service for murdering his wife and three children. Magistrates said there were special reasons not to impose a custodial sentence, saying it would be excessive in view of Disney's duties and employment as a Home Secretary.

SUNRISE Smith, 31, of Chlamydiagate, Whoft, was fined £100 with £1 costs, but received £350,000 compensation due to a clerical error at Framley Magistrates Court on Wednesday.

PRINCE Schoolboy, 22, of The Alarm, Sockford, was fined six years' interest for inflating himself to the size of an ambulance and releasing radioactive gases outside Here Be Turnips on May 21.

AMANDA Childsniffer, 12, of Golliwog Prom, Whoft, was fined £5 with £3 costs for possessing enough pickled onions in her loft to make a 4.5kg vomit bomb.

Less than the warm welcome

by Adam Wrent

POLICE had to be called to a a street in Chutney at the weekend after a fighting threatened to become a rioting.

Residents of Waxworm Reach took to the streets en masse at the weekend in protest at the arrival of a further dozen foreign asylum-seekers. Bricks were thrown and locals demanded the removal of the newcomers, the third immigrant family to move into the area in the last six moths.

Ever since their country was torn apart by wars between rival fractions, immigrants seeking to escape the *trouble and strife* have been flooding into Britain at the rate of check this figure.

The displaced families, many of whom cannot speak English, are finding it difficult to integrate into their chosen communities. Chutney Social Services director, Concept Nicolas, pointed me that, because Waxworm Reach is predominantly white, "the new red, yellow, mauve and green faces are easy targets" for a well-deserved punch in the head.

Amid cries of "send them back" and the throwing of pots, the twelve migrants were escorted from their flat. They were then taken to Chutney Police Station for their own safety, where they were given toast and custard.

"They're trouble," said one bigot [>flag: LEGAL. Ed.]. "This used to b e a niceneighbourhood."

And, you know what? The violence isn't just coming from people who belong here, either. In Batley, where most of the immigrants have washed up, the refugee community is dangerously split along tribal lines.

A household of twenty-eight green refugees was deported home last week after they pleaded sorry for burning a maisonette full of yellow ones to the ground.

A spokesfax from Framley's immigration department yesterday read, "we make every effort to welcome new arrivals to the area, and see that they settle and integrate comfortably into Chutney. We are

Look at the little bleeder, waving like an Englishman.
PHOTO BY BALLIOL SASQUATCH

horrified by the events of the weekend, but shit happens."

The Framley Examiner is pleased to announce it will again be sponsoring next Wednesday's anti-immigrant riots. Come along and bring a bottle.

Man attacked by nerds

BRAVE Stanley Poubelle was last night recovering in Framley General Hospital after being attacked in Shirtshrift Street on Saturday night by a gang of nerds.

Umemployed builder Stan, 56, said he felt lucky to be "alive, and" appealed to Framley Examiner readers to help apprehend his culprits.

"I was a-strolling home from the pub," he went, "and all of a sudden I sees these six nerds on the other side of the street, whereupon they laid into me, like. It was with words at first, you see."

After berating their terrified victim for not knowing that the atomic number of Iridium was 77, the nerds ran across the road. One of them was heard to shout, "it's the most corrosion-resistant metal known to man, you bag of old farts."

All six of the social misterfits then took off their spectacles and started hitting Mr Poubelle with them.

The violent intellectuals attacked Stan with eancylopaediaes, inserted chess pieces, and kicked him to within a sixpence of his life under a torrent of machine code abuse. "One of them called me a FF1G 5H178AG3FF00," said Mr P, shaking and sobbing.

Police are appealing to anybody with information to come as far forward as possible, since some policemen are short-sighted and are professionally obliged to wear glasses.

A spokesman for The Encyclopaedia Brittanica last night pointed out that the corrosion index of Iridium is only slighter lower than that of Osmium.

Plan refused

PLANS for a new fire station in Wripple have been rejected by the borough's planners.

Staggerback Rollerby Properties had submitted plans for a 109-storey development including a vibrating restaurant at the top, and a load of shops at the bottom, with 28-storey wings extending from either side as far as the church and the WI hall, in case the building ever needed to fly.

A representative of Framley Borough Council told local paper The Framley Examiner reporter me that Wripple village green was "not even slightly the right place for this enormous thing. The firepole alone was over 1100 feet long."

The developers are planning an appeal which the council plans to reject.

WEEKEND TV

SATURDAY

PICK OF THE WEEK

With Ursula Claybeam

READERS WILL be excited to discover that this week I am choosing a programme originally shown several weeks ago! Yes, you're not dreaming, my pick of the week is episode 6 of *Hospital Corners* (with Michael Flipflops) which, on Wednesday evening, after fish fingers, tinned carrots and angel delight, I will be watching for the seventh time! And I encourage you to do the same! Of course, to join in, you'll need to have one of these new VCRs or Video Channel Recorders like me and Denis, but Roberts Radios sell them at reasonable prices and they're not too heavy! You won't want to get left behind when everybody's talking about episode 6 of *Hospital Corners* at work the next day! VCRs are the future and stuffy old televisions are the past. I've already thrown my set away, and I know you will too, when you see episode 6 of *Hospital Corners*. **That's my pick.**

BBC

8.30 Pages From Gagfax

8.35 Scrappy Doo, Why Are You?

9.00 The Saturday Speedboat Sarah Smith & Keith Philbin steer randomly at Newton-le-Willows and the Prime Minister interviews Roman Holliday.

12.12 Weathercock Bill Giles

12.15 Olympic Sportsnest including (approx. times)
12.20 Miniature Swimming
1.05 Equus
3.25 Men's Sanderson (Final)
3.50 Women's 100x4m Relay (Semi-Finals)
4.10 The Adventure Game
4.50 Table Dancing

5.5 News (8,589/53,112) A bomb goes off in Ulster and Jan announces a royal engagement.

5.20 'Ello 'Ello Jack Warner and Gorden Kayo pound the beat.

5.45 Jim'll Unnerve You

The weekend starts here! There's plenty of fun for younger viewers when Sarah Smith and cheeky puppet friend Mr Cabbages meet the secretary of the Transport & General Workers Union and Emu

SATURDAY SPEEDBOAT
9.00am BBC

6.20 The Two Ronnies of Hazzard Unpopular spin-off with Barbara Dickson as the Balladeer.

7.10 The Late Late Breakfast Time Selina Scott and Debbie Greenwood attempt to jump over eighteen double-decker buses in a double-decker bus.

8.05 Summertime Nuisance Laughter with Keith Harris and his new puppet, Wasp's Nest.

9.05 Carrott's Shtick Jasper beats his donkey of an audience.

9.35 News (as 5.05) (rpt)

9.50 Match of the Unexpected Highlights of Brighton & Hove Albion.

10.25 The Big Saturday Big Night Movie:
Carry On Freaking Out (1968)
Television premier of Nixon-era rock opera
Bongo Star ... Jim Dale
Sid Dylan ... Sid James
The Acid Queen ... Kenneth Williams
Pearl Necklace ... Barbara Windsor
Swami Yogi Bear ... Charles Hawtrey
Kyoko Ego ... Joan Sims
Dr Robert ... Kenneth Connor
Keith Animal ... Peter Butterworth
Cynthia Plastercaster ... herself
Paul McCarthorse ... Terry Scott
Screenplay: Talbot Rothwell & Terry Southern
Dir.: Jack Nicholson

12.00 Penisbobs Yukkie uses his scampi fingers to help him get wood.

12.15 Last Orders

12.25 Closedown (rpt)

BBC "2"

6.25 Open Polytechnic
6.25 The Politics of the Penis
6.50 Nuclear Holocaust: Newton-le-Willows 7.15 Two Plus Two Is Maths
7.40 How Green Is My Yellow?
8.05 Italian Pour Les Anglais
8.30 Shakespeare's Many Lesbians
8.55 Biscuits in Edwardian Britain
9.20 I Fancy You, Joyce
9.45 Management Is The Eighties
10.10 How to Photograph Your Insides 10.35 Does Tennis Work?
11.0 The Miracle of Fluff
11.25 Games Sans Waring
11.50 Important in September
12.15 The Duvet of Christ 12.40 How We Used To Think We Lived
1.05 Dividing a Horse

1.30 Saturday Cinema:
The Brevet Bunch (1943)
War drama. Disgruntled, underpaid tommies wish that for them the war was nearly over.
Brevet Major Rufus ... Jack Hawkins (dubbed by Marni Nixon)
Brevet Sergeant Grimshaw ... William Hartnell
Brevet Private Lavender ... and introducing James Perry
Dir.: William Joyce

3.20 Playing Away Brian Cant & Toni Arthur spend the weekend in Brighton.

3.45 One Man And His Mary Poppins More competitive kite-flying, bird-feeding and making an anagram out of Dick Van Dyke's name at the end, with Phil Drabble.

4.35 Labour Party Conference 1982 Day 6 of the continued live coverage, including the retrospective Denis Healey 'Silly-Billy' montage. Presented by Robin Day.

6.05 The Old Grey Whispering Test Bob Harris struggling to make himself heard above the music of Cabaret Voltaire.

6.45 Weather and Sport A look back at the week's forecasts with Bill Giles.

7.05 Live From The Albert Proms The London Sinfonietta plays John Adams' *Fast Ride In A Short Machine* and a specially commissioned work for parrot and orchestra by Alwyn Tittershear.

8.40 One Foot In The Future Young Scottish researcher, Kirsty Wark, investigates how British architecture will be represented on television in the 1990s.

9.10 So You Think You Want To Be... Made Into A Ball

10.00 Pissed-Up Nannies Quarter-final action introduced by David Vine.

11.05 Newsnight At The Zoo

11.10 Third Degree Burns Gordon Burns meets Sheila Ferguson.

11.50 Alfred Hitchcock Presents Agatha Christie's Michael Cimino's "Sir Arthur Conan Doyle's The Chinese Detective Investigates Barbara Taylor Bradford's Strange Case of Columbo vs Gerry Anderson's The Mysterons" Double Bill

12.45 Last Orders

12.55 Closedown (first shown on BBC1)

ITV

6.25 Open Sesame
6.25 Counting 1-2-3 Cookies ah-ah-ah
6.55 Spanish For Junior: *Agua*

7.25 The Mike Morris Breakfast Hour Celebrities refuse to wake up for their interviews.

8.25 The Amazing Underwater World of Captain Nimmo Animation.

8.30 The Grizzly Life and Times Of Douglas Adams Lazy author Adams worries that Denver Pyle will sell the last remaining Siberian-toothed bear as a pelt.

9.30 Today Is Saturday, Where's Our Speedboat? More or less fun with TV doctors Graeme Garden and Magnus Pike. Phone in to offer your organ swaps or to swear at Buck's Fizz on 01 999 8055.

12.25 Moustache of Sport including live coverage of the Winter Olympics
12.30 Snowballing
1.10 Bob The Slayer
1.55 Speed Snorting
2.45 Ice Hockney
3.45 Skier Jumping

4.00 Kent's Big Granny Haystacks

4.45 Score Drawer Dickie can't quite hear Brian's match report from Upton Park.

5.05 Weekend News Leonard Parkin washes his car and takes his mother shopping.

5.15 Metal Machine Mickey Locked groove feedback.

5.45 The InCrediBle CHiPs Jon & Mr Punch get angry and turn into a big green motorbike.

6.40 Russ Meyer's Pussycathouse With special guest Bella Emberg.

7.15 That's My Typecasting Mollie Sugden acts all posh.

7.45 3-2-0-2-7 The quiz that makes no sense with Dusty Springfield.

8.45 Weekend News (as 5.05) (rpt) Followed by a nice cup of tea and a sit down

9.00 It Was Actually Alright On The Night 3 Denis Norden introduces more of the final, transmitted versions of the outtakes we know and love. Peter Sellers delivers a line in a lift and a man says "Not one thing" without moving his head from side to side.

10.00 An Audience With Harold Macmillan (B&W) (rpt)

10.45 Over The TISWOS Carolgees gets into a drunken fistfight with Gorman over James. *Not Whoft.*

11.15 Last Night Movie:
No Sex Please, I'm Not Robin Askwith! (1972)
Television premiere of Heath-era simulated comedy-sex comedy.
Robin Askwith's boss ... Tony Booth
Mary Pentagon ... June Whitfield
Arthur Lowe ... Robin Askwith
The Wife of Bath ... Valerie Leon
Dir.: Allan Smithee (Alan Smithy)

12.45 God, Why Hast Thou Foresaken Insomniacs?

12.55 Closedown (first shown on BBC1)

TEDDYBOY MARTIN

175 YEARS OF EXCELLENCE

01999 865465
www.tedbozmaz.com

GOOD OPPORTUNITY TO OWN THIS HOUSE

MOLFORD ST MALCOLM
£450,000 Teddyboy Martin are pleased to offer this rarely sought after property for sale.
A magnificent Tudor, four-storey Georgian style house set in 8 acres of unspoilt, rolling lounge, belonging to another, larger house.
On market unexpectedly due to owners currently being on holiday in Magaluf. Quick sale preferred.

GRAEHAEME GARDENS, FM12

SASQUATCH HEIGHTS
£82,950 Mind-expanding semi-detached rotating Edwardian residential swimming pool, retaining many period features.
This pool is offered fully furnished, with wall to wall carpets and functioning fire place.
Pool floor hatch leads to thatched cellar with wine storage, parking and mains electrical points. Also wave machine and flume to loft.

NIGHTMARE COTTAGE

BATLEY £225,000oro
Grossly underrated House In A Mood. Doors always slamming, water always too hot (except in shower), windows mysteriously wide open when you get home. Draughty when jealous. Doesn't like you having your friends round.

NICE ONE, CYRIL

£64,395 GASCOIGNE, PLINTH
One way house with "In" door and "Out" door ("Out" door switchable to second "In" door via exterior switch). Please arrange viewing well in advance, allowing plenty of time to get out.

LOFT CONVERSION

£46,550 THE POPS, BELLAIRE
We are disappointed to offer this former house, converted into seventeen lofts. A baffling property which would be ideal for, I don't know, an ambitious loft-lover with seventeen lofts' worth of stuff.

£155,000 OREO

THE BUTTOCKS, SOCKFORD
Superbly converted flat. No windows, no lights, radios all over the place. Ideal for extreme antisocial type. Or blind person.

£78,000

TRIREME CIRCUS, WHOFT
Beautiful 5-bedroom detached house on unfortunate electrical ley line. Taps occasionally live, carpets occasionally standing on end. Some chance of strobe lighting and hard disk erasal. But at the moment, worth a look, to be honest.

HIGHLY TALKED AFTER PROPERTY

THE TRUMPTONS, WHOFT
£113,500 Badly thought out 14th century maisonette situated conveniently on the fold of the map. 4ft ceilings, no doors on ground floor, fluffmill-powered windows, greenhouse cellar, that sort of thing. This is your last and own only chance to own yourself your own highly talk-provoking home. NB Susie it's ALSO on the flight path!!! Me and Paul PISSED ourselfs

Altogether & Hopscotch

LETTING AGENTS
01999 966 862 www.....co.uk

KITCHENETTE WAY, FRAMLEY FR2 £323 weekly (£1400pcm) A well-presented first floor flat ideal for professional couple willing to share with other professional couple unwilling to move out. Bring a sword.

THE BLUETONES, SOCKFORD FR3 £1200pcm Aerial flat, loosely tethered above this desirable warehouse development. Ribbed steel structure, hydrogen / helium mix. Excellent views, but unsuitable for vertigo sufferers, the elderly or smokers.

FALTERMEYER'S WHARF, FRAMLEY (£1 million pounds pcm) Light, spacious whorehouse conversion, built over the middle of the Wharf's historic 15th century bascule bridge. All fittings bolted to floor. Living area splits and tips to allow passage of tall ships. Some warning given.

Le POP-POP, WHOFT (£1,500pcm) Architect designed, thermometer-shaped house. 1st floor bedroom leading to 10th storey bathroom in hot weather.

BATTLECAT, MOLFORD. (£1100 pcm) Unconventional 2 dimensional apartment (depth and height, no width) situated right up against left hand wall of 3-dimensional victorian townhouse. Security guard and counsellor. Must be seen (by standing at angle).

GRAND COLONNADE, WHOFT (£15,000pcm) Over-bright last floor roof in this ever populated crescent. Commanding views of the moon and the elements. GCH, loft, pets.

GOING, GOING, GOING

£170,950 MOLFORD ST GAVIN
Traditional French bungalow with circumflex glass roof and fully fitted neighbours. Gas fired spiral escalators and easily movable windows. Fashionably situated on the underneath of the town, with commanding upskirt views.

£36,000

Teddyboy Martin are pleased to offer this modern, 2 bed house, with a door, windows one, two, three, four. Full GCH, garage, garden, cavity wall insulation. One window contains film about two dogs visiting a biscuit factory.

SOLD

SHILILLINGBURY LILLINGBURY ILLINGBURY ON INGBURY, FM12

£1.1M Gobstoppingly, filling-looseningly vulgar mansion. Everything bright pink, including giant glass pissing flamingo waterfall feature in living room. Several bathrooms wallpapered in royalty cheques. Home of former newsreader.

ALTOGETHER & HOPSCOTCH "WE LET IT ALL OUT..."

Ron's new poems are sheer poetry !

by Ursula Cloybeam

Ron gets his inspiration from the natural world around him, and likes gravy.

PHOTOGRAPH BY FRANK CHICKENS

THOXTOXETER resident and amateur poet Ron Plural has his eyes set on the biggest prize in poetry, the Poet Laureate Prize.

I met Ron, who has been writing since he retired from professional wrestling in 1998, on a park bench in Thoxtoxeter, where he was having a Forest Fruits drink and inventing a ballad. Ron told me he thinks his newest poems are exactly the sort of thing that Poet Laureates ought to be writing.

"These two new poems are the best things I've done, far better than either of my previous poems. Acquiring all the skills of poetry was hard, I'll admit, but I've got it now, and I'd like to be Poet Laureate please."

POETRY IN MOTION

Ron has written both his new poems out and sent them to the Queen, accompanied by a short couplet (written in January) explaining in ten words or less why he wants to be Poet Laureate.

"I done them in a binder," he explained as he rolled me a menthol cigarette on his poet's notebook. "Her Majesty can't fail to notice that."

Ron's poems are personal, he says, but he sees no reason why he couldn't turn his hand to grander, national themes, like Coronations or the state of the railways.

"How hard can it be? I've done four poems, that's true, but I've got loads of words left."

The current Poet Laureate, Andrew somebody, was not in the phone book.

HERE ARE RON'S TWO NEW POEMS

The Old Man With A Drawer
There was an old man with a drawer
Who decided to open the drawer
So he opened the drawer
And inside the drawer
There was an old man with a drawer

The Old Man Who Was Old
There was an old man who was old
Who was asked by an old man "How old?"
"How old am I old?"
said that old man so old,
"I'm as old as those old men of old."

© Ron Plural 2002

What's on...

Oliver Mouth, *Oils*
KEYSEL GALLERY

Review by Amy Llarona

THIS NEW EXHIBITION of oils by Fracton artist Oliver Mouth is just the sort of thing to take your kids to this half term. And if they complain that they'd rather

"More Bloody Boats" oil on canvas, Mouth 2001.

be playing *Battlebat* on their PlayCylinders, explain, as patiently as you can, that these oil paintings of boats KICK ARSE.

Let them know who is PAINTING BOSS. Let them know that Oliver Mouth is KING OF BRUSHES, and that every time he picks up this BRUSH, of which he is KING, and every time he chooses a subject, as long as that subject is boats, you can rest assured that the painting which he makes is going to KICK ARSE.

Write it large, across the clouds of the sky, that Oliver Mouth is THE MAN WHO PAINTS BOATS. Let no child wake, crying in the night, saying, "Mummy! Who will paint boats for me?", for the answer will be known. Whenever boats need painting, one man will always be there, and that man is OLIVER MOUTH and his boat paintings, in oils at the Keysel Gallery until the 5th, KICK ARSE.

(our regular art columnist, Delawarr Louche, is on holiday.)

Theatre audience "extremely patient"

BY BUNCO BOOTH

THE OWNER OF CLINTON'S Promenade Theatre paid tribute to the patience of his audience this week.

Bob Catapult showed me round the auditorium, where a full house has been waiting for a matinee performance by genteel TV drag act Hinge and Bracket since October 1998.

"I come out onstage every few months to explain that the performance was cancelled long ago due to ill health, but the ladies and gentlemen always tell me they don't mind waiting a bit longer. You know. Just in case."

The happy theatregoers have been surviving on a diet of Neapolitan ice cream and interval drinks for four years now, and although several audience members have died from scurvy and liver failure, Bob says the crowd's enthusiasm shows no sign of flagging.

"People round here love a good show, and, although most of them are now aware that Patrick Fyffe (who played Hilda Brackett and not the piano) died earlier this year, they're convinced this will still be a fine entertainment, if and when it ever happens."

There was excitement last week when news reached the rear stalls that the late Mr Fyffe had been replaced by 1980s Rubik's Cube expert Patrick Bossert. Hopes are now high that a new "Hinge & Bossert" show may be underway by spring.

A poster advertising the show.
PHOTO BY LESLEY OGRE

I may not know much about about about art but I know what I'm like!

by Adam Wrent

LOCAL ARTIST Fabien Giraffe was last week sensationally fired by the subject of his latest portrait.

Giraffe, 35, of Television Spinney, Whoft, has described his dismissal as "a thundering blow to the balls of what was to be my finest work."

Cpt Giraffe started his self-portrait last Autumn, but only two weeks ago called work to a halt when he announced, in a shock to the art world, that he was the wrong man for the job.

"I've been a bit hard on myself, but I just wasn't cutting the mustard," he metaphored yesterday. "I'd been working from a photo, since I wouldn't be able to be present at all the sittings, and unfortunately the process didn't afford me a decent level of detail.

"So, after much thought and some more thought, I fired myself. It's the first time I've been sacked, and I have to admit, it's the worst thing that's ever happened to me."

APPALLING MESS

However, his subject, local artist Fabien Giraffe, remains unrepentant.

"It doesn't look anything like me," the artist and subject explained clearly. "And I'm not paying £3000

(From left to right) Fabien Giraffe.
PHOTOGRAPH BY HOTPANTS COLORADO

for a load of square-jawed rubbish that I wouldn't even hang in my dog's bathroom."

But Giraffe was quick to retort. "The fee isn't important, although I will miss paying myself. The picture is rubbish, I'm right," he argued, "but I quite like it. It's got a certain smirk. If I had any sense, I'd be proud of it, rightly and wrongly."

The self-portrait, which has a "certain smirk" (according to one source) is now likely to be completed by another artist, who may paint some of his own features onto Giraffe's face. Should be interesting.

Police stay tough on drugs

FRAMLEY POLICE Chief Constable Rupert Bone yesterday attributed his team's tireless hardline stance against crime to the excellent quality of the amphetamine sulphate they had recently confiscated.

"This is some of the most binging gear my boys have ever got their germans on," said Ch Con Bone through bloodshot eyes.

"I feel invincible."

The show must have gone on

The Framley Pagoda is shutting its theatrical doors for the first ever time tonight in order for essential renovations to take place.

The theatre has famously kept a twenty-four hour open-door policy throughout its colourful history. This was intended by its original owners to provide a constant cultural focus for the local community.

After much deliberation over when the renovations would begin, it has been decided to close the doors, somewhat surprisingly, midway during the first performance of the *The Cocktail Sailor*, Framley's Newest Show in Town. The cast and crew are delighted.

"What better way of celebrating this historical theatre than to be playing while it's closed for stage repairs?", said one sailor.

Our roving reporter meets Framley's refuse men, and learns how sanitation is a dirty job but somebody's...

A dirty job but got to do it

The daunting piles of rubbish I had to face in my job. I couldn't believe my eyes!
PHOTOGRAPH BY HESELTINE GRENADE

FRAMLEY FACES RUBBISH PROBLEMS

WHILE FRAMLEY itself is planning to adopt the controversial Maxi Bin scheme, most other collection zones in the borough have rejected the idea. Here's how the rubbish is dealt with elsewhere...

FRACTON	turned into feed for cattle and old people
SOCKFORD	shot from a gun towards France
CHUTNEY	denial
WHOFT	hidden under a big bed in an enormous room just over the district border
WRIPPLE	fed to a giant iron beast that lives in a hill
MOLFORD	ski-bins pushed downhill towards less prosperous districts, where residents use the contents as currency

Crime awareness week

By Katie Blirdsnest

FRAMLEY POLICE have announced a Crime Awareness Week as part of their Community Outreach programme, to take place between the 5th and June. Plain-clothes officer, Jemmy Guvnor, popped into The Framley Examiner offices to give us the low-down on protecting your property.

The week will include a "Bogus Callers Blitz", with Jemmy's team knocking persistently on the doors of many of the community's elderly residents.

They will prove how ineffective door chains can be and will be offering to open a high interest savings account for bewildered pensioners if they'd like to bring that wad of notes out from the tea caddy. No hiding place is safe from Jemmy, it's like taking caddy from a baby!

FANCY PARKING

There will also be a chance for young drivers to undertake an intensive course in road skills, to be run by Guvnor's right-hand, Driver Maurice. Young men with no other way out will be able to learn ancient handling methods in the 2-day "Drive! Drive!! Drive!!!" course, which Maurice himself learned off his old man.

Modules include 0-70 In 8 Seconds, Cornering Under Pressure and Dumping The Wheels In A Bit Of A Hurry. And Jemmy tells me that a one-off job may be on offer for any sprog what proves their bottle.

BURGLARY WORRY

And if you're worried about house-breaking, Framley Police are happy for concerned residents to pop into Jemmy Guvnor's local nick, which is somewhere in the north of Scotland apparently.

"Just give my boys a bell on 07999 762237 when you get there, and don't forget to give them your address with a rough estimate of value of contents," rubbing his hands together.

---

by Katie Blirdsnest

WHEN THEY TOLD me what my report was going to be about this week, I couldn't believe my eyes! Me? Join the dustbin men and pick up rubbish, like a dustman? I couldn't believe my eyes.

But when I turned up for work with the Sockford Refuse Disposal Crew (1 Team), I just had to "muck in" with the rest of the boys, even though I was a girl, which makes things quite different, in a man's world!

I met team manager Mike Roulade for my first shift, and asked him what the job was like. For instance how were the binmen treated by the people they served?

"We're like Marmite, us," he told me.

I asked him if he meant that people either loved dustmen or hated them.

"No," he replied patiently but sternly. "We're *exactly* like Marmite."

FIRST SHIFT

We pulled up for our first stop in our dustcart, and I began loading rubbish out of the alley behind Watterson Avenue. I couldn't believe my eyes!

"People throw away the oddest things," said Mike, laughing at my reaction.

He wasn't joking. There was what looked like a tar-baby in one bin, and the bottom half of a statue of Ronnie Barker poking out of the top of another. I asked Mike what was the worst thing he'd ever found in a bin. He paused to think.

"A dead leprechaun," he said eventually. "They're always trouble. It's the paperwork."

CONTROVERSY

Conversation was heated on the way

to the next pick up. Everyone had their own views on the controversial MaxiBin scheme that has made the headlines recently. These new king-sized bins are emptied every six months and have found few friends among the public, but are surprisingly popular with the dustmen.

"I'm off to Cyprus with the lads from 2 Team, for the next eight weeks," Mike said. "It's a straight choice. My lads are coming round twice a year, no more, no less. Now do you want one big skip full of rubbish blocking your driveway or forty-five wheeliebins? The choice is yours."

The binmen themselves seem unconcerned about public disapproval of the scheme.

"It's just like it was with the alphabetical rubbish idea," said Keith Mumbles of 3 Team. "At first people resisted it, and made our lives difficult, throwing away potato peelings into the bin for P for potato, rather than P for peeling, but they soon got used to it."

He lit me a fag, and we laughed.

THE WASTE LAND

At the end of a hard day's graft, I rode with the bin lorry back to the landfill site where all Framleys' rubbish is dumped.

It was an amazing site. I walked round, trying to take it in.. As I climbed to the highest point of the pile, it felt like I was literally wading through a pile of rubbish. Crows were ranged along the perimeter fence like birds, and the stench was overwhelming, rich, and creamy, like salt.

My journey was at an end, and I knew with every roly-poly I did down the pile, I knew it would take longer to wash the smell from my clothes.

I had joined the binmen.

Your first stop for value

Framley prepares to try and remember war dead

Framley's War Memorial is gathering crowds again.
PHOTOGRAPH BY JACKPOT CONNOISEUR

By TAUNTON MISHAP

AFTER YEARS of neglect, Framley's War Memorial is expected to attract large crowds again this Sunday.

The suddenly-popular obelisk was until recently scheduled for demolition, but a sudden resurgence in interest has gained it a stay of execution.

The monument commemorates the men of the Framley Rifle Regiment - the local batallion who were completely wiped out on the night before the historic battle of Limoges, in 1917. According to British Army records, the entire regiment was shot in the back while attempting to desert, a statistic unique in the history of warfare.

The regiment, most of whom, the memorial reveals, had German names, was disbanded immediately afterwards, when Framley declared itself neutral. The mayor of the time said he was not prepared to send any further men "to certain death at the hands of the merciless guns of the British Military Police".

Attempting to explain the appeal of the monument, Sockford entrepreneur Capston Cacton told me that many people feel it is time to acknowledge the sacrifices of the war years.

"If we do not learn from the past, we are doomed to repeat the future," he explained. "This memorial is important to Framley, which is why I have bought up the land surrounding it and, every Sunday lunchtime, will be screening popular films onto the marble sides of the needle."

This week memorialgoers will have a chance to see the middle third of Wayne's World 2, and next Sunday there will be a showing of the left hand side of Carry On Spying.

Redaing week a success

A READING WEEK at Newby's cannery supervised by Molford Library was judged a "great success" according to event organiser Lumpy Jungle.

"This is part of our community outreach programme," she said. "We chose books, which would have relevance to local people, and made them available in a way that would exist in harmony with their lives."

The books - *Under The Greenwood Tree* and *Firefox* - were printed in two paragraph installments onto the labels of tins of skipjack tuna, allowing employees to read while they worked.

A similar scheme has been proposed for Oriel Fruit Farms in Sockford but experts have warned that growing the text on to the sides of grapes will take considerably longer.

Take up your egg and leg and walk

THERE WAS GOOD news for local drug addict Mowbray Melton when doctors at Framley General Hospital gave him the good news: "You will walk again."

Surgeons had amputated the Sockford thrillseeker's left leg two weeks ago, due to complications arising from long term intra-venus herion use. Pre-operative X-Rays showed that one of Melton's leg veins had become blocked by an object - later revealed to be a scotch egg.

"I was starving, so I nicked it from a garage. I couldn't wait to eat, so I just jacked up and spiked myself with egg," he explained at length at a presconference at the hospital at the time.

LIMB SALVAGE

But now, thanks to a revolutionary new procedure, the junkie may be able to kiss his old leg hello again.

"We still have Mr Melton's leg on ice," said Chief Speculative Surgeon Dr Torben Bumhammer, "and have successfully removed the scotch egg. Though reattaching the severed limb is impossible, we are proposing to liquify the leg, and simply inject it back into Mr Melton's body."

Doctors say they are pretty certain that injecting the bad leg into Mowbray's one remaining good leg will enable him, within days, to walk faster than ever before.

"Four hundred miles an hour," Dr Bumhammer insisted, revving his blender.

by Pharaoh Clutchstraw

Mr Melton, in happier times.
PHOTOGRAPH BY RICTUS LIPS

Charity fat

THE CHAIRMAN of Chutney Parish Council has set himself a "countdown conundrum" of a sticky wicket. Stuart McO'Shea, 1947, is asking his parishioners to guess how much weight he willl lose during the month of Lent.

After the challenge is over, Stewart will put the weight back on before having the exact same amount removed again via the liposuction process. The extracted human fat will then be presented in a commemorative soup-bowl to the lucky guesser of the closest guess.

Mr McO'Shea, 54, has said he's determined to beat last year's total, when his poor dieting skills led to a weight gain of 17lb. As promised, he was then forced to undergo the standard fundraising failure forfeit of drinking a pint of cat bile through a straw full of dead skin.

Permission OK'yed

PLANNING PERMISSION has been granted by Framley Council for a new commemorative statue to be built in Van Dyke Park.

The proposed monument has been described by its artist as a "religious work", and depicts a scout pack eating their packed lunch on a rollercoaster, from the opening titles of *Jim'll Fix It*.

The statue, which was designed by bedbound Sockford sculptor Ibrahim Bethsheveth, will be built and opened by TV funnymen Bill Oddie and Mica Paris in the the spring.

A Man Is Being Questioned By Police (right, inside the police station) yesterday.
PHOTOGRAPH BY POMPIDOU CENTAUR

Man questioned

BY PIGSHIT NELSON

A MAN IS BEING questioned by police in Wripple after changing his name to A Man Is Being Questioned By Police, it was revealed yesterday.

The man in question, whose name is too complicated to use again in this article, claims he is being constantly questioned by police, in a series of spurious arrests designed to wind him up.

"Last week, they had me in for seventy-two hours while we went through the spellings of 3000 famous men. I got about half of them wrong.

Saint-Saëns took me nearly three quarters of an hour. It's a disgrace."

Chief Constable Ruuuuuuuuuuuuuuuuuupert Bone, himself a champion shotputter, said that "the spelling incident" had been hugely exaggerated, and that "we just needed to check the name Ayman Al Zawahiri for a charge sheet."

He also insisted that his conviction that there was "something not right" about the man in question, which had led him to set up 14 separate lines of heavily policed enquiry, would eventually bare fruit.

Molford St Malcolm

A Humorous View

MOLFORD ST MALCOLM TWINNING ASSOCIATION. - An exciting talk got this month's meetings off to a cracking start. The association welcomed guest speaker Jean Pierre Richelieu and tea was served. An attendance of more than 8 members came along to hear Jean Pierre who had travelled all the way from St Eyots. He gave a humorous view of the typical French year starting with the clearing of the hedgerows and the barrow decorating and the eating of grouse at Whitsuntide, the winner being the one whose grouse contains the coin and becomes king for a day. Members then had a short interval, with refreshments, during which they calmed down. Next week's meeting will be cancelled due to unforseen circumstances.

Beard With Sauce

MOLFORD LUNCH CLUB. - A delightful luncheon of smoked salmon with lemon sauce was enjoyed by all at last week's meeting. Treasurer Trevor Treasureton kept everyone royally entertained by growing a full beard in 20 minutes which, for the third year in a row, was long enough to reach his lunch. He then astonished members by picking up his piece of salmon with his beard and tossing it in the air. A motion was passed to applaud Mr Treasureton, and clapping and coffee followed. Apologies were received from Sgt Lowther and Mrs Appleby, who are having an affair.

Whoft

Anniversary celebrated

WOMEN'S INSTITUTE To mark the 75th anniversary of the Whoft Women's Institute, president elect Mrs Prudence Juris re-enacted the full minutes of the very first meeting, culminating with the act of institution of the WI. As a result, there are now two Women's Institutes in Whoft. Anyone wishing to help draw up new rotas for use of the hall, or to join either WI, or move from one WI to the other, should contact Mrs Juris or the Department of The Environment and ask for a leaflet.

Enjoyable Trip

DARBY & JOAN. - Mrs Swain presided at the meeting held in The Running Mayor and everyone agreed that the trip to Wovlingham had been enjoyable with agreeable weather. A considerate driver took members on a countryside tour of all the pubs between Wripple and the coast, ending with a delightful meal at The Squirrel's Problems. The driver was sentenced to a lifetime ban and 8 years' imprisonment.

Triangle Cheered Up

PARISH FELLOWSHIP. - Tertiary meeting. Twelve members of the inner council were in attendance. Minutes were read, and a triangle of grass just outside the church was cheered up by taking it to the zoo.

Creme

Harvest Supper

A CHURCH. - A harvest supper with games and competitions arranged by members of the congregation was held on Friday in St Saint's Hall. The service was a harvest festival and nine courses, led by Mary Josephs. Harvest For The Hungry boxes destined for Bulgaria and Macedonia and a collection for the Framley night shelter were blessed by the Rev Phantom Brown, and everything was eaten. Three recently baptised children were welcomed into the church, but ran screaming when they saw a horse struggling on a spit.

1970s Housewife Day

UNITED FELLOWHOOD CHURCH. - Morning worship last Sunday was '1970s Housewife Day.' All members of the church who had been housewives in the 1970s took parts of the service, and Maureen Barber gave the address. Readings were taken from Fanny Cradock's *Puff*

LOCAL CONSUMER RIGHTS campaigner Baj Curtins is at it again! He's taking Clinton seafront ice cream vendor Roger DeBear to court for false advertising. Apparently, although the ice cream cones pictured on the side of Roger's van appear to be over a yard tall, and filled with up to a gallon of ice cream, the actual cones Roger is selling turn out to be much smaller. "And another thing. His 99s cost a quid." Mr Curtins has contacted his Euro MP and hopes to force Mr DeBear to attend a war crimes tribunal in the Hague to account for his blatant deception.

PHOTO BY SCOTT CHEGG

Pastry Bible and *The Reader's Digest Book of Hoovering*. The guest was the bearded man from *The Joy Of Sex*, who was very very very popular.

Window on the world

PHOTOGRAPHIC SOCIETY The new season's programme of meetings got of to an eye-opening start with a display and talk by local photographer Galleon Prompt. Mr Prompt showed photographs of faraway places with exotic names like "America" and "Hart-le-Pool", all of which made members feel dizzy with possibility. The talk was followed by a sit down and glasses of water. Next week's talk will be by associate member Jumbo Rheims, who will show his world-famous photographs of grass.

Wripple

Silent tribute

WRIPPLE WOMEN'S INSTITUTE. - The meeting opened with a minute's silence in memory of the still late Jim Henson. This was followed by Noah Cudihogs who offered us 'Something Different' in the form of a cookery demonstration. The theme was one of speed of preparation, simplicity of flavours and overall tastelessness of the finished product. He certainly managed to achieve this as he produced dishes ranging from a potato sandwich to strawberry mouse. During social time there was an opportunity to sample the dishes but members remained unimpressed. Elizabeth Benteene won the evening's competition with her 'Easy Pie & Pea' and a fierce left hook. In-form challengers are invited to the group's next meeting at the Wripple Arena where Mrs Benteene will be defending her title.

Lively meeting

DARBY & JOAN & MANDY. - The September meeting of the over 55s wing of the Wripple Bigamists was held on Tuesday, with the admission of new member Mr Tony Biscuits and his wives almost doubling the attendance. A motion to move to a bigger hall was passed. Coffee and houmous.

Flower Arranging

WRIPPLE VILLAGE HALL. - Enrolments are being taken for two new courses starting soon at the Village Hall. These are very friendly, informal sessions, this summer focussing on 'Transforming A Front Garden' and 'Transforming A Back Garden.' The course will be led by Julia Poveney, whose front and back gardens will be converted by students into 'a glowing and brilliant riot of colour' while Ms Poveney makes tea and looks on from her recently restored oak kitchen. Classes may last all day.

A rare treat

WRIPPLE ARSONISTS. - The new chairman of the Wripple Arsonists was sworn in using the traditional brazier and sirens, while petrol was

Framley Town Plans

119 Kimberley Row, construction of single-storey sex annex at the rear. **48 Cox Street**, display of free-standing boards, flags and swastikas. **20 Urban Myth**, Molford, resiting of public payphone facility to second bedroom. **Orchard Cottages, Cigarettes Lane**, conversion of four existing cottages to provide accommodation for six elephants in a line. **108 Mill Road, Whoft**, replace existing bungalow with identical bungalow. **Bakers Arms, Sockford**, raising a section of the northern boundary wall from a height of 1ft to a height of 170ft to stop the people on the 13th and 14th floors of the neighbouring tower block from seeing any of the property. **43 Pestle Close, Little Godley**, to retain existing satellite dish, rocket silos and perimeter fencing. **High Street, Molford St Malcolm**, conversion of police station to art gallery. **22 King**

Creole Terrace, Chutney, lifting of concrete slabs from rear patio, burial of two unpleasant adults, hyperactive 4-year old child and noisy dog all belonging to 20 King Creole Terrace, relaying of patio. **Wallaby Kirk, Molford St Gavin**, redevelopment of existing single-storey lean-to to provide forecourt (including canopies, pumps, underground tanks, car wash and parking for 2500 cars). **St Margaret's Church, Whoft**, installation of two-storey half-pipe in graveyard. **77 Cotton Fields**, Sockford, construction of a PROPER toilet to replace the existing overflowing monstrosity. **St Merton's Church**, Thoxtoxeter, conversion of existing church building to forty-five foot sealed concrete cube containing two of each kind from the congregation. **18 Welwyn Garden Gardens, Framley & 19 Welwyn Garden Gardens**, linking monorail.

6 Eugene Terreblanche House, Batley, addition of 14th Century church tower housing 23cwt tenor bell to front door. **236 Pencil Street, Sockford**, single storey extension to first storey, suspended by cables from geostationary dirigible in low orbit. **Junction of Millichope Ridge and Pethig Arch**, conversion of unexploded WWII rocket propelled bomb to two 1-bed flats with garden access. **Urchin Road, Clinton**, replacement of existing flat roof with party susan containing 48,000 picnic eggs and ¾ metric tonne of dry roasted peanuts. Celery. **207 Animal Crescent**, erection of a 22ft statue of Moby on roof gable **St Greavesie's Christian Community Centre, Awkward Lane, Codge**, painting of go-faster stripes along east and west walls. **139, Cunard Heights, Molford St Gavin**, re-siting of chicken goujons from freezer to fridge.

Zephyr 1375 am

TENBY
Midday Madness

THE COLONEL
Coffee Time Request Show

ROBBIE NOUGAT
Breakfast with Nougat

GREGORY ROBERTS
An Evening with 'The King'

TRINA OXGLOVE
Weather Hour

TOM BELT
'Don't Ask Me!'

DAVID VALVE
Housewife's Choice

RON BOVRIL
4am Breakfast with Bovril

CLAIRE KINVIG
The Best Recent Playlists

CHRIS BIDDEFORD
News Argument

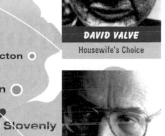

ADRIAN MATCHBOX
The Matchstick Report

ROSIE CHAMPION
The Sound of the Eighties

Fracton
Clinton
Wotten Plodney
Creme
Slovenly
Little Godley
Whott
St Eyot's
Wripple
Urling
Sockford
Chutney
Framley
Molford
Molford St Gavin
Lessbury Moreborough
Molford St Malcolm
Durbiton
Codge
Molford St Arahim Ramal
Rubmy
Effing Sodbury
Bellaire
Prince's Freshborough

The great sound of Framley

History on your doorknob

with Arbroath Smokie

EVER SINCE THE DAYS of William the Conqueror, when "Franley" was first recorded in the Doomsday Book, and registered for tax purposes as a "ditche or ponde", history has been being made every day right here under our doorsteps.

Though many of the buildings and people of the past are now sadly no longer with us, their remains still remain.

So let's take a closer look back in time round the area in which we live in, today in this day and age, and peep behind the curtain, to discover the history that lies under everyone, right here in Franley, at the end of the day, at this point in time, when all's said and done.

It's like history on your doorknob!

EFFING SODBURY WALRUS MILL

THIS FAMOUS MILL, colonised by families of walruses (not walrii, I checked) delighted and mystified visitors and tourists to Effing Sodbury during the latter half of the 19th century.

With its remote hilltop setting and no visible entrance, the old corn mill was generally assumed to be empty. This was to be the case until 1852 when legend takes a turn for the fuller mill.

In spring of that year, a passing traveller spotted a lone walrus barking from a single window situated in the roof. A cloud of blue smoke was then said to have emerged from the mill's flues and chased the petrified fellow down the hill.

Over the next 30 years sightings of window walruses became commonplace, and the alternate clouds of blue and orange smoke emerging from the chimney could be seen from as far away as Whotten Plodney and Durbiton.

In 1899, however, the building was demolished to make way for a new corn mill and walrus sanctuary. Within the walls, Victorian construction workers were delighted to discover two children playing. They were never discovered.

FRAMLEY SEAFRONT

IT'S A SOURCE of great local displeasure that Framley's historic seafront now lies in ruins.

Until 1958, Framley had much-sought-after Seaside Status. The designation had been granted to the town by King George III who loved holidaying here, but only because he was a mentalist. (According to the diary entry covering his 1774 visit to the town, he thought he was in a balloon).

However, an in-depth study into Framley's suitability for the role of Seaside Town was commissioned in 1957 after HM Queen Elizabeth II spent a "disappointing" two weeks on Framley seafront. The study revealed that Framley was landlocked, and Seaside Status was rescinded by royal decree. This was a huge blow to the then mayor, who had, in a spirit of coastalness, brought in four buses of gulls for the royal visit, beached a dolphin outside the Queen's hotel, and manned the reception desk with crabs.

In recent years there have been moves to pressure the Royal Family to reverse their judgement. Councillors and representatives of the Framley tourist industry have said they are willing to do whatever it takes to comply with the terms of the original ruling, even as far as moving every single resident, street and building 20 miles up the FR404 to the coast.

Although the glory days of Framley-on-Sea are long gone, you can still get a flavour of how the town used to be. Many reminders of Framley's glorious maritime heritage do still remain - Adam Faith the donkey still gives rides up and down the high street, and the last candyfluff stall only closed in 1998. Sadly, Framley's beautiful grass pier (pictured) now has an estate under it, and is usually on fire.

CHUTNEY VIADUCT

ASK ANYONE who was at the Great Exhibition of 1851 what their favourite bit of British engineering is and, chances are, they'll still say the same thing - The Viaduct between Chutney and Lessbury Moreborough.

The construction of the huge viaduct took place on the 16th of February 1850. The speed of the building process was largely due to the utilisation of Victorian 'Steam Mules' to propel the engineers up and down the side of the viaduct to work.

However it was the groundbreaking 'Suspension Engine' that marked this as a triumph of early Victorian engineering. This hydraulic pump raised the viaduct essential inches in clement weather to allow passage underneath to top-hatted gentlefolk. The toll? A penny.

An interesting side-effect of the suspension engine was that it allowed water to travel uphill across the viaduct. It was so efficient that flooding occurred twice daily at Lessbury Moreborough, creating an inland tidal system and successful summer tourist attraction.

Unfortunately, the viaduct fell ill in 1921 and had to be put to no further use. It can only be seen now in memory.

FRAMLEY MONUMENT

THIS QUIET memorial at the corner of Belling Street and Wharf Parade is the only reminder today of the catastrophic 1994 fire which destroyed much of Old Framley.

At the time, historians say, most of Framley's buildings were wooden framed, meaning that the whole town "must have gone up like a tramp". Contemporary accounts describe a "conflagracioun of greate ferocitee and fearsome vigorous as if the mouthe of helle itself were agape upon the streetes" *(Smash Hits)*.

Although the fire flattened much of Framley, it did clear the plague that had been raging through the town, and, parish records also note, cleared a backlog of suspected witches awaiting processing in the district pens.

Studies show that the blaze started in a monastery kitchen in Cake Walk, and spread quickly down Butter Lane, as far as Hat Street, destroying 90% of the town over four days, before firemen were called not a moment too soon. A statue of some water was erected in Cake Street to mark the aversion of disaster but it burnt down almost immediately and was replaced by the current monument depicting a monk reading the safety instructions for a Breville Sandwich toaster.

Time to run!

By Pigshit Nelson

RECORDS FELL like clumsy rain last Thursday, at the annual Framley and District Athletics Club "Race Against Time".

As usual, the challenging road race attracted both experienced athletes and strange plush-covered man-beasts, all competing to see who could reach the 6.00pm finish line first.

This year's winner, with an impressive time of 5.57pm, was Strimony Bimmelmann, a prizewinning temporal steeplechaser from Crème. Spectators watched as a faint ghost of the runner streaked past the six o'clock mark a full three minutes early, eyes bleeding with the strain.

The popular race started from outside the Bruce Dickinson Memorial Fencing Lounge in Denegate, and ended, as is traditional, at six. Crowds lined the route, waving clocks and appropriate pictures, many of former Six O'Clock Show hosts Michael Aspel and Kenny Baker.

WINNING TIMES	
1st: Bimmelmann, S	5.57:00
2nd: Wendigo, B	5.59:26
3rd: Big plush wolf	5.59:28

There was, however, a worrying moment of controversy towards the middle of the race, when bad signposting along the route led to seven competitors finishing at 3.38am the previous day. Fortunately, having been forewarned,

Runster Bimmelmann smashes a record.
PHOTOGRAPH BY BENETTON PRELLT

course officials were able to rectify the problem so it had never happened.

Bimmelmann's new record smashes the 5.58 six o'clock barrier set by Sir Roger Bannister in the Molford Hundreds in 1962. The record had stood for so long that many were beginning to think it unbreakable. In 1976, sports physicist Richards Richard declared, "If man had been meant to arrive at 6.00 at 5.57, God would have created him three minutes earlier."

Local MP, Ianbeale Steeplecocque, who picketed the event with a sign, has promised race fans that next year's event will be cancelled.

A match with something for everything

WHOFT BERBERS...........................1
MOLFORD BUTTERFLIES.............1
(Electric Entertainment League)

By BARBOUR ZADAGIO

SATURDAY saw Whoft come within a tantalising 1 points of their first ever victory.

Actually winning a game is still nothing more than a sweet little nightmare for the Berbers, but this, their first game of the season, was also their best so far.

Conditions were messy underfoot after two weeks of torrential fluff, making handling difficult and sneezing inevitable.

A row before the kick-off failed to resolve the matter of whether this was a league or union game, and Molford insisted on playing 15 league men against Whoft's 13-strong union side. As a compromise, each team was allowed to bring its own referee.

Molford kicked off and immediately started winning - a strong position on which they disappointingly failed to build on for the rest of the match. The players all started running around shouting numbers at each other, which I found rather distracting above the noise of the 8-strong crowd.

The Butterflies, fresh from their

astonishing 2-1 win against the Sockford Clownes, stormed into the match, their referee awarding them no fewer than 28 penalties in the first five minutes alone.

After further struggling and a fist fight between the two refs, Whoft goalie Adrian Rugby (what an amusing name for a rugby player, isn't it!) made a valiant save from the crossbar onto which he'd climbed, although in doing so, he clumsily avoided not falling off and rupturing two of his famous kidneys.

Butterflies centre winger God Johnson then sent the ball on to skipper Sir Frostie Canuderbitch who passed to left hook Ravenal Showboat on the blind side who powered his way to a showstopping try, landing the ball right in middle of the face of spreadeagled Adrian Rugby, who was by now being attended to by beleaguered ambulancemen.

Rugby was declared dead minutes later, just as four of the flagging Berbers found themselves locked in a scrum. They continued to play as an indivisible sixteen-legged mess for the rest of the game.

The second half whizzed by in a flapping of arms and more shouting of numbers (which I found less distracting because I left at half time) and apparently it was a drawer.

SPORTS extra

Sports day means sport

St **BARRABAS' Infants' School** sports day went with its usual bang, this Saturday, writes one of our staff.

Parents and children cheered as pupils lurched about the lower field, confused by the rules of the Knife & Fork race, until teachers intervened.

The 110 Metre Hurtles also hospitalised several young competitors. Eventually, after hurtling through a nose-breaking eight sheets of plywood, a victorious and bloody Gawain Bethlem, 8, was helped to the podium by his mother.

At the Optical Course, designed for the school in 1946 by Mauritz Escher, hot favourite Oliver Hans fell at the "Neverending Staircase". With the field wide open, year 3's Maysie Ballon stormed to victory after a stunning "Which Line Is Longer?".

The Three-Legged Pole Vault was won with the bar at 47'6" by the unseeded Sorcha Cockrill and Evan Elevan, after their chief rivals were disqualified for going "one under - one over", a foul in the rules, I'm led to understand.

The great-grandparents' race went to Mr Wisty Memorial, 84, after great-grandmother Mrs Eileen Thoth came over all faint and sicked up in the last few yards.

Molford District Darts League Results

The Drink & Drive	11-4	The Fluff Lion
The Broken Arms	9-6	The Famous BBC2
The Chandelier & Grandad	6-9	The Naked Landlord
The Prince of Peas	2-13	The Goldilocks & Bear & Two Bears
The Drummer Out Of Def Leppard Who's Only Got One Arm's Arm	7-8	The Knitting Noodle
The Eighteen Bees	1-14	The People On Fire
The Frank Finlay & Firkin	6-9	Here Be Turnips
The Carry On Abroad	9-6	A Anchor
The Crush & Grape	4-11	The Warm Zippy
The My Family And Other & Groom	0-15	The Simply Not Good Enough
The Chitty Chitty Bang	10-5	The Old Lady And Broken Kite

Television treasures are found in treasure trove

by Taunton Mishap

TV BOSSES WHO PUT out a call for lost episodes of classic television shows from the golden age of television were shocked and stunned by what has turned up in a loft in Whoft - a treasure trove of television previously thought lost forever.

Mahabarat Robinson, 52, found the unlabelled film cans amongst the effects of his late dead father, a former Comedy Classic wiper for the BBC.

"We'd presumed these rare historical artefacts had been wiped. But, goddamn it," said a BBC spokesphilistine yesterday, "we were wrong."

THE GOOD LIFE

The hoard, which contains the forgotten pilot episode of popular seventies survivalist documentary *The Good Lives* has shocked media historians, particularly in the many subtle ways this early draft differs from the hit show as we now know it.

In the newly rediscovered pilot, the title role of Tom Life is taken by

Mr Robinson is delighted that his finds have been found.
PHOTOGRAPH BY ANDREW DEFINITELY

much-missed adulterer Leonard Rossiter.

,

In the show, Rossiter, together with his wife Barbarah (Diane Keen), decides to build a farm in his lounge, much to the annoyance of stuck-up neighbours Jerry (*Rising Damp*-star Don Warrington) and Hanna (Minnie Riperton). Soul legend Riperton also performs a medley of her smash hits *Les Fleurs* and *Inside My Love* in the middle of the programme, backed by The Mike

Sammes Quantity, while Rossiter delivers a pig.

Warrington, who claims to not remember recording the show, was delighted that it had turned up. "What do I do in it? Oh, good."

Also in Mr Robinson's nostalgia haul were the missing Christmas episode of *Fawlty Towers*, where the cast go to Barcelona to stay in Manuel's brother's guest house; the final episode of *The Sweeney*, in which Denis Waterman gets eaten by a seal; and Arnold Ridley - Private Godfrey out of *Dad's Army*.

All the forgotten gems will be returned to the BBC archives, where they will be taped over with weather reports and closed circuit footage of the car park. Mr Ridley will be humanely destroyed on the June 13th edition of *Rolf's Animal Hospice*.

News In Brief

PENSIONERS RAIDED

A retirement home in Fracton was raided by police from Framley Drugs Squad in the early hours of Saturday morning.

Drugs worth a pavement price of £58,000 were seized, mainly aspirin, paracetamol and mogadon. 35 frail and infirm people were arrested and further 113 harassed. Unconfirmed reports say there are no survivors.

HOUSE HAUNTED HOUSE

Whoft resident Grammaticus Throttle has called in experts following claims that his house is haunted.

Throttle, 59, is convinced that his house is being haunted not by ghosts, but by living people. Exorcist Fulton Wonderful, however, says the so-called ghosts are Mr Throttle's upstairs neighbours, whom Grammaticus has been trying to evict since they installed glass floors and a 76-trombone doorbell.

JEFF'S WEDDING STORY

A woman whose husband fell asleep during their wedding vows has filed for annulment. "It was so embarrassing," says 23-year old stunner Lorraine Plums. "He was supposed to be saying 'I do', but all we could hear was him snoring." Her new soon to be ex-husband, Victor, later explained he was "bored".

Time for a wash

FRAMLEY TOWN hall's famous 20th century astronomical clock is to have its face washed for the first time since its construction almost as many years ago.

The huge clock, which is rumoured to only be fully visible from space, has been a favourite amongst old residents since it was built into the shopping precinct roof in 1968.

The passing hours are marked with a chime from one of the twelve bell towers scattered around the town. Every quarter hour, a wooden joust takes place above the clock face between the mediaeval characters of 'Jack o' the Hours' and 'Molly o' the Minutes', the result of which determines the length of the following hour.

By request of local MP Ianbeale Steeplecocque the essential

The clock figures who will have a special bath.
PHOTOGRAPH BY KEVVIN CHIPS

renovation works are to be undertaken while the clock mechanism is still running. This procedure will involve careful hand holding and numeral lifting during cleaning to avoid "time standing still".

to leave the hotel for three weeks now, because of the snipers. This is the only phone number I can remember, so I hope this gets through. Jenny, I love you and miss you terribly. Look after the kids. Donald.

COLANDER that lets the lumps out but leaves the liquid in. £15. Box FE8741. And no, I don't know how it works.

ETCHASKETCH "Curves" edition. Only draws curves. A giant leap sideways. 01999 722444.

LP for sale, 50p. 01999 240971.

FORD TURNIP 3.0 Touring, R-reg, very clean, fsh but no reverse gear or brakes. £3,000 asap because I've been driving round the block for 2 months and I want to get out. Tel 0906 480991.

HOSTESS TROLLEY. Fits two hostesses or one hostess and one client. £120 after 6pm.

TRAMPOLINE REQUIRED Any condition accepted. Mine's been stolen. Please hurry, I'll be coming down in a minute. 01999 733 008

STANNAH stairlift, lifts your stairs so you can't get onto them, vgc, £3500. Box FE8440.

INVISIBLE MAN, good nicker, £500. First to see will buy. 01999 673382.

CAN PEOPLE TELL by the way you use your walk that you are a woman's man? Do you have time to talk? We've helped six people like you. Call 01999 450981.

JOE & PETUNIA

THE FACT THAT I SMOKE IS YOUR FAULT forehead-mounted 3ft placard. £10 ten pound a tenner. 01999 460171.

HAYNES MANUALS for sale: Vauxhall Cioo 1985-89, Zanussi Z101 pocket fridge, Robin CurlyGirly hairdryer 1990-92, IKEA cutlery (new shape) and wallpaper. 01999 871298.

BLACK & WHITE MICROWAVE oven. £75. 01999 238664.

KEITH HARRIS ventriloquist's dummy. Comes with Orville ventriloquist's dummy ventriloquist's dummy. Call 01999 648 877 any time before the item is sold.

ROOFING CONTRACTORS, guttering and points. Will frot. Discreet service. Box FE8300.

BABY, Winnie The Pooh design, vgc, £10. 01999 313453.

INCOMPLETE KITCHEN. Bits of wood, bits of tiles, plughole, some other things, rest somewhere (might get round to finding bits). 01999 688140.

WICKER RADIO, geuine twiggy sound, AM only. £15. 01999 429420 am only.

250 x 2 piece jigsaw puzzles, each showing scenes of bits of harbour/sky. £1 each. Will separate. Box FE 01999 454120.

WHEELCHAIR, lightweight, folding for a car, little used. Good fun while it lasts. £45. 01999 866426.

PINK FLOYD'S Dark Side Of The Moon. Royalty cheques not quite as large these days, hence quick sale. Other satellite properties also available. Phone Roger on 01999 878 930

HOLY CRAB

GLASS GARAGES, self-assemble, show off your stuff to burglars, 8ft x 6in x ft, £8000. Freephone 09999 100600 (calls charged at £35 per min at all other times).

CAN'T SLEEP at night? Get up. £35. 01999 238117.

DANNY BAKER VIDEO "Football's Craziest Linesmen Vol 3". Still in box. £1. 01999 896 033

01999 845763. Offers 01999 863741.

INEXPENSIVE CHILD-MINDER required to look after sensitive 6 year old (Josie) while rest of family go on 3-week holiday to Disneyworld. References / experience not essential. Call Mr Hollyhock on 01999 482762

PINSTRIPE chimney pots, 32" waist, £20 each or £20 the pair.

RAWSORE Breast Pump & 50 litre feeding churn with Nipple Replacers. Box FE8280 after 6pm.

SLEEP-EASY INFLATABLE QUILT. Fully inflated forms 4' patchwork sphere floating eight inches above mattress. £15. 01999 560125.

FRAMLEY EXAMINERS for sale. Complete set 1978-2012. £offers Call Prof. Arthur Bostrom on 01999 429006. Experiment successful.

The Framley Examiner

"I sold my bicycle to the firth person who bought it. Thanks, Framley Examiner."

Mr Ing, Molford St Gavin

DANCING TABLECLOTH. Ashtray Polka / Cutlery 2-Step / Flower Arrangement Cha-Cha-Cha-Cha-Cha. £20. Box FE8631

"MRS COD" Ladies' Fish-n-Chips Umbrella. Take your mind off the weather by letting it rain delicious fish and chips straight onto your head! Wrapped, or open. £12, pickled onions 50p. 01999 852 872

IRON-ON GENTLEMAN'S PENILE TATTOO for urethra wall. Reads "Get In Lane". No longer required. £8. Whoft 855 341.

LOFT LADDERS, £135. Use your loft! We have thousands of ladders and nowhere to put them. We'll pay you £135 to store a few dozen in your loft. 01999 866 400

VOLKSWAGEN QUAGWAT 2.0E, not right from day one, handles like a rowing boat full of drugged children, £6,790 if necessary. Tel David (not "Dave") 01999 520998.

CHOCOLATE LOG effect electric fire. Just turn it on and it melts all over carpet. Already melted so £2. 01999 705590.

SIDEBOARDS. Italian. Job lot, 2 doors blown off, you're only supposed to bloody phone 01999 290000.

The Framley Examiner

"My spiral travel scissors sold within 24 hours!"

Mrs Eth, Wripple sold for £50*
(* spiral travel scissors sold for £75)

1930s dinner service. Complete: 74 spoons, 3 forks, half a knife, tureen, gravy boat and soup yacht, £120. 01999 420425 after £120pm.

MY EX-WIFE'S NEW MAN'S MOBILE PHONE NUMBER IS 0999 766 533. Call it anytime between 1am and 4.20am and ask for Mr Cunt. That's 0999 766 533 and "Mr Cunt".

PAIR OF 18th Century "Bad Kitty" cat handcuffs. £200 or what? 01999 871289.

PUSH / WHEEL CHAIR, £45. No phone so write.

RYVITA? / RIBENA?

3-BEAN BAG. Tiny. £1. 01999 811111.

EVER WONDERED how a magician saws a lady in half? I think I can show you how. Box FE8311.

COFFEE TABLE, tea towel, Bovril slippers. The kettle's just boiling, pop round any time! 01999 552170.

NOVELTY CHESS SET Pieces representing Burger King (Dovercourt branch) relief staff. Board and Jessica Leonard (white bishop) missing, hence £35. 01999 885490.

CHILD'S three-quarter length grown-up, never used, £350ono. Box FE8230.

DOG BISCUITS, 3 flavours, Poodle, Labrador and Custard St Bernard. £5 a box or £5 a box. 01999 219335.

CLASSICAL GAS

INTENSIVE CARE BEARS Full set of upsettingly realistic children's toys, including Sunshine Coma Bear and Love-a-Lot Serious But Stable Bear. IV capoc drips on furry stands, and Wolf Nurse. Offers. Box FE8166

400 CONDOMS. All pink. Inappropriate gift. Obviosuly for girls. Will swap for blue ones for boys. Box FE8982.

DODGIMIX food processor with blender, 4 blades & 28 recipes. Requires some emptying, hence £no idea. 01999 885166.

VAUXHALL SPASMA 1.3L F-reg, vgc, no paperwork except MOT valid until 2047. £3,000 and no questions. Tel 01999 859120.

DOWNRIGHT PIANO. So piano. Really piano. £450 after 01999 381150pm.

SET OF SIX novelty cycling helmets. Sombrero, deerstalker, topper, fez, porkpie and scotch egg. Owner to collect. £8 each except £12. 01999 631408.

GIRLS mountain penny farthing. Used once. Also chest of girls clothes and effects. £yes. Box FE8137.

TIRED OF GOING UNNOTICED? Try one of our 'Stare At Me And Win £1000' t-shirts. M, XM, XXM. Call Vince 01999 450887 after today.

LAURA ASHLEY wetsuit, size 14. Black velvet bodice, long sleeves, with crepe de chine skirt. Bargain, £2000. Box FE8086.

HORIZONTAL baby bouncer, fits most halls, £45. 01999 882531.

MORPHY RICHARDS BeardMaker. Watch your beards grow and rise! £35. 01999 838440.

TABLE TENNIS table, half size, no receiving end, £65. 01999 352920.

ALL SCOTLAND'S BUTTERFLIES. You wondered where they'd gone. I've got them in my garage. £150 the lot. 01999 842 098

ELVIS COSTELLO This Year's Model train set, £15. 01999 487101.

"FUZZY PUMPER PUBERTY SHOP" TOY. Supplied with "Brunette", "Mousey" and "Ginger" Play-Doh tubs. Box FE8922.

NAN VARNISH, 5 litres, £30. 01999 328600.

GENUINE Victorian television cabinet. Mahogany with ormolu brass handles and ivory aerial attachment. £350. Will sell to the first person who calls, whether they like it or not. 01999 461023.

UNCONVENTIONAL DINNER SERVICE. Jack knives, tuning forks, satellite dishes, crown green bowls, that sort of thing £60. 01999 713382

BABYGAP maternity dress. Ages 4-5. £70. 01999 681290.

THE CORN LAWS

LADIES' EROTIC ACCESSORY. Battery-operated vaginal swingball. Stimulates and bruises. Comes (every time) with two fanny racquets. £25. 01999 844 812

SINGLE "Z" BED, will fold out into double "N" bed or a pile of I's. £12. Box FE8533

Last year,
The Framley Examiner
readers sold more than
22,000
rare birds' eggs through our classified pages.

OAK EFFECT pine-style dining table with elm-plated mahogany finish, £200. 01999 862380.

TOTTENHAM HOTSPUR bedroom accessories, including bedlinen, pitch, turnstiles & bunkbed shaped like Pat Jennings tipping one over the bar. £offers. Box FE8385.

SALT & VIAGRA CRISPS, for nibbles that keep you up ALL NIGHT LONG! Also Dry Rohypnol Peanuts. 01999 Box FE 230886.

MATSUI digital nappies, with action replay and 10x macro, £300 each. 01999 300500 (T).

1967, lovingly restored in glass pack. Fiancée beginning to embrace free love, hence quick sale. £43 quickly - now nearly December. Box FE8109.

SLIPSHOD

SNOOKER BOARD, complete set of six balls, Jocky Reardon signature flights, Jim Bowen's "Bull Pocket" quiz book, £45. 01999 841971.

ALUMINIUM LADDER, 13ft long, 3 rungs, up only, £15. 01999 837414.

COLLECTION OF EARLY prototype vinyl CDs (1979-83). "Lexicon of Luxury", "Drat!", "Legionnaire - Just The Hits", "Nik Snood Live At The Blackheath Oregano", "Infrastructure IV", "Ickenham Dartboard - Sharp Pants and Piano Ties", "Walnut Whip" and "More Shillingbury Tales". Also half jar of jam and one six-inch nail. Acquired through work. £20 the lot. Call 01999 866 732 and ask for Michael Rodd or Judith Hann.

WEBSITE SOILED CLOTHING? Crusty with bollock marmalade? You're not coming in. Framley 895 544

PORT DECANTER and set of six solid Stilton glasses. Ripe. 01999 827454.

DICK VAN DICK

NISSAN THROATGRIPPER 4x2, terrifying 7.0L 3-gearbox, 6-wheel chrome and reinforced leather nightmare covered in roo bars and spotlights. The worst investment I ever made. I only needed it for the school run. £12,000 or anything. Tel Linda (not her real name) 01999 492217.

BARBIE ROLLERSKATES, will fit Barbie aged 6-9. £13.29ono. 01999 830987.

FRONT DOOR. Single panelled 77" x 35" glazed white uPVC door leading to my house and all my possessions, £35 the lot. 01999 901999.

GOODMANS Slightly Too Personal CD Player, plays songs relating to your life and details those areas in which you have failed miserably to live up to your own expectations or the expectations of those around you. Unwanted gift. Box FE8377.

SINGLE BED with mattress, storage drawers and me in it. £30, or £10 with annual hand-job. 01999 842151.

SCENES FROM HOLY BOOKS CRISPS, available in Bible, Koran, Bhagavad Gita and Chokey Bacon. Also, turn your visions of the blessed virgin into crisps. 01999 963 371.

TOILET DUCK. Turns water blue but pecked my arse. Removes crust under rim. £4. 01999 863 373

SPEAKING CLOCK RADIO, tells the time every 10 seconds. 2 (very insistent) voice settings: Naughtie / Wogan. £0. 01999 352133. Need not collect.

CLIPART CD "Saluting Fried Eggs". Over 240,000 images of fried eggs in a variety of saluting poses, including cub, National Socialist, senior officer, RAC, twelve gun and high-five. 01999 822 920

The Framley Examiner

"I got excellent results from The Framley Examiner. I sold everything I own except what I advertised."

Mrs Roophie, St Eyot's

COCKER SPANIEL KITTENS, superb temperament, quizzical look. 01999 480161.

PINE CD STORAGE towers, 14ft tall, store 4 CDs in luxurious splendour. En suite bathroom. £4500 each. 01999 381666.

PAIR OF galvanised haystacks, £15 each the lot each per pair. 01999 492294.

INCOMPETENTLY DRAWN hand-made Father's Day card depicting some sort of blue square holding hands with larger green shape (possibly car?). Message inside reads "Please Love Me Daddy from Josie", but spelt wrong. £offers. Unwanted gift. Call Mr Hollyhock on 01999 482762.

ARMITAGE SHANKS handbasin on pedestal. Ivory, with skid marks, £85. Box FE8626.

CAMCORDER WANTED, must be in good working order. Needed ASAP - baby about to fall out of high chair. 01999 829737.

Last year,
The Framley Examiner
readers sold more than
13,000
feet of purloined rushes from Star Wars Episode 8

CROWD SUBBUTEO. 48,000 pieces. Extremely slow play. Kenneth Wolstenholme's "Some People Are On The Pitch" Edition (1966). £12 in original box. 01999 872 421

BILLS. Gas. Water. Council Tax. £387 the lot. 01999 8

CHILDSPLAY™ carrier bag. Safe for putting over head. Fully breathable. £6 Also Wendy Abandoned Freezer. £45. Tel 01999 848 221

CUB SCOUT uniform, size 16 with 38" bust, £30. 01999 761443onn.

MELTED CHEDDAR bubble bath foam. 50cl. Produces one huge bubble. Do NOT pop. £3 01999 855 188

PRINGLES JUMPER. Full of crisps, very itchy and I just can't stop wearing it. Will swap for Pickled Onion Monster Munch jockey shorts. 01999 844 902

A final slice of the pie

by Bowery Tarpaulin

Britain's oldest pie is about to serve its last slice. Clinton Pie, baked in 1951 as an exhibihit for the Festival of Britain and relocated to Clinton seafront in 1952 is now down to its last portion.

For the last 50 years the pie has provided, in total, hour after hour of enjoyment to visitors and local residents and visitors alike.

The first slice, served on Saturday 5th June to King George VI by Winston Churchill, became a symbol of hope, prosperity and nourishment for the nation.

After this, slice after slice was served, until the following year,

The pavillion housing the pie.
PHOTO BY HARRISON COMPARISON

when the pie was relocated to the jetty on Clinton seafront to act as a "Pastry Beacon of Peace".

Since then until now, hundreds of visitors have visited the 25m diameter savoury tart, including

some celebrities and some politicals.

That is until next Saturday, when the last few morsels of the pie will be auctioned off to local charities with the intention of funding a "Save The Pie Trust".

The Trust will endeavour to protect the last few crumbs of the famous pie, and return the jetty to the ocean as a memorial.

"It'll be a great and tragic day for all of us who come to Clinton, year after year for the Pie", says Pie enthusier, Canard Leghorn

"I've been coming here since I was 30, and that's twenty-three times. My daughter's still missing and where will the pie be when it's gone?".

Donations and concerned relatives can contact Mr. Leghorn on his Pie Helpline during low tide.

Train man dies

A DEPRESSED train driver who was on the verge of bankruptcy has committed suicide by throwing himself under a passenger.

Rufus Boing, 31, was said to be at "both ends of his tether," according to his doctor, when he deliberately dived under the front wheels of Carolyn Morphene's Vauxhall Average as she drove through the town centre.

Ms Morphene, who is suffering from post traumatic stock, was a regular passenger on Mr Boing's 0732 from Framley station, and had even accidentally slept with him on "one or two" occasions.

A spokesmen from MidCentral Journeys offered Mr Boing's family his deepest sympathy, and presented Ms Morphene with new wheels. There was a strike that day which explains why he wasn't working and she wasn't on a train.

In Court

BALLYHOO Bullknuckle, 46, of Manic Street Preacher Street, Molford, was hanged and banned from driving after he admitted parking all over 65-year old Denise Poverty in the Arnhem Contre one day.

MY MOTHER, 54, of My Family Home, Framley, heaped shame upon the family by being found guilty of parking a vomit bomb outside Framley General Hospital on All Saints' Night.

REG Edit, 43, The Address, Crème, was fined £50 for paying a previous £50 fine without due care and attention.

ANNIE Pandy, 27, of Slag Heap, Molford, was fined £35 with FF68,00 costs and A$200 compensation for possessing 8.1g of marshmallow at his address on October.

KERRY Perry, 23, of Boysenberry Spiral, St Eyot's, received a 35-year conditional discharge for damaging the corner of an envelope belonging to Glans Cliffcakes on July 14. He was ordered to cough up £400 compensation and his first born child (as yet unborn) in costs.

PAUL Discovery, 29, of Hexagon Rhomboid, Thoxtoxeter, was raised two metres and blown through an open window for 'becoming lighter than air' on two separate occasions during the Summer of '69. He was asked to pay a heavy fine.

EVEREST Blessed, 19, of Manilow Retreat, Effing Sodbury, had his head separated from his shoulders for assaulting a grizzly bear at Framley District Zoo on the sixth Friday of May last year. An additional fine of £80 remains unpaid.

VIOLET Complexity, 76, of Cake St, Whimsy, was returned by second-class mail after being inadvertently posted to an illegal address. Her statuatory rights remain, as ever, unaffected.

BESTHEMANE Fisticuff, 31, of Steam Crescent, Fracton, was released into the wilderness last Friday as part of an experiment to determine the shelf life of lime cordial. She may never return.

ELEPHANT McCartney, 24, of The Dodecahedron, St Eyot's, received a damning 3 minute summation of his shitty life after being lowered on top of Justice Constant Waxy during Big Court. His sentence is being punctuated.

School concert "far too loud"

By not Our Arts Correspondent, TAUNTON MISHAP

THIRTY-TWO children from Molford Children's School are recovering in hospital after a school concert went disastrously wrong last week.

The end of term jamboree had been organised by head of music Nigel Merry, who was due to conduct the senior orchestra through a medley of light popular hits from the 1960s, using his favourite 5-inch-long conductor's baton.

However, a sudden outbreak of flu caught Mr Merry off the hop, and his place was taken on the night of the concert by his deputy, Sally Quaskling. Parents are blaming the tragedy on this decision.

ENORMOUS VOLUME

"It was terrible," said the mother of one of the trumpeters, "Miss Quaskling had a huge baton, nearly a yard long, much bigger than Mr Merry ever used. When she started conducting, the children just followed, but her baton... Her baton was far too big..." She broke down.

Another parent told emergency services that the piece was so loud that "people started to run screaming from the hall in fear of their lives."

"The children were only following orders," said another mother's brother. "But... too... too loud..."

Within moments the band striking up Petula Clark's *Downtown*, windows in neighbouring streets started to shatter and the earth was momentarily tipped off its axis.

The concert was called to a premature halt when a have-a-go hero attacked Miss Quaskling with a fire extinguisher, killing her.

The horn section's eardrums burst painfully.
PHOTO BY MORDRED FRONT

Children were reportedly led away with burst bloodvessels and bleeding mouths. A CD of the concert will not be available ever.

Developments announced in missing charabanc case

The coach party in the road outside The Running Mayor public house, shortly before they set off for Fracton and vanished.
PHOTOGRAPH BY MOGADON SPOOK

by Jesus Chigley

POLICE WHO HAVE BEEN INVESTIGATING the mysterious disappearance in 1953 of a charabanc full of holidaymakers have announced that the bus and its passengers can now be officially declared "presumed missing".

In a neatly typed press release, released to the press last Thursday, chief investigating officer Det Sgt Ronald Sodastream said that his team were now almost 99% certain that the coach was no longer on its way to Fracton, and that there was no reason not to assume that it was probably missing.

"In police work, it's important not to jump to any hasty conclusions," the sergeant's statement read. "We couldn't rule out the possibility that the charabanc was just taking the long way round. I assure the public that my officers have been watching the main Fracton arterial road for the last fifty years like hawks, just in case."

WHERE IS THE BUS?

Having redesignated the errant pantechnicon's status from "late" to "presumed missing", the police are confident that enquiries into its whereabouts can now begin in earnest.

"I'm glad that, after all these years of uncertainty, the anguish is over for the families and friends of the unaccounted for holidaymakers,"

Sodastream told me yesterday.

"To those patient people, I say take comfort from the knowledge that your loved ones are undoubtedly missing."

And things are already moving fast. A special group of detectives are looking into the possibility that the coach and passengers may have simply gone invisible, while other experts are searching all the drawers in the police station to see if someone just filed the bus away somewhere and forgot where they put it.

New paving stone

A new paving stone is to be laid to replace a damaged one. The stone, made by Dabney & Dabney Brick Works, will occupy 45cm of the pavement at the corner of Slops Steps and Prefab Way in Sockford. The stone will be laid by a top pavementer rushed in by contractors Wonham Foreign de Foreigner. Saturday is expected.

This month's LOTTERY PREDICTION from Megalithic Meg

6

"I predict 6"

Voter apathy to blame

BY BUNCO BOOTH

THE LOWEST EVER turnout in Framley at last week's local election is being blamed on voter apathy.

The council elections, held on Thursday, broke all records for turnout, percentages and majorities, in a surprise that psephologists (who are people who study voting trends)* weren't expecting.

One of Framley's most famous political faces, Cllr Geoffrey Cauchaugh, managed to poll the most votes in his ward, with the returning officer declaring him elected with a majority and total of 1 vote. All the other candidates polled none.

"I only put in my vote for a photo opportunity, and naturally, I voted for myself," shouted Cllr Cauchaugh from his fifth-floor office as I interviewed him from the car park.

ROCK THE VOTE

When asked why they did not even vote for themselves, Cauchaugh's rivals remained unapologetic.

"Politics doesn't really interest me," said one. "It doesn't have any effect on my life. And anyway, you can't really change anything, so what's the point?"

Exit pollsters at a polling station in Whoft find it easy to cope with an influx of no voters.
PHOTOGRAPH BY FORGETMENOT EVANS

Perhaps more surprisingly, others did not even know the election was taking place.

"That's perhaps even more of a surprise - I didn't even know the election was taking place," said others.

ANARCHY FOR THE UK

None of Cllr Cauchaugh's 15 opponents lost their deposit, luckily, thanks to the D'Ainty Poll Act Bye-Law 1997, which states that "a candidate need only poll no (0) votes to be deemed legitimate."

The act, which the High Court and House of Lords have declared "illegal, unethical, undemocratic, overtly and unfairly partisan and entirely empirically contradictory" has been declared "awesome" by Mayor D'Ainty.

* *Source: British Airways in-flight dictionary.*

Mayor stoned

BY BUNCO BOOTH

QUESTIONS are being asked about the future of the mayor, Mr William de D'Ainty, after claims that he was stoned last week in his office.

Mr Mayor, 44, was found slumped over his desk in hysterics by his secretary, Herod Williams, on Friday lunchtime.

Miss Williams, who famously won the boat race in 1960, also claims that she had to cancel the mayor's appointments for the rest of the day because he thought his fingers were ten little milkmen. Mayor D'Ainty spent the rest of the afternoon happily practising his signature on a blotting pad.

"He was blapped," she illuminated.

When questioned about the events by interested reporters, Mr Mayor admitted that his memories of Friday afternoon were "hazy, at best," but insisted that he had no recollection of anybody throwing stones at him.

In Court

Conman made pensioner get him a glass of water

A MAN DESCRIBED AS "a dangerous conman by police", tricked his way into the home of Wripple pensioner Jerome Leading, 72, last Thursday and persuaded the unsuspecting old man to get him a glass of water.

The conman then sat down in Mr Leading's lounge, drank the water, and left.

Police say this is one of the oldest scams in the book, and have warned all pensioners to be particularly vigilant, remembering to check the identification of all callers.

The glass of water, filled from the cold tap in Mr Leading's kitchen, was yesterday being ground into a fine powder by forensics experts in case it turns out to be full of clues.

Scott is certainly a top of the class!

by Jesus Chigley

SCOTT JOPPPLIN, a Year 12 pupil from St Gahan's School For Boys in Framley, is definitely top of the class! His record-breaking haul of SIXTY-FIVE! A-Levels has made him become the most successful pupil in the school's three hundred year history.

Normal pupils at the school usually take no more than three A-Levels, with an optional fourth for swots. Scott made special arrangements with the examination board in order to achieve his achievement, often sitting two exams at once and, in one case, entering the same set of answers for three papers in different subjects.

It was unconventional examing by anyone's standard, but the results speak for themselves.

"I was nervous before the results envelope arrived," he told our reporter when I phoned him, "but when I saw I'd passed nearly all of them, it was a huge relief and I got drunk."

The only subject that proved too tricky for the exam mastermind was Geography, in which he did worse than me. "I'd been up for eight days' straight by that point, and could only draw circles," he said in his defence.

Scott, whose father is married to local TV weatherman Gareth Smee, is to be immortalised by a tapestry draped over the west wing of the school like a blanket over a parrot's cage.

Here are the exam results that made Scott the cleverest boy in the world:

English (D)	Spirograph (A)	The Farm (A)
Maths (D)	Pub Quiz (B)	Showing Off (A*)
French (D)	Woodwork Oral (C)	Crumb (Robert) (A)
Geography (U)	StickleBricks (A)	Crumb (Charles) (A*)
History of Soup (A)	Jugs (A*)	Marijuana Cuisine (B)
Tommy Cooper (A)	Rugs (C)	The Unbelievable (A)
Whisk (B)	Burning It (C)	Alphaboni Rigatoni (C)
Mouse Hunt (C)	Homebrew (C)	Write Anything You Like (A*)
Stopping (A)	Somebody On A Beach (A)	If... Then... (B)
Kettle Maintenance (A)	Umbrella (Opening) (A)	Lucky Dip (A)
Hiding a Bus (B)	Umbrella (Closing) (C)	Fire Exits (B)
Manchester (C)	Cannonball Run 2 (B)	Walking In A Straight Line (C)
Playtime (A)	Big Coins (C)	GCSE (A)
Applied Carpets (B)	Surprise (A)	Pure Maths (Best In Show)
Captain Sensible (B)	The Blustery Day (B)	Worm Husbandry (B)
French Smiling (A)	French Kissing (A)	Sandwich Spread (B)
Mud Wrestling (B)	Pin The Tail On The Answer (B)	Showboat (A)
Body Popping (A*)	Roundie or Squarie (A*)	Bullshitting (A)
Hula Hoop (A)	Dominoes (B)	I Spy Roadsigns (A*)
Measles (A)	Guinea Pigs (B)	When I Grow Up (B)
Shoegazing (B)	Fancy (A)	Battleships (B)
Practical Kitten (A)	Highland Fling (B)	Lists (B)

So, think you could do better? Try our sample questions from some of Scott's papers and see if you could beat Framley's own Stephen Hawkings!*

1. In one word describe how long it takes for the sun to travel the sky.

2. Two men start walking towards each other at the same speed on different days. When will they learn?

3. "Discuss the significance of 'Trial By Eating Sweetcorn Niblets With A Cocktail Stick' in *Gawain and The Green Giant*." Discuss.

4. Now close the box.

5. What is the essential difference between a web spun by a cat and that spun by a mouse?

6. A triangle has four sides. The sum of the internal angles is 270°. Using this information, rearrange the sides to spell the word "Hut", without breaking any of the matchsticks.

7. "There is light at the end of the tunnel." How do you know this?

8. Make an ox-bow lake.

9. Use both sides of the paper if necessary.

*These questions are for fun only, and are not exchangeable for A-Levels.

Ernhold Swiss (Left), the headmaster of Teapop Prep School, expressed concern at the hygeine of the Sewerside Leisure Centre (Above)

PICTURES BY TESCO DICKBARTON

Big bug

by Pharaoh Clutchstraw

FRAMLEY ENVIRONMENTAL HEALTH OFFICERS closed a local leisure centre and took samples of school canteen food after a mystery bug hit pupils at Teapop Preparatory School on Monday.

The children, aged between 11, complained of "feeling all sick" after attending a schools' fishing gala at Framley's Sewerside Leisuredrome on Friday evening.

The leisure centre, which attracts more than 14 visitors a day, was sealed off with gaily coloured sellotape. Urine samples were taken from all three mezzanine pools and one was put in the outdoor pool as a control.

Teapop School head Ernholt Swiss said: "I knew that something was terribly up when every one of my 90 children failed to be at my school on

Monday. All but 86 of them were back in my classroom the next day so that's alright then."

The source of the contanimation is not yet known. Teachers first thought that the Sewerside pool was to blame because pupils had attended the Friday gala and fished there the day before Friday. Leisure centre staff, on the other hand, insisted the infection had started from improperly cooked school dinners, such as Sloppy Semolina and Spotted Dick With Dead Flies In.

Council Health officials say they are keeping an open mind until all the samples have been looked at, with results expected to be available at the end.

A Framley Borough Council press officer said, "If samples from both the pool and the canteen turn out negative, we may have to conclude that the bug was brought into the school by an infected pupil, perhaps one carried into the playground on a gust of wind."

Day raises £250

PUPILS AT Gregory's Girl's School in Molford St Malcolm have raised £250 towards the cost of new textbooks during a sponsored fancy dress day.

"This year we chose a special theme," said Headmistress Wendy Redrobin. "Everyone, staff and pupils, came dressed as Stephanie Webster from Year Nine."

"We wish Stephanie a speedy recovery. In retrospect, maybe we should have warned her."

Stephanie, who is currently lying in a trauma-induced coma in Framley General Hospital, was the only pupil not to dress up specially for the day.

Stephanie's music teacher, Miss Brie, has prepared a special tape, which doctors say may help bring her out of her catatonic state.

"It's a recording of her favourite song, sung by the whole school, doing an impression of exactly the way Stephanie used to sing it."

Good levels

A Year 12 pupil from St Tuscadero's County High School For Girls has passed 94 A-Levels. Yasmin Strost, is, according to the pictures editor of a local newspaper, an unphotogenic bespectacled goink.

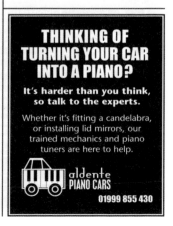

READER'S OFFERS

BBC

9.00 Joliffe The cloth crab descends from his cloud and tells the story of a hand grenade that falls in love with a bunch of keys. Narrated by Oliver Postgate.

9.15 Hey You! Yes, You God! It's Sunday! Leviticus 11:2 sung for under-10s.

9.40 Worship On One The playful choirboys of Winchester Cathedral. Narrated by David Attenborough.

10.10 Aslan Magazine A look back at this week's events in Narnia.

10.40 Does He Take Sugar? (6/10)

10.55 Hear Say! Programme for the tone-deaf.

11.20 We Are Experiencing Technical Difficulties (18/26) (rpt)

12.35 The Computer Programme Fred Harris investigates the government's pledge to get a BBC Microcomputer into every home by the year 2000.

1.00 Farm The kids from The New York School of The Farming Arts get upset when heifer Doris is sent to the abbatoir. followed by **Farming for Weathermen** with Jonathan Bell

1.25 Thousand Island Discs Roy Plomley methodically dips all Barry Cryer's favourite records in salad dressing.

1.50 News Headlines A look ahead at next week's storylines.

1.55 Film Après-Midiée:
Whistling at Hayley Wind (1959) When children discover a rapist on the run hidden in a barn, circumstances cause 12-year-old Hayley to believe that the stranger means her no harm.
Mills ... John Wind
Hayley ... Hayley Wind
Man ... Oliver Casterbridge
Billy ... Frank Sorry
Dir.: Bryan Numan

3.30 The All-New Adventures of Foghorn Rabbit

3.40 Alias Stephenson & Atkinson (rpt) Comedy western adventure series with Bob Goody and Chris Langham

4.25 Julian Balloon The storyteller (Michael Gambon) weaves another yarn using his fridge magnets.

4.35 Go With Groom Simon Groom returns to his family's Dethwick farm for the eighth time this series.

5.05 Charlie's Gordon Army Gordon Honeycombe, Hannah Gordon and Buster Crabbe are pressed into service by Captain Drake.

5.55 News (8,590/53,112) Jan grows suspicious when she has to cover Kenneth's shift for the third time in eight weeks.

6.05 The Edwin Drood Mysteries By Andrew Davies, dramatised in six parts by somebody Dickens

6.35 Stanley Lebor appeals on behalf of the Neighbourhood Watch.

6.40 Screams of Praise Human sacrifice.

7.15 Sweet Jesus Sitcom. Audrey (Penelope Keith) falls for the teenage Christ.

7.45 Polpot Drama. Ross goes into hiding in the tin mine when Angharad finds the ditch full of bespectacled skulls.

8.35 It Ain't 'Alf Cramped, Mum Wartime sitcom with Melvyn Hayes as Anne Frank and Windsor Davies as Obergruppenführer Stertzlitz.

9.05 That's Enough Sausage-shaped vegetables, dogs allegedly saying 'sausage-shaped vegetables' and Cyril Smith reading us one of his Odd Odes in which he apologizes for breaking Cyril Fletcher's armchair.

9.50 Magnusmind Specialist subjects include Specialist Subject Questions I Asked During the Last Series of Mastermind and Little Known Facts About Iceland.

10.20 News (as 5.55) (rpt)

10.30 The Heart of the Thinking-Man's Crumpet Nude studio discussion. David Jessel disappointingly stands in for Joan Bakewell.

11.05 What Tastes Salty And Slithers Across The Dancefloor? David Jacobs and Terry Wogan cha-cha-cha to find out who will be Host of The Next Series.

11.45 The Sky Tonight Patrick Moore accidentally swallows the sky and Chicken-Licken can't remember if he or she is in the wrong story or not.

12.10 Phil Silvers as Steve Biko

12.35 Weathercock Michael Fish's

12.40 Last Orders

12.50 Closedown (first shown on BBC2)

BBC "2"

8.05 The Pope Pope Karol Wojtyla I returns to his birthplace where he will be facing penalty kicks from General Jaruzelski and Lech Walesa.

10.10 Open Polytechnic
10.10 This Lime's Bleedin' Diabolical **10.35** Squat Betty **11.00** The Rock n Roll Years: *1927* **11.25** I Cried When Charlie Got Blown Away **11.50** Collecting Crabs **12.15** The Littlest Homo

12.40 Sviatenski Plays Ravel *Quarter-final.*

1.05 That's a Queer Sort of Ball, Mother Opinioned England v Twickenham. Highlights from yesterday's international in New Zealand with commentary by Alan Bennett.

1.55 Indoors Indoors Annie Farmhouse cooks lunch for James Burke.

2.20 Vertical. Science. James Burke eats his Sunday lunch.

THE OLD FLANNEL FUNNEL
BBC2 4.45am

Post-closedown music show. Late night tunes from Kawasaki Wetbike, The Collective, and Organ Dispute, plus an exclusive play of the new Hudsons' single. Presented by Ellen McArthur

3.10 Rather Be Lord Olivier says he'd rather be Osvaldo Ardiles, Peter Purves or Justin Fashanu. (B/W) (rpt)

3.40 The Second World War In Crisps (rpt) (6/26) Wotsits over Berlin.

4.30 The Great Crisp Race Three more teams of engineers attempt to drive a Ringo across the ocean floor. With Professor Heinz Siebenundfunfzig.

5.05 Whicker's Lounge This week Alan talks us through his magazine rack.

5.40 Around With Alice Another of Czech animator Jan Svankmajer's subversive anti-state golfing films. Jan's guest this week is Dennis Waterman.

6.10 News Review Ludovic Kennedy and his panel look back at this week's events in White City.

6.30 The Monkey Programme Tripitaka gets it on with Valerie Singleton.

7.15 The Natural World About Us The life cycle of *homo sapiens* filmed over the course of seventy-four years by a dedicated team of Brazilian rain forest ants. Narrated by Roy Skelton.

8.05 Bent Coppers In 1974 producer Paul Watson produced an extraordinary fly on the wall documentary series about two of Britain's top policemen. Tonight he revisits the pair to discover if their dishonesty has been exposed eight years after his documentary that no one watched first exposed their dishonesty.

9.00 Jack High The world's best flat-green bowlers compete to score the world's worst poker hand. Semi-final: David Bryant v Bill Moseley.

9.30 35 Minutes: *The Harlem Bogtrotters* Film following a dismal Irish basketball team trying to get a cartoon series made about their non-existent exploits.

10.10 Samuel Beckett Season: *Not Yet* A close up of a woman's mouth as she cycles up the steep slopes of the Alpe d'Huez, chasing the peloton. Billie Whitelaw gives a tour de france performance.

10.45 Betjeman in Birmingham (rpt) Buying a spade in the Bullring.

11.30 Your Socks Are Giving Me The Horn

11.40 Kirk Douglas Season:
Falling Down (1961) Psychopathic sympatheth I-SPRCS, goes on the rampage in ancient Rome after his wife abandons him on the cross. May be badly edited for bad language.
Ian Spartacus ... Kirk Douglas
Maggie Spartacus ... Lee Remick
Det Sgt St Matthew ... Shelley Duvall
Persian shopkeeper ... Karl Malden
Dir.: Stickley Brick

1.10 Last Orders

1.20 Closedown (first shown on BBC1)

ITV

6.00 I Am-TV David Frost.

9.25 Bob The Biscuit (rpt)

9.30 Minipopska 8-year old Marek Strzelecki dresses up as the Pope and makes a pronouncement on chocolate biscuits.

10.00 Sport Dickie

10.30 Good Morning Faith from St Nedwell's Chapel, Shillingbury Illingbury with readings from Percy Filth.

11.30 Pant Along With Nancy Lamaze class.

12.00 Weekend Waldheim Former UN Secretary-General Kurt Waldheim denies direct knowledge of any of this week's alleged events in "Europe".

1.00 Out Of African Township Meryl Streep and Jack Hargreaves fall in love with a carthorse.

1.30 Les Schtroumpfs Hergé's Aventures de Tintin Schtroumpf et Hercule Schtroumpf test Papa Schtroumpfette's little grey beards. Translated by Eric Thompson.

2.00 Mork & Dawber Documentary. Robin and Pam take a break from filming but, even though the cameras aren't rolling, Robin can't stop performing.

2.30 The Big Moth Highlights of Brian Moore eating a jumper.

3.30 Major Charles Winchester & The Bear

4.30 Just Catworzel Geoffrey Bayldon scratches his head as the eleventh-century scarecrow gets into more trouble with his dog, Jumble.

5.00 Sunday Flipping Sunday hosted by Gloria Beaumont.

6.00 Brasseye Top darts players are made to look foolish by Jim Bowen in the seemingly innocuous quiz.

6.30 Weekend News And finally, Martyn Lewis reads a newspaper and potters about his flowerbeds in a sunhat.

6.40 Steve Heighway Harry Secombe sings *You'll Never Walk Alone* and recreates his classic goal from the 1971 FA Cup final.

Hard-hitting current affairs. Britain's clown community faces its toughest crisis yet with the closure of Rillings' Circus, laying off over 14,000 full-time and 6,500 part-time clowns. Tonight Berys Jorvis talks to every single one of them.

WORLDABOUT
BBC1 10.30pm

7.15 Me & Me & My Girl Sitcom. Simon (Richard O'Sullivan) is unable to finish his new libretto after Samantha (Stephen Fry) steals his credit card.

7.45 You're 'Aving A Laugh Practical jokes backfire on presenters Rusty Lee and Martin *Say "Yes, Father"* Daniels as they visit the East End.

8.45 Fingers Crossed At Her Majesty's Veteran entertainers in more death-defying performances.

9.45 Weekend News (as 6.30) (rpt) Followed by a nice pot of tea and a really long sit down. Lovely.

10.00 Clive James On IV Drip-feeding endurance show with the least hungry man on television.

10.30 The South-East Show Melvyn Bragg proposes that culture should only be available in London.

11.30 It's Not Like The Old Days An invited panel laments the unfestive feel of today's Christmas Day schedule.

12.00 Christmas Meditation Lord Rabbi Lionel Bluebird of Happiness offers some of his own thought.

12.10 The Queen Repeat of her message to the nation after one and a half bottles of Gordon's.

12.20 Oh No! It's The Moomins Nightmare-inducing animation. Narrated very, very quietly by Nick Ross.

12.30 Closedown (first shown on BBC1)

B/W indicates Black & White
Rpt indicates a repeat
Times indicate times

Fireman rescued from big tree by cats

By Odgar Cushion

A WHOFT FIREMAN had a lucky escape on Wednesday when a routine cat rescue operation turned out to be a lot more!

The cat's owner, Mrs R. Webster, had called Whoft Fire Services after hearing plaintive miaowing from a tree high in her garden.

"At first I thought it was the wind, miaowing through the leaves, but then I realised that my cat, Lucky Webster was up in the tree," she said.

I ran to the kitchen, where she continued, "I ran to the kitchen and phoned the Fire Brigade. A neighbour had told me they'd be the men for the job. Firemen can climb trees, just like cats, you know."

HOORAY FOR FIREMEN

On receiving the call, the Whoft Fireman bundled into their engine. Within minutes they were at the scene, laughing and joking and doing skids.

Mr Sautée takes up the story.

"The lads offered me a ladder, but I turned it down. I was pretty sure I'd heard somewhere that when cats in trees see ladders they expand to fill

The cat and (inset) the fire engine responsible.
PHOTO BY MARY MARTHA O'GOD

the branches. That sort of thing would just make our job twice as hard.

"So I put on my new climbing boots and got stuck in!"

The plucky fireman then began his careful ascent, breaking branch after branch in a clumsy, inconsiderate fashion.

"I thought it'd never end,", Trevor recalled, "by the time I'd reached the top of the tree I decided that I'd had enough and stopped climbing."

Unfortunately his final resting location had put him tantalisingly 'just-

out-of-reach' of the kitten, who was busy pawing honey out of a bee pot.

BUTTERFLY LUCK

The other firemen, realising that their ladddders simply weren't long enough to reach man or cat, quickly admitted defeat and ate a slice of cake and mackerel sandwich.

"I can't move."

"Come down!"

"Miaowwww!"

And so it would have gone on, had not a group of local cats started gathering around the base of the tree.

"It was quite beautiful to watch," said the pets' owners. "Our cats were getting excited. They must have been attracted by the matching butterfly designs on the bottom of the trapped fireman's shoes."

The cats, who had been following the fluttering shoe motion, suddenly pounced, bringing the broken fireman down to earth with a terrified ankle.

Said Fire Chief Keith Cimbalom, "Cats love butterflies and it was fortunate that the soles of my fireman's shoes depicted two such wonderful specimens, The Red Admiral and The Cabbage White'

Lucky Webster floated down from the tree some time later on a breeze.

Fig Friday is a figging success!!!!

A Framley mother and daughter have been drawn closer together after a school 'role-swap' charity event left them unable to fig-ure out who was who.

Shannon Cannon and her daughter Duke swapped places last Friday - Shannon attending classes at St Icklebrick's Primary, while Duke stayed home doing the household chores and reading *Bella* - in order to raise money for awareness.

Both of them adjusted to their new duties so quickly and effortlessly that they're considering changing for good.

"School's a piece of piss", Shannon declared, "much easier than it was first time around, when I was at school."

"I never realised how much work my mother did, it's great! More! More!" Duke let on later.

Shannon's husband, Thomas agrees. "I wasn't convinced at first, but the swap has left me feeling like a new man too. This is too wonderful for words."

The school is considering cancelling 'Fig Friday' in future, since the success of the event has raised the average school leaving age in the area to thirty-three.

School prize day congratulates pupils

By THE CREDITS

KING TUBBY VI Grammar School, Framley held its annual prizegiving this week, honouring the achievements of boys and girls from all years of the school.

The prizes were presented by local celebrity, ex-TV AM weatherman Cmmdr David Philpott. Philpott stood in at the last minute for absent guest of honour, Mayor William D'Ainty, who was unable to attend due to an urgent breakdancing appointment.

Special prizewinners, who all got copies of The Framley Examiner book are listed on the right. There were also loads of A-Levels and

excellence in sport and lemon squash.

Thanks were offered to all those who had helped make the event such a success, particularly those who had generously given photographs, or agreed to be photographs themselves.

Framley Examiner Prize for completing their book project	Robin Halstead Jason Hazeley Alex Morris Joel Morris
Year 7 Divinity Prize	Rowland White
Year 8 Good Conduct	John Hamilton
Baden Schleissgarten Friendschip Medal	Cat Ledger
Class of '68	Jonathan Gibbs, Philip Morris, Jason Whyte, Ben Parker, Mark Whitehead, Jonathan Parkyn, Simon Ansell, Andy Waterworth, Wendy Albiston, Nick Sommerlad, John Sparkes, Bob Lock, Bo Bloke, Bobby Locque, B O'Block, Robert Lock, Robin of Loxley, Lucky Bob, Bobert Blockington, Robbie L'Oc, Bob Block, B. Oblong, Rock Bollock
your comments here	

News In Brief

SIAMESE TWINS BIRTH

Whoft's famous conjoined twins, Paul & Deniece Sharpe, are celebrating the safe arrival of their ninth child, Harvey. The Sharpes, who have been conjoined at the genitals since birth, became famous after featuring in a Desmond Wilcox documentary on BBC1 in 1984. Harvey, who shares a lung with Paul, is not expected to survive.

WHAT A STORY

1000 local children have raised £1 million for the Mayor's charity, which has something to do with hospitals and the by-pass. At the day-long event, which may become an annual fixture if successful, 100 huge cheques were presented by policemen dressed as clowns, who then gave everybody a balloon and a complimentary puppy. Then there were fireworks. Journalists and photogrophers who omitted to attend the event were said to have been "sacked".

CAR STOLEN

A car stolen from the Asda car park in Whoft was found three minutes later in the Asda carpark in Molford, full of shopping. The car continues.

Meet Zebedee!

Say hello to Zebedee, the zebra! He's our new mascot, and he's recently been transferred from local premiership side Framley Zabadak, following an incident.

You'll see him at every Framley Imaginaire match from now on, cheering from the touchline, or maybe in the wall if there's a free kick on the edge of the eighteen yard box and we're down to ten men. Zebedee will always give 110% over the full ninety minutes!

*artist's impression

FRAMLEY IMAGINAIRE FOCUS ON FACT FILE

HOWARD ANTHITLER

Date of Born: April 13th, 2002
Place of Birth: The Mirror End Stand, The Imaginaire Stadium o'Flight
Height: 4'12"
Previous Clubs: Tufty, Chip
Position: TBA
Squad Number: 83
Joined Imaginaire: October 1996.
Debut: TBA
International Debut: NA
Played: 0
Goals: 0

Howard has suffered badly from injury ever since the idea of playing football for a living was first suggested to him. With his 28st frame, chronic asthma and prosthetic legs, eyebrows were raised at the time of his £2.4m transfer from Whoft Hospice reserves in 1997.

However, he soon proved his critics right with an unbroken run of seasons brilliantly spent at home with his feet up. Though playing in this position naturally made him more of a backroom boy than a star of the field, cometh the time, cometh the man, and many fans fondly remember his stunning display of sitting quietly on the bench against Molford Incredible during the historic 1-0 victory that prevented Framley Imaginaire's expulsion from the World of Football.

Sadly, a combination of injury and related loss of form has denied Imaginaire fans the chance to see their hero's inaction, confining Howard to the saloon bar of The Warm Zippy for the past season, from where he relays the other football results to the stadium via the pub payphone (authenticity subject to random teletext reception).

Membership

Imaginaire Junior Supporter's Club members get lots of benefits and free gifts! Look what membership could get you...

0 - 5yrs
- **Standing tickets to all home matches.**
- **Complimentary, personalized packet of 20 Bensons signed by Mr Shaq Tehrani, reserve team physio and proprietor of Tehrani's News.**
  (no more than 2 schoolchildren at one time)

5 - 16yrs
- **Complimentary set of 11 Framley Imaginaire first team butt-plugs, courtesy of Blackjack's Shagshack, sponsors of Imaginaire since 1932.**
- **Eligibility for half-price knuckle-duster & nunchakas gift set**
- **Discounts on Junior Away-Days**
- **Priority waiting list for membership of the Imaginaire Hardcru (includes The Cute Hooligan badge with real fur and moving eyes).**

IMAGINAIRE BIRTHDAY CLUB

Zebedee says HAPPY BIRTHDAY to this week's Junior Imaginer : Subraminiya Raj who will be 3 on Wednesday

Happy Birthday!

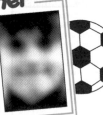

NEW FACES!

Good news for fans of *The Imaginaries*, Framley Imaginaire have just signed a new spectator!

Diego Malvinas, who cost £8m, is an exciting signing for the club because he also supports Argentina. He caught the selectors' eye after a fantastic couple of seasons at the home end at Boca Juniors.

Imaginaire's new hot property is much in demand, and there is talk of him supporting England next year, if he impresses at his new home.

Competition Corner

Last week's competition was won by Johnny Ann Miller, 6, of Molford St Gavin, who correctly guessed that Framley Imaginaire had scored seven away goals between 1995 and 2001.

Johnny's prize was to get to sit on the lap of Imaginaire's goalkeeper during the penalty shoot-out at the end of Thursday's vital qualifying match for the FA Cup.

If you want to join the Framley Imaginaire Junior Supporter's Club, just send a banker's draft for £175.99 to JSC, Framley Imaginaire, Administrative Office, Stadium O'Flight, Embankment Way, Framley FR1 6LS. Remember to write your name, age and address clearly on the back of the banker's draft. Please allow up to 6 months to receive your badge.

FOCUS on Roy Newby

A promotional cut-out of Roy stands outside the very first of his shops, now Newby's Bulbs and Screws.
PHOTOGRAPH BY HARRIET FILLIGREE

He's king of shops

by Beaky Coxwain

ROY NEWBY is one of the area's best known figures. Over 90% of the shops in Molford bear the Newby's logo, and his name appears above street signs, on bin bags and within the curlicues of every £20 note spent in the town.

The debonair philanthropist vegetarian entrepreneur millionaire is a long way from the humble immigrant refugee who first arrived in Molford in the late 1950s, but Roy has never forgotten his roots as a humble immigrant refugee who first arrived in Molford in the late 1950s, but Roy.

So, this week, we take a look at the career of Framley's very own Roy Newby, Roy Newby.

Roy's autobiography "From Rakes To Riches" is published by Newby's Books and is available from all Newby's bookshops, and in the bedside drawer of every hotel room in the Framley area, priced £12.99.

Roy Newby TIMELINE

1949	Roy born, Prestatyn, aged 0.
1958	9-year old Roy becomes a refugee, leaving Wales after being chased out by a dog. He settles in Molford, claiming political asylum.
1959	Young Roy starts his own business, doing chalk drawings of himself cutting out silhouettes of people in the park.
1960	Roy secures a lucrative government contract to supply his drawings to the Middle East.
1967	Having made his fortune, Roy invests in commercial property in the Molford area, buying a vacant retail space on the corner of Hooky Street and Youave Avenue.
1968	Roy's shop "Just Rakes" fails to entice the public, and closes.
1970	Undeterred, Roy opens a new shop on the site, "Simply Rakes".
1971	After the failure of his second shop, Roy takes stock and raises investment capital for a new project.
1972	"Roy's Rakes" opens.
1973	Roy has reason to celebrate. His shop is a roaring success. The store's Unique Selling Point - that every rake has Roy's face carved into the handle - really pulls in the punters. It's a practice that he continues to this day - Roy's face can still be found on every Newby's product, on the side of every dinghy, in the heart of every cabbage.
1973-4	Roy opens twelve more "Roy's Rakes" shops, all in Molford High Street. They are a huge success.
1975	Roy's luck runs out. His prestige 13th branch of "Roy's Rakes" in Molford High Street fails to attract customers, and remains derelict to this day.
1976-7	Sensing that the time has come to try something different, Roy labours day and night to open a revolutionary new shop.
1978	"Newby's Rakes" opens.
1979	Success! Roy's new "Newby's" brand takes the area by storm. The money rolls in.
1980	Newby's Airport opens.
1981	First branch of Newby's Grocery and Newsagents opens, cashing in on the public appetite for grapes and magazines, popularised by glamorous movies such as the James Bond series and *Glitterball*.
1983	Newby's Toys opens
1985	Newby's Hats starts business
1986	First branch of Newby's Cushions
1987	Newby's Cushion Hats opens
1989	Newby's Walk-In-Hospital opens
1990	First branch of NcNewby's
1991	Newby's Swank Fashions
1994	Newby's 24-7-51

SAFETY FIRST

With Chief Fire Officer Kenneth Blan

This week:
The Cup Of Tea Code

We all enjoy having a cup of tea this time of year, but although they can be exciting and fun, they can also be dangerous. So this November, be SAFE not SORRY

1. always keep cups of tea in a dry tin box with a lid
2. hold the cup of tea at arm's length, well away from others
3. never return to a tea pot once the tea has brewed
4. never throw cups of tea or indulge in 'horseplay'
5. never put a cup of tea in your pocket
6. keep pets locked safely outside while you're making a cup of tea
7. better still, go to a well organised cup of tea making party rather than trying to do it yourself

remember, remember, the fifth of november, teabag, kettle, and pot

---

HERE'S HOW TO ERECT YOUR ROY NEWBY FACT PYRAMID!

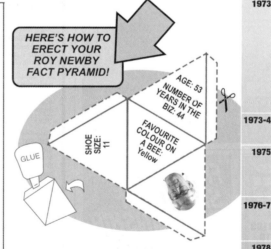

GLUE

AGE: 53
NUMBER OF YEARS IN THE BIZ: 44
SHOE SIZE: 11
FAVOURITE COLOUR ON A BEE: Yellow

The Framley Examiner

Framley's Traditional Favourite since 1978

PRICE 45p

KIDS

Meet your sporting heroes

PROPERTY

Plans for town centre

STYLE

Make the most of your shadow

Framley MP is caught with his hand in the packet

"CRISPS FOR QUESTIONS" ROW HITS FRAMLEY MP

by Taunton Mishap

DYNAMIC local MP Ianbeale Steeplecocque was last night in hiding in his expensive Wripple home, after the Parliamentary Behaviour Committee (in London) put the controversial member under official scrutiny.

The knucklebattering follows a string of revelations about his business dealings with Framley millionaire entrepreneur and former bankrupt Lee Organisn.

SLEAZE

Steeplecocque, 23, has found himself at the centre of the so-called "Crisps For Questions" scandal. Documents leaked to The Framley Examiner (Framley's Traditional Favourite since 1978) suggest that the MP has been accepting "bungs" in return for asking questions in the House of Commons.

The portfolio of smoking guns shows that Mr Steeplecocque was paid a total of £19,000 over six months by local crisp magnate Lee Organisn.

LIES

Mr Organisn, owner of Turn Your

Memories Into Crisps (The 'Turn Your Memories' Into People), denies any wrongdoing, and denies handing over crisps in little blue envelopes to the beleaguered MP.

But, since Steeplecocque spent most of the same six months asking questions in parliament about the crisp industry, Organisn's denials have so far fallen on thin ears.

BULLSHIT

"This looks smelly," said Mayor William D'Ainty in a press release, "and sleaze should confine itself to the kitchen. But, until the parliamentary committee has published its report, Ianbeale Steeplecocque should be presumed innocent, no matter how badly I treat him in private."

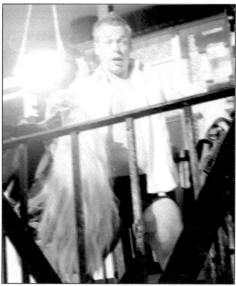
Mr Steeplecocque MP flees the scene of a crime.
PICTURE BY GERALDINE SKINHEAD

The soon-to-be-disgraced MP has not made himself available for comment, and refused to speak to unexpected reporters early this morning as he trouserlessly fled a prostitute's flat.

The case continues to continue.

Taxi driver attacked

TAXI DRIVERS in Framley have been warned to be on their guard after a minicab was boarded by pirates.

Stanley Bogwig, 42, had just dropped off a foul-mouthed customer at Here Be Turnips, a pub known as a popular pirate haunt, at 8.30pm on Saturday when the attack took place.

Three men armed with cutlasses boarded the dark blue Vauxhall Average and ordered Mr Bogwig to drive to a quiet car park on Stuffing Lane.

They threatened to make him walk the plank if he didn't do what he was told. One of the men blindfolded Mr Bogwig with two eye patches while the other two seized maps, tissues, beaded seat covers and boxes of traffic-light-style air fresheners.

The three bearded corsairs then tied up Mr Bogwig with towing rope and made off in the direction of Madagascar.

INTERROGATION

Police have applied to magistrates for a extra 24 hours to question the parrot they took into custody two days ago.

Detective Constable Inspector Gregan McHough yesterday told waiting reporters that although the brightly-feathered suspect had been helpful at first, it was now refusing to say anything other than "hello, Sarge" and "for the benefit of the tape."

LENTILS P19 & 20   PARK RANGER FASHION P61   NOSE CLUES P11   SPORT P69 - 79   BRAS P51-112

Sockford .W.I take step into a future

THE LADIES OF Sockford Women's Institute are sending a message into the future, by using a time capsule to preserve a snapshot of how local life is at the moment, in this day and age.

The historic capsule will be buried on the waste ground behind Tibb's Angling Supplies, with instructions not to open it for twenty-five years, by which time the future will have arrived. Sealed inside the 6 foot by 4 foot box will be all the members of the Sockford W.I., except Mrs Arglesocks who has offered to stay behind and nail the lid shut.

Mrs Beryl Cormorance, who came up with the idea for the project, described to me how the buried ladies will be the perfect way for the moon men of the 21st Century to understand our current world as it is today in this day and age.

"Inside the capsule, we will adopt a variety of poses, representing all the richness and diversity of life on earth. For example, Mrs Ardennes will be dressed as a rainforest, and Mrs Please is going to be playing the bassoon."

TWENTY-FIVE YEARS

Although the chief purpose of the capsule is to allow the people of the future to see how we used to live, Mrs Cormorance explained there was another eriment to the expelement.

"I can't wait to get dug up, so I can see how the world has changed in twenty-five years," she enthused. "I would imagine there will be rockets. Everyone will probably be blue and have wrinkly foreheads, and,

by Adam Wrent

hopefully, they might be able to do something about my hip."

BUCK ROGERS

Learning from the disastrous experiences of other time capsule makers has been important for the W.I. time-travellers, Beryl told me.

"There's always the chance that, by the time the people of the far future unearth our capsule, the container may have become waterlogged, destroying the contents. Just in case, we are going to make a video of us getting into the box, which the astro citizens of 2027 will be able to watch, should they crack open the capsule and find it's just full of sludge.

"We've also asked the TV people to show the video of us climbing into the tin once a year, on *Focus On Framley*, so our great, great grandchildren will be able to see that too. We think we've thought of everything."

● *If you'd like to suggest a representative pose for the W.I. ladies to adopt in their plastic coffin of doom, call Mrs B.Cormorance on 01999 843 877.*

Mrs Cormorance stands next to the capsule that will take her into the future.
PHOTOGRAPH BY ABRAM TUMULT

Minstrel arrested

BY BUNCO BOOTH

FRAMLEY POLICE were glad to move quickly on Tuesday, reacting to reports of a public disturbance outside Clots Estate Agents in Denegate Parade.

Fourteen officers piled out of a lovely big van and arrested the troublemaker, a Mr Conerry Seuss, 38, from Neu Funfundseibzigstrasse, St Eyots. Seuss, who had been singing *Sweet Georgia Brown* to passersby, was then put in the lovely big van and driven to Framley Police Station, brrrm brrrm where he was charged with minstrelcy.

At a press conference, held in the snug of The Warm Zippy, DCI Gregan McHough indicated the straw boater, five string banjo and white gloves that Mr Seuss had used in his act.

"With only these simple tools and a tin of Cherry Blossom bootpolish, Mr Seuss was not only able to perform random acts of senseless

minstrelcy, but also indulge in fol-de-rol and public displays of razzmatazz.

"Some witnesses insisted they had even seen evidence of bojangling,

Conerry Seuss
PHOTO BY BO OWLS

but this cannot be confirmed at this time."

This is not the first time Mr Seuss has come to the constabular attentions of Framley police. In 1996, after reports of a jesting incident, police raided his flat and seized several belled hats and a pig's bladder on a stick.

"We don't need this sort of thing in Framley," summed up DCI McHough, wiping beer froth from his moustache. "For goodness sake, this isn't the medieval ages, this is the twentieth century."

Mayor visits new ward

FRAMLEY'S INDOMITABLE Mayor, William D'Ainty visited Framley General Hospital's new Intensive Care ward this Tuesday.

The ward provides beds for 97 critically ill patients, all of whom were stacked in the corner while Mayor D'Ainty tried all their beds to see which one was his favourite.

While 27 of the beds were "too soft" and 69 of them were "too hard", the final bed, belonging to the late Harald Whipsnow, 71, was "just right".

The Mayor will be staying in the bed until he's sucked all the butterscotch Angel Delight out of a specially erected intravenous drip.

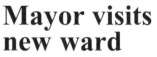

Funday Examiner!

WITH DAMIUN CLAVALIER

HELLO GANG! Well! What a week it's been at the Funday Examiner for your Uncle Damiun!

I've been asked to write some really big stories for the grown-ups, and, phew! If it hasn't worn me out! And it hasn't left me much time to come up with new things for you to do, I'm afraid.

So, if some of this week's puzzles seem to be the same as last week's, don't worry. I'm sure you'll have just as much fun working out the brainteasers and finishing the puzzles again as you did last time.

I've had some letters from your mums and dads too! To all of you who sent their pocket money for the Funday Examiner badges and codebooks, thanks!

I give you my word that this week, I will send them. And if it's not this week, it might be next week! If you really need yours, you might want to try sending the money again.

Happy waiting!

COLOURING-IN PICTURE PUZZLE

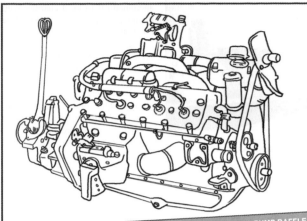

Colour in the COLLETS red and the SUMP FEED blue. Make the OIL PUMP BAFFLE a nice, clear yellow. Now, what do you think is wrong with Uncle Damiun's car? Send your completed pictures to me at the Funday Examiner, and try and get it right this time.

GAME ZONE

Here's some more hot new tips and cheats for the Nintendo PlayCylinder II...

PLANET OF DACHSHUNDS
From options screen press L, R1, R2, D, R, □, O, ⊠, L, L, L, R, R and game will change to "Submarine of Dachshunds".

PRINGLE MOUSTACHEMAN AND THE WOTSITS OF DISAPPOINTMENT
The fewer crumbs you get in your moustache, the higher your garlic bonus.

SUPERMARIOWARD
To avoid a malpractice suit, make sure you're hiding under the ambulance whilst the princess miscarries. The security guards can't see you there.

SONIC THE ROADKILL
On level 1, to avoid getting crushed the moment you leave your burrow, press L2, R1, power off.

METAL MICKEY SOLID
To make Irene Handl "Boogie Boogie", use the Fruitbat from the tank bunker.

FUN FOR THE HOLIDAYS

WHY NOT come along to Framley Town Hall (floor 6, avoid using the lift) and have some fun on one of the council's Kids' Kourses this holidays?*

ARSE PAINTING
Back by popular demand. £150 + meals. (Tue-Sat, residential, 9am prompt check out.)

TXT MESSAGING
Includes oral tuition and day trip to Portugal. One day course, last few places. £3. (Mondays, Wednesdays)

ACCOUNTANCY
Ages 5-11. To BACA standard. Guaranteed placement at local firm. (Mon-Fri. 10am)

*only two schoolchildren at any one time.

HURGÉ'S ADVENTURES OF CANCAN

Tintin is on holiday.

HURGÉ'S AVENTURES DE PÔP-POP

Tintin est toujours en vacances.

DAMIUN'S SEA WORD SEARCH

```
I A M S I C K O F T H I S J O B I M
T R E A T E D L I K E A N A P E I F
I H A D A P O U N D F O R E V E R Y
C O L L E A G U E I V E D R E A M E
D O F D R O W N I N G I N S T A R V
I N G P I R A N H A I D B E A M I L
L I O N A I R E G O D K N O W S I D
R A T H E R B E S T U C K O N A S P
I K E T H A N S P E N D A N O T H E
R H O U R S T A R I N G A T A S T U
P I D B L O O D Y G R I D O R D R A
W I N G A N O T H E R M I C R O S C
O P I C M A P O F H O W T O F I N D
A F U R N I T U R E S A L E I M I G
H T F E E D T H E E D I T O R T O H
I M S E L F A N D A F I V E R S A Y
S I M T H E O N L Y H A C K H E R E
W H O C A N S P E L L P I R A N H A
```

LORD
OVAL
SOON
CAT
FOREVER
DUNN
FINE
SPRY
OFF
VET
THERM
RIPE
IF
BRA
WISE
GIN
IKEA
HERB
GOSH
BAA
PWOAH
EUK
IAN
SARI
DOGWAR
TAO
FERG
LADA
HRH
HERO
MEAL
OAT
OATS
GOT
NONE
TUB
NEST
COGNEAT
BONT
HARWUNK

ROGER THE HORRID BEAR

10455 "Roger The Babysitter"

Roger is watching *Under Siege*. Which triplet has the worst colic?

Last week's solution: The cut-and-shut was made from cars 1 and 5.

Just what they wanted

DOCTOR COBWEB'S COBWEB FACTORY £18.99
Spin miles and miles of real cobwebs... Make a cobweb picture! Build a cobweb bike! Fill your bedroom! But don't make Doctor Cobweb angry or it's no more cobwebs!

"BILLY BRAGG" HANDHELD WATCH-A-GAME GAME £14.99
LCD game based on the popular singer songwriter.

WALLET & GRIMACE TALKING ALAMRM CLOCK £11.99
Wakes you up with a choice of four phrases. "You owe me big time" / "Time's up" / "In your dreams, pal" / "About fucking time". Distressingly persistent.

BATTENBERG THE GAME OF CAKE £31.99
With over 5,000 questions, battenberg-shaped question box and 36 pieces of cake.

BLUNT INSTRUMENTS' SPICK & SPAN £27.99
Talking educational toy.
"Do it again"
"Those aren't hospital corners"
"You could eat your dinner off that"
"Spell 'Clean'"

GUESS WHEN £17.99
The mystery time game
"Are you nearly dinnertime?"
"Am I up yet? Why am I here?"
Guess your opponent's time before they guess yours.
Oh yes, it's never too late to play Guess When, the family fun game that'll have you in clocks!

DAVID BRYANT SUBBOWLEO £21.99
Reproducing all the thrills of real tournament bowls by fingertip control. With OO scale self-balancing teams, bowls, jacks, pipes, slacks etc.

BUGGEROO £16.99
The game of anal stuffing.
"Take an object
Try and stick
It up the arse...
...But watch it kick!"
Not suitable for anyone.

WHO WANTS TO ANSWER THE SAME QUESTION A MILLION TIMES? £24.99
Try the challenge of a lifetime! Based on the long-running TV show. "Are those all your final answers?" "Do you want to phone a hospital?" "And I understand your wife's a welder." "Hurry up, I haven't got all day..."

with christmas toys from
NEWBY'S bookshops
15 High St, Molford

into gold, cures all known diseases, makes possible unaided human flight. No trade enquiries, no police, no customs & excise. £15 a bottle. Box FE8741

LARGER THAN LIFE pottery dog collection. Dog collection beautifully rendered in pottery. Owner to collect. £200 01999 266698

'HOW TO STOP TALKING HUNGARIAN', book and tape set. Ideal gift for anyone not planning on visiting Hungary. £12. Tel 01999 865 433

HUGE GONGS

KID'S Hungry Onions game complete with sack of onions and time-locked isolation chamber. Who will eat the most onions over a month? 30 days' silent pleasure £150. Tel 01999 577889

PAIR of DJ turntable mats for twin mixing deck. Logos: "Mrs Mills" and "Rock-a-doodle-dandy!" Strangely timeless. Call Maxy on 01999 752 129

LOST: Cream coloured shoulder bag. Answers to the name of Sooty. 01999 731 403

BOOKS REQUIRED to complete collection. I require paperback copies of "Bridget Jones' Diary" and "Ainsley's Barbecue Bible" to complete my collection of all the books ever written. Good prices paid. 01999 499 313

BABY HARNESS and adult chariot. £22. Tel 01999 844 621.

MEAT, MEAT, MEAT! Pantomime Horse Steaks. £22 a kilo. Tastes a bit like pork, but wrapped in polkadot fabric. Delicious with golden eggs. Contact Milham's Pantomime Farm Produce Plc 01999 835 200

LONELY BOFFIN Great Night Out kit. Includes inflatable club, drunk tablets, taxi bedspread, 20 Bensons and a dressing gown with "All Back To Mine" embroidered on the breast pocket. Still in box. £65. 01999 701 904

HANDLEBAR moustache. Fits most bikes. £14. 01999 855 596

BED WETTING KIT with three refill packs. Two liquids, one solids. Ultra realistic and completely random. Offers? 01999 131124

SNOW TREES. In bloom and covered in blizzards. Deciduous and evergreen. £32 each. 01999 800 345

NOVELTY PUBIC LICE. Real lice, novelty gift idea. £10. Wripple 875

THE COMPLETE Underwater Chef. Volumes 1-5 bound in waterproof coating (Asparagus to Barbequing). £15. Fram 446523

HOME BREWERY Kit. Planning permission required. £3000 Freehold. BOX FR52234

GIANT BATH TAPS. Half the length of your bath, eight foot tall, two foot diameter. Fill your bath in seconds. £80 a pair. 01999 730 811

SIR SPINALOT™ TOP HAT. The original and still the best. Powerful clockwork brim. With No-Grip shoes for full spinning action. £40. Tel 01999 865532

BLACK & Decker 0.33" hammer drill with 500W amplifier and two 12" speakers. Council injunction pending, hence quick sale. £90. Mike on 01999 722 932

WATERTIGHT alibi. Used hundreds of times. £50 BOX FR57883

STAR TREK Collectibles, including trading cards, videos, books, action figures and Nichelle Nicholls' (Uhura) right hand. Pre-imprisonment sale of effects. Offers. 01999 501 765

JACK-IN-THE-MOUTH jack-in-the-box. A real surprise for the victim. "A laugh riot" The Catholic Herald. £45. 01999 612 633

PAIR OF fat ladies £88 Whoft 81490

ALMOST infinite number of manuscripts full of monkey typing. Left over from recent project. Experiment successful. Contact Prof Arthur Bostrom via BOX FE8664

SET OF 3 ornamental garden gases. Oxygen, Helium and Radon, all beautifully rendered in Helium. £40 ono Framley 357753

DRIED ORGASMS, available in handy tablets. Take effect immediately. The only swallowing you need ever do. MANDY'S PERSONALS, 01999 362118.

AUTHENTIC 1940s Republic Serials' "King Of The Rocket Men" gimp mask and straps. £200 Dave 01999 433 820

ROGER SLOMAN

GOOD Cop / Bad Cop Slippers. Break your right ankle, while massaging your left instep. £15. 01999 711 838

RARE BLUEPRINT of abandoned MoD sand castle project (1953). Great tablecloth. 01999 920 165.

FOUR SUITS for ventriloquist's doll. Doll now outgrown them, so no longer required. £130 Tel 01999 754 120

BLANKETY BLANK chequebook and bank account. Contains millions of pounds of undeclared, untraceable BBC money from the late 1970s. 01999 355 429

X-RAY PHOTOGRAPHS. Ladies' Day at Ascot, Roedean Prizegiving and What's Really Inside Your Travelcard. £40 each. 01999 410 933

IT'S PROBABLY MINE

EDIBLE chess pieces, with Yorkie knights, carrot pawns and a Weetabix king. Great game. Disgusting meal. Eaten (but thrown up again almost whole), hence only £5. 01999 621 199

ELECTRIC COT FENCE. £300. "Now Junior ain't going nowhere!". Unique American design. Slightly frightening at European voltage, but they only need find out once to learn. Contact Jeavons and Fitch Kid Control Ltd Box FE8021

"QUINCY, The Batman Years". Video collection. £32. 01999 622 095

FOUR HUNDRED AND NINETY-NINE "I'm Leaving You, Geoffrey" T-shirts. Minimum print run, but slightly excess to requirements. Call 01999 876 431, but hang up if Geoffrey answers.

SUNGLASSES, many designs. Also Moonmugs, Jupiterjugs and Plutothimbles. Also from £10. Also 01999 438660 and also ask for Patrick.

FALSE EYELASHES made from black shuttlecocks. Property of the late Dame Barbara Cartland. £65. 01999 707 844

ENORMOUS back-mounted hourglass that ticks away the passing seconds of your life with grains of inexorably falling sand. Would suit someone born on 4th April 1972, in reasonably good shape, light smoker, with family history of heart disease. Freaking me out, hence quick sale. £offers. 01999 831 911

10 LITTLE PILCHARDS™ children's lunchbox and flask. £5. 01999 398 766

HAND-KNITTED brown, purple and orange jumper, with slogan "I KNITED MY JUMPER". £25. Tel 01999 864 812

FIELD OF DREAMS for sale. ¾ acre. Some nasty back-at-school bits in the lower corner. £offers. 01999 622 988

POCKET Billiards table. Slight tear in baize. Balls need attention. £290 Chutney 689

14FT CARDBOARD CUT-OUT of Alice Beer. Used once (ie covered in sick), hence £3. 01999 327555.

INCOMPLETE set of bound partwork magazines. "Sew Today With Bruce Springsteen" Vols 1-4 (Cross stitch) and 14-16 (Denim). £10 the lot. 01999 633 097

10 Pilot's Licences. Genuine. Make your stag night go with a bang. 01999 755 490

FLASH-ME bathroom lighthouse. Guides you safely out of the bath and back into the bathroom. £200. Fr 833 112

TEAPOT, T-shirt and T-Bird for sale. Also T-bone, Teepee and black and white TV. Call Mr T on 01999 755 301

SELECTED ANAGRAMS £50, A Grandma's Celeste £05, A Gent's Crème Salad 5£0, Grade Salesmen Etc. FR. 01999 90199

ALONE? Join Date-A-Gibbon and meet the moron of your dreams! Partners you can manipulate, partners who never say a thing, partners who make you look like a casual professional brilliant hilarious billionaire sexual athlete compared to them. Call today! 01999 657657.

T-SHIRTS T-SHIRTS T-SHIRTS £150 the lot. Also F-Shirts (for one-armed people with colostomy bags) £35 each. Grey, yellow, foil. Box FE8473.

DANCING on The Ceiling, Turn Back Time, Live Forever and other well-kept secrets revealed in this fascinating set of instruction manuals. £20 each. 01999 800 735. Also available "Help!".

MOBILE PHONE. £30. Hairbrush, £5, driving licence, £150 nice wallet, £10. 07999 930919.

E.T. SCARF. Head at one end, body at the other. Very long neck. Simply grotesque. I had nightmares, now it's your turn. £12. 01999 624 320

EVERYTHING you've ever dreamed of. In underbed storage boxes. £45. 01999 300 976

FOUR BARS OF INTRO (drums, trumpet, Nelson Riddle). Unsuitable. Will swap for half a middle eight (steel guitar, congas, duelling banjos). Box FE8211

FOR THE love of God, get out of my way. 01999 855 176

TEBL Teacher required (Teaching English as A Belgian Language) to help confuse and bewilder home-schooled child. Call Mr Hollyhock on 01999 482762.

OX-BOW LAKES

'THE THREE LITTLE PIGS and the Big Bad Three Little Pigs', Subtle moral tale for advanced toddlers. £5 Framley 01999 822324

TRADITIONAL rustic bongs made from wellington boots and gunbarrels. Horseshoe handles. Haystack lids. £80 each. Box FE8755

IDEAL GIFT for him! Treat your boyfriend or husband to five laps of Silverstone on the back of a goose! Prices from £250. 01999 844 099

REAL FRUIT in imitation wax bowl. £15. 01999 755 400

SECOND HAND HOLIDAY. 4 days in Ibiza with a blonde girl called Liz. August 1998. It was alright, I suppose. Used once. Call Dan on Fr 743 822

SIMPLY RED airbrush kit. "Disguise Your Full Potential". Doesn't work, hence £1 / Works hence £100. 01999 735 404

HANGING BASKET. 1955 collectable Ruth Ellis souvenir wicker basket. £25. Fram975458

BABY BOUNCER. 18 months old. 8 weeks' experience handling Friday night crowds. Comes with double breasted babygrow and clip-on bib. £30 p/hr 01999 802 133

POLTERGEIST chef. Makes unwanted dinners at quarter to three in the morning. £400. 01999 661 892

23 BOXES of Pickled Onion All Bran. Didn't take that much to get everyone vomiting and shitting themselves. Plenty left over. £offers. Box FE8640 (>FLAG: Who ARE these people, Julie? This bloke's rung up before)

'PERRY COMO Live and On Fire, Again'. The album that started it all. %offers BOX FR73343

JUST BECAUSE I'm having dinner with you, it doesn't mean you're in my pants. Cut this out and stick it to the menu. Failing that, try shutting his dick in a drawer. 01999 377 651

AEROPLANE GLUE

KEVIN ROWLAND's mind, encoded in COBOL. Now your home computer can think, dance and sing just like the Dexy's Midnight Runners frontman. Extraordinary. £20. 01999 599 320

BOOGIE WOOGIE

BABIES' ELECTRIC RAZOR, with rattles and Petra The Pig charger, £100. May have been used once. Box FE8673.

4' diameter child's swimming pool shaped like an open mouth. Forms centrepiece of 18' diameter "Screaming Face" garden feature. £75. Melinda on 01999 761 433

FOR SALE. Classified advert advertising set of six saucepans, vgc, £25. £15. 01999 650 388

SWORD of light. Shield of truth. Bag of crisps. Will not separate. £30. Box FE8720

INSTRUCTION CASSETTES. 6 vols: "How To Eat Spiders". 3 vols: "How To Eat Everything Except Spiders". £20. 01999 776 800

ELECTRIC SOCKS. Deliciously warm when you climb into them. £9. Whoft 8431

PIRATE FLAG, cannon and grappling irons. Redundancy sale. £30. Also assorted plunder. £15. Call Mr Tillotson on 01999 601 511

COFFIN DODGERS. No job to big or small. Other containers avoided. Call us for complete pricelist BOX FR5498

COLLECTOR'S SETS of certified bone china artistic wall plates. "Reach For The Pot - NAAFI Canteens of The Battle of Britain", "100 Years of Carsickness", "Scenes From The Life of The Infant Bresslaw", "The Milli Vanilli Files" £150 each, or £600 the lot. Call Elsie on 01999 411 902

HUMPTY FROG designer cardigan. Web-spinning cuffs, wooden underflaps the lot. Worn once (while writing this advert). Fucking uncomfortable. 01999 788828

MAN & VAN. A man with a van. Anything. 07999 923441.

ALARM CLOCK that wakes you up with the sound of people burning to death. Lacks charm but I was never late for work once in the three months preceding my nervous breakdown. £18. Tel 01999 655 451 after 5am.

VINTAGE FLIGHTS to 1960's New York. Two discount tickets to visit the States during this exciting and liberating period. Couple must be over 50 and accompanied by a piano. £10 Whoft 594

BOY'S NAVY BLUE. Dad's Army Green. When I am king, dilly dilly, you shall be £50 ono. 01999 844 754

WET-LOOK bowler hat. Extra saucy. Adults only. £16. 01999 344 811

HAVE YOU got a novel in you? Most people have. We remove them using the latest techniques. General anasthetic and no scarring. Private consultations, $65. 01999 299951.

ACTUAL SIZE Morris Minor made out of cigars. All my own work. What on earth was I thinking! £45. Tel 01999 633 209

WEDDING DRESS, black and yellow, fuzzy velvet, with four huge crepe wings, calico pollen sac and 'compound eye' style veil fitted with delightful 3ft antennae, £400oao. Box FE8630.

SOFA shaped like Salvador Dali's moustache. Formerly the property of Mae West. £offers. 01999 740 843

JOSS STICKS. Various exotic scents: Teacher's Breath, Auntie's Duvet, Pub and When Did You Buy This Chicken? Packs of 12, £4 each. Call Rainchild on 01999 855 491

LEISUREKING Abdominal Teaser, £35. Comes with tummyrubber and timing pants. Box FE8182.

"PAIR" of ladies' shoes (one orthopedic boot, one stilt). £12. Tel 01999 508 729

MICROSOFT WARDROBE 3.0. Sorts your clothes into type, colour or alphabetically. Except trousers. £25. Framley 850 046

CAPTAIN FLIPTABULOUS

DECK OF CARDS. Spades slightly aggressive (some biting). Also Queen of 9s missing. Otherwise vgc. £2 01999 722 960

DOORBELL, 12 string acoustic. bass, kit. You pay, we play. Covers or original material., Will travel. 01999 654 377

"MR SAFARI" self-adhesive windscreen lion. Fits Vauxhall Nova, obscuring most of your view with lion. £30. 01999 744 300

SOAP ZEPPELIN. Flies and cleans. £400. Box FE8562.

BLACKCURRANT CORDIAL Moustaches - I will model three different styles for you. All at once or separately. I await your call. 01999 909099

BAKING POWDER, tons and tons of it. Went through a phase of thinking I was a baker. Realise now I was a judge. £offers/medicine, 01999 347796.

MIKE OLDFIELD'S old suit. 32" Inside leg. 3" sleeves. Not what you'd expect. Can be played as Bodhran. £185. Box FE8976

TWENTY-THREE PIECE SUITE in velour with duckdown cushions and seat belts, vgc, £350. 01999 227865.

MOTHERS HELP. 01999 354792. I'll help your mum.

ECHO & THE BINMEN

ALL CENTRAL HEATING, boilers, radiators, tanks etc removed discretely while your ex is on holiday. Call Gavin 07999 419872.

FRANK ZAPPA sex doll. With Moon Unit / Dweezil costumes. £30. 01999 851 934

BAKED ALASKA - the greatest cover-up of the last century? Cold and hot? I think not. What aren't they telling us? www.thebiggestconspiracyintheknownworld.ac.fr

THERE IS NO GOD and I've got the proof: wasps. £12 per 100. 01999 582239.

PACK OF THREE tournament quality ping pong balls. Ideal for enthusiastic player, or that trick girls do with their bits. 01999 733 218

GINGER BABY with black and white scan photo. £35. Will not separate. 01999 766 511

AMAZING saucy party trick. "Chipolata" which expands to size of bratwurst and sprouts two meatballs when bitten. Embarrasses and delights. £11 ono. 01999 855 210

SET OF FRAMED PHOTOS of Brian Blessed building a kite. £30 ono. 01999 733 701

AROUND & AROUND

taking a closer glance at rural Framley with Arbroath Smokey

Country Walks

WALK 132

Thoxtoxeter to Glibley

APPROXIMATE DURATION OF WALK 4 HOURS
DISTANCE COVERED 20-30 MILES

Butcher's Old Field at Ovenly   PHOTO: MALCOLM HOUDINI

THIS IS a mildly diverting stroll of between twenty to thirty miles, mainly in woods but with some farmland, from Thoxtoxeter to Ovenly and Boxing-Glove Mt Bellround, returning by Cloxted Farm and the edge of North-South Heath to Glibley.

Starting the walk from the top-floor of the multi-storey car park in Thoxtoxeter's main street, an easy jump takes you to the flat roof of The Cauliflowery Public House. Turn 90 degrees to your right and slide down the building's historic 15th century hexagonal drainpiping.

About four hundred yards to your in front, you should see a tall field. Turn right on marked path over stile into field, keeping fence on right.

Go under the pond and then up and over the top of the trees beyond (use a compass if you wish). This should take you to an opening and a leisurely amble across the FR404.

Turn right for an hour (it is safe to err on the side of caution here), then finally turn left into Ovenly Billiards Course and, keeping off the astrobaize, follow the signpost into the top left hole.

The next part of the trip takes in some hard walking, including an overwater sprint of approx. 500m, in the approach to Boxing-Glove Mt Bellround.

Walk vertically upwards, then right and finally down again, landing to the left of where you were originally. This tricky manoeuvre requires practice but looks great and should be no trouble to the seasoned country walker.

You should now be in the kitchen of Cloxted Farm. Make your apologies and leave by the nearest exit (usually the stove). Turn left uphill, and, when the path divides in two after six or so steps, take the righteous fork.

The pure of heart will emerge on North-South Heath. Follow the track North or South (it doesn't matter) and after a couple of days you should emerge outside the Pig and Valve public house at Glibley. Reward yourself with an evening in the company of one of their many celebrated whores. *You've earned it!*

A trip into your memory lanes

DO YOU REMEMBER when Whotten Plodney was bordered by Whoft on one side and Spain on the other?

If so, you're probably old enough to remember the first *Around and Around* feature I did on the dangers of crop migration.

Crop migration, for those of you unfamiliar with traditional country practices, is where a field of produce is herded to a new location nearer its target market.

In the days before steam, this significantly reduced transportation costs. Good farmers could direct whole orchards to new locations, while more mature crops could be left to relocate themselves.

Unfortunately, as is often the case with unfortunately, the increase in crop migration often led to whole areas relocating and huge gaps opening up around the countryside.

The Association of Wheat Walkers was set up in the late 18th century to oversee the practice of crop migration and ensure that any gaps left in the land were refilled as soon as possible.

It was Dr. Brian Bolland, however, who was to come up with the true solution to this conundrum.

By discovering that seeds are far lighter and more obedient than sprawling fields of produce, he found where certain crops were required and planted them there.

Crop migration is still practised in certain areas, but these days it's done under controlled conditions and for enjoyment rather than profit.

So next time you eat a wheat, *think where it may have come from!*

Storing nuts for winter

WITH AUTUMN still ringing in one's ears and the excitement of Christmas children spinning smashingly into focus, it's all too easy to forget about preparations for the festive season.

I've been collecting a few wise country tips on how to plan for and survive the Christmas season. All from the country, *of course!*

When hens start burying their eggs, it's time for you to stock up on plenty of hot soup and warming cocoa because it's more than likely to be a cold month ahead.

Look out for broken twigs and bruised leaves. We can always learn from our arboreal cousins. This usually means *red sky at night, shepherd's delight.*

Domestic animals' behaviour can also guide you during this period. Dancing cats and whistling dogs indicate a white Christmas, while stinging hamsters often spell rain.

Look in your garden. If you find wroms, then dig them out of the soil and measure them. Generally, the longer the wrom, the better.

In short, don't get caught out this winter. The clues are in the countryside around you, *just listen.*

Sheep Marathon cancelleda gain

THE ANNUAL St Eyots to Glibley Sheep Marathon has been cancelled for the 50th year running due to growing pressure from angry Cloxted residents.

The route, which follows an almost perfect straight line between start and finish, traditionally meanders in the middle.

"The sheep have usually lost interest in the race by the time they reach Cloxted and graze.", one organiser said. "That's why we have trouble with this event time after time. Maybe next year."

tv guide saturday   july 6th 2002

bbc one

7.45 The News at Ten Babies (rpt) Sandy Gall and the Blustery Day

8.10 Dr Who (rpt) Animated series

8.35 Rolf's Cartoon Hospital (rpt) Rolf helps a kitten squashed flat by an anvil.

9.00 SMBBC with PY & Duncan Avec Pierre-Yves Gerbeau et Duncan Goodhew.

12.15 Sportsnest including (approx. times)
12.20 Football Mucus
1.05 Pillow Fighting from Lingfield
1.25 First Bollard Back
1.40 Second Bollard Back
2.35 Half-Time
2.45 Ice Eisteddfod
3.40 Who Ate All The Pies?
4.00 The Adventure Game *with Sue Barker, Steve Rider and Lesley Judd.*

5.05 News (16,061 / 53,112) Huw refuses to wear a tie at Peter's funeral.

5.25 Cartoon 80:20 it's a mouse of some sort.

5.35 Hi-De-Hi-De-Hi-De-Ho (rpt) With Simon Cadell as Cab Calloway and Ruth Madoc as Minnie The Moocher.

6.05 Jim Davidson's Generation X Slacker fun with guests Ethan Hawke and Daniel Clowes.

7.05 Better On The Radio Inappropriate TV transfer of previously endearing comedy

7.35 Only Thing That David Jason Does That Isn't On ITV And Horses (rpt)

8.10 BorehamwoodEnders Local residents complain about the nearby late-night filming of a popular soap opera.

9.00 No. THIS Is Your Life Aggressive reappraisal of the life of wind-up merchant Trevor Bayliss.

9.30 News (as 5.05) (rpt)

9.50 Parkinson Classic interview with "The Greatest", Ali Bongo

10.40 FILM: Don't Tell Mom The Baby's Dead (1990) Harrowing screwball comedy

12.05 Top Of The Pops 1 with Manuel's Pyjamas, Twoozer, The Outstandings, Vulnerable and Kid Shit (rpt)

12.35 Are You Being Repeated? John Humphries sitcom (rpt)

1.50 Panoramic Last week's Panorama resized in 16:9 for widescreen TVs.

2.50 Last Orders

3.00 Closedown

REGIONAL VARIATIONS

ITV 4.00pm - 5.00pm **FRAMLEY NORTH EAST** Farming Week **WHOFT** Building an Igloo **FRAMLEY SOUTH** Roger The Horrid Bear **ST EYOT'S** Factory Club **FRAMLEY NORTH WEST** Interviewabout: The Framley Barrier **WRIPPLE** The Mrs Susan Wiltham Show **CODGE** Biscuit Time **CHUTNEY** The World Cup Final (LIVE) **SOCKFORD** Agaton Sax And The Sockford Computer Plot **MOLFORD ST MALCOLM** The Story of Cork **MOLFORD ST GAVIN** FILM: Ai No Corrida **FRACTON** Summerside Special **CLINTON** Tides (LIVE) **SLOVENLY** Closedown

bbc two

7.00 News 24/7 Rolling news service piped directly from MTV Europe.

8.00 Open Polytechnic
8.00 How To Get Out of a Loft
8.30 Valves (unit 4)
9.00 Gestetner Maintenance
9.20 Tidying Your Telephone
9.40 Gasthaus Glockenspiel

10.00 Saturday Cuisine. Cookery. Monty Rissole rustles up something involving bacon and tea to kill the pounding behind his eyes.

10.35 The Sexist Gourmet (6/8) Where in blue blazes is my bleeding dinner, woman?

11.10 Ant Kitchen A colony from Peru make a finger buffet.

11.40 You Only Live Once Incest and country dancing.

12.15 Wildlife On Toast David Attenborough pops some tree frogs under the grill

1.05 FILM: A Black & White Film (1930s-40s) Series of 11-minute scenes of women crying on railway stations and men in flying helmets. (B/W)

2.45 The Middlebrow Mysteries Det Insp Jack Middlebrow investigates the mysterious appearance of a line manager. (rpt from Sunday)

3.35 Labour Party Conference 1982 Day 7478 of the continued live coverage including Barbara Castle being interviewed by Sir Robin Day.

4.30 TOTP7 Gary Davies introduces the very best of his links from 1985.

5.10 Last Of The Summer Olympics Britain's gold medal hopes rest with Bill Owen in the Bathsleigh.

5.40 Robert Wars X-treme Robinson vs Hardy. Presented by Lord Charles.

6.10 They Think It's All News For You Public School vs State School.

6.40 Good Weather Isobel Lang

6.45 Bad Weather Christopher Walken

7.00 Yes, Paul Eddington Sitcom. Paul (Don Warrington) agrees to appear in a new political sitcom (rpt)

7.30 CrimeWave UK Nick Ross wraps a stolen GTi round a phonebox.

8.05 England Inch-By-Inch Bill Oddie's painstaking odyssey reaches 100657'N, 001765'E.

8.35 World's Strongest Young Musician of the Year Semi-final: Emma Johnson v Adrian Spillett.

9.05 I Don't ♥ Staying In On Saturday Nights Celebrity sofa reminiscences

10.35 Reputations A look behind the public façade of Changing Rooms' Mr Fixit, Handrew Andrew. Narrated by God.

11.05 I'm Andy Partridge The regional entertainer's abrasive style gets him into conflict with his producer again.

11.35 When Louis Met... Louis Louis Theroux spends three days with Louis Theroux impersonator Louis Laroux. (Edited for language and violence)

12.25 Last Orders

12.35 Closedown

itv one

4.35 GM-AM Environmentalists protest at the enormous, unnatural size of Lorraine Kelly's breakfast.

9.25 Tiswos 2000 Bob Carolgees and Spank the Monkey get the kids all sticky. Also starring Den Hegarty in a leather skirt as Sally James.

11.30 CD on Saturday... OK? Cat Deeley asks more pop stars if they can tell what it is yet.

12.30 World Really Championships

2.00 Framley Fortunes Local quiz

2.30 Fen Practice PC Muffin finds an owl. (rpt).

3.30 You've Been Patronised

4.00 Magpie P.I. Tom Selleck shows children how to make a coconut bird feeder. (rpt)

5.00 Weekend News John Suchet trolls round IKEA looking for 60W pearl bayonet-fitting bulbs

5.20 Lily Savage's Blank Attack

6.00 The Death Of... Another chance to see Jeremy Spake drive a tube train into the sea.

6.30 Data Entry Idol After eighteen weeks Ant & Dec are down to the last 12 contestants. Will Darius finally make it big?

7.30 Cilla's Surprise Date Cilla's in for a real surprise surprise when her blind date is with former manager Brian Epstein.

Stoner Zone BBC1, 3.10am

8.30 Pyramid Game 2000 Archive footage of Steve Jones poses the same questions he asked in 1983 to new contestants who can win the chance to repossess the prizes from their original winners.

9.00 Who Wants To Earn c11K pa? Chris Tarrant introduces three more lucky contestants who want a job in a petrol station.

10.40 I Know Absolutely Everything About Footballs Two comedians in a sofa

11.10 PICK OF THE DAY FILM: The Real Morph: Through The Table (1991) Biopic depicting the amazing adventures of the stop-motion plasticene homunculus. Morph's career is in the ascendant until he and Chas fall out over a racist comment. *Morphine Lord* - Richard Pryor *Charles Sproxton* - Gene Wilder *Mr Bennett* - Wallace & Gromitt *Anthony Hart* - Robert Lindsay *Grandmorph* - Peter Cook
Dir: Brian Cosgrove & Mark Hall

2.40 Movieline This week's releases reviewed by their own press departments.

3.10 Stoner Zone Unedited close up footage of a plate of spaghetti bolognese. (rpt)

3.50 Witch Hunts Live US sport

four

8.00 Transglobal Underground Baseball with Natacha Atlas

9.00 Tnage4 Cross-stitch.

11.00 Political Behaviour Last year's General Election re-staged as an eviction-based phone vote talent contest in order to interest all the 18-21 year olds who otherwise can't see the point in voting for anything. John Prescott performs *Mack The Knife* and Oliver Letwin has trouble with the chickens.

11.55 Enough Graham Norton! Graham meets J.D. Salinger, Joel & Ethan Coen, Chris Morris, Captain Beefheart and Lord Lucan. With music from The Beatles.

12.00 Littlejohn On The Prairie Uncompromising views on frontier grassland from the outspoken journalist (rpt)

1.00 Returning New series in which celebrities revisit their old haunts. This week Courtney Love returns to Liverpool to get off with the two people she missed last time. With Pete Burns and Cilla Black

2.00 I Love Lucy Speed Vintage comedy with Desi Arnez and Sean Williamson Jr (B/W) (rpt)

2.30 Aintree from Newmarket

4.00 The Bronze Age Kitchen (6/8) Bones

4.30 Clockword Baffling quiz presented by HRH Prince Edward. Magdalen College vs Blur.

5.05 Merseyside *Omnibus*. Sandra is concerned that Maggie is turning into a bear again until Reg flies by with his new friends from the galaxy of Andromeda to help open the leisure centre. Phil expects an audience-friendly explosion soon.

6.30 Big Baby Highlights from week four. The poor side refuse to share the nappy (rpt).

7.00 Trading Places Spagger, an HIV+ heroin dealer from Hastings swaps jobs with dental nurse Godiva Shuffle

7.30 Holding It In The series visits three more people whose jobs prevent them from regularly going to the lavatory. Narrated by Michael Kitchen.

8.00 The Upside-Down House The Gibson family continue their attempt to spend six months living upside-down. This week, Colin falls out of bed again and Marianne's bath floods the attic.

9.00 David Blane: Making The Sky Disappear Spectacularly special US TV special.

9.50 Heroes Of Comedy André Preview.

10.00 The 1000 Greatest 'Had An Accident Lately?' Adverts Of All Time

11.35 Boxcar The Bastard Cripple Cat Animation from the makers of South Park.

12.05 Ally McCoist Single, Scottish and falling apart. (rpt)

1.00 Late Night Sculpture Semi Final. "Cowgirl" Hepworth vs Jac Ometti.

1.50 Sparrows (rpt) Hard-hitting drama by Jimmy Truthwright set in 1978, about the IRA's breakaway birdwatching ring.

chanel no 5

7.50 Little Mr Men and The Mr Men Mr Small Uppity and Mr Uppity.

8.05 The All New Adventures of The Same Old Popeye

9.00 Front Of The Year Charlotte Church and Eastbourne are the finalists.

10.00 FILM: That Darn Walrus! (1969) Disney comedy including (approx. times)
10.10 Rollerskate chase
10.22 Mechanical breakfast maker
11.16 Parent struck with cream pie
11.29 Villains dunked in harbour

11.35 Ratdog Unappealing cartoon

11.50 The World's Worst... Television series

Clockword C4, 4.30pm

12.45 Lord Peter Wimsey The Vampire Slayer (B/W) (rpt)

1.40 David Dickinson's Manhunt Newton-Le-Willows (rpt)

2.10 Xerox Warrior Princess Unoriginal fantasy series.

3.00 News at Ten A classic episode from the much loved third series. (First shown on ITV)

3.30 FILM: Tupelo Ass Station Gizz Guzzler (1987) Pammy Cum and Rocky Neville star in this family matinee. (Edited for bad language)

4.55 Bollocks To Bathtime Up-to-the-minute current affairs show for the under fours.

5.10 Lovejoy: The Next Generation *Into The Ormolu Quadrant.* Captain Tinker flies the USS Chippendale into danger.

6.05 Knight Fever Suggs and his singing car.

7.00 Millionaires Want To Be The Who *I Can See For Miles* and *Boris the Spider* rehearsed and performed by Stelios Haji-Ioannou and Michael Winner.

7.30 Harry Enfield And Less Sketch comedy without Kathy Burke or Paul Whitehouse.

8.00 The UK's Worst... Breath

9.00 FILM: 3 Men & Syd Little & A Lady (1991) Malone, Magnum and Mahoney look after the straight-man when his wife goes away on business.

10.45 FILM: Night Mail (1993) Hollywood remake of W.H.Auden's 1930s GPO promotional film. Sylvester Stallone attempts to thwart Lance Henriksen's plans to plough a hijacked mail train through Grand Central Station on Christmas Eve. *Score by Benjamin Britpop.*

12.35 FILM: Dark Side (1974) Pink Floyd's memorable live performance from the surface of the moon, with guest vocals from Michael Collins.

Big, bigger, and bigger!

Judy's sunflower towers above the corner of Alphabet Street and Maxink Way.
PHOTOGRAPH BY HERBIE FOWLERS

BY TAUNTON MISHAP

A sunflower growing race at The Teapop School has proved to be a blooming marvellous success as one of the plants entered has grown really large!

The flower, named 'Sonny' by its owner Judy Sausages, has grown at least tenty times higher and wider than its friends and the growth shows no signs of stopping there.

"At first I thought it would stop as soon as it reached the top of my garden fence," Ms Sausages told me,

"but now it looks like it has only one destination in mind. The moon."

Horticultural experts have been called in to try and curb the plant's relentless self-enlargement using kitchen scissors, but to no avail. If anything the plant seems more determined than ever to grow.

"You cut one stem and two grow in its place. Our only hope is that this thing's not intelligent," said one 'expert' as layer after layer of hot pollen ate through his jacket.

The winner will be announced on Thursday.

ROADWORKS NIGHTMARE

by Challenger Putney

FRAMLEY motorists have voiced their extreme concern over the 'nightmare' state of roadworks at junction 12 of the FR403 motorway.

Over a period of three days, over 2000 individual complaints were registered with Framley Borough Council concerning the 'essential' repairs.

"It was a nightmare," said one happy motorist, "I was driving along and then all of a sudden the road surface was replaced by what seemed to be nothing. It felt like I was falling through the earth's crust, but unpleasant."

Other car users reported seeing Cornish road cones, strobe warning lights and crazy tarmac.

"It was quite literally just a nightmare. I was driving my father home from the all-night garage when all of a sudden we were being chased over a waterfall by a swarm of bats", said ten-year-old Elverton Crest.

However, when council officials were called to investigate the situation, they claimed that no roadworks were present, or had ever

A road, like the one in the story
PHOTOGRAPH BY SUE PUTNEY

been present, at the stated location.

"We're currently investigating the situation, but these roadworks never existed", one of them said yesterday.

The motorists seem to agree. "Yes," said one later today, "My journey to work took me 2 hours longer than normal, thanks to these nightmare roadworks, but then I woke up and it was all a dream".

All charges against the roadworks have now been dropped and an out of court settlement now seems likely.

Police discover the same body again and again

POLICE investigating the discovery of a body on wasteground near Cossett Park Industrial Estate have identified it as 38-year old Samantha de Tricycle of Honeyman Circus, Whoft.

However, they have also opened an immediate investigation into the investigation, since DNA tests had already positively identified Ms de Tricycle when she was found dead on a bench in Cossett Park three years ago.

"I just don't understand it," said police forensics expert Foster Nice when I started asking him things, "people can't die twice, they just can't. It simply isn't possible."

Events took a further extraordinary turn on Friday when a third de Tricycle corpse was discovered during a sponsored police treasure hunt by a field near some trees in a ditch.

by Taunton Mishap

At the post mortem, Mr Nice broke down in tears, falling to his knees and challenging the Almighty for proof or denial of resurrection.

"His faith has been sorely tested by this," admitted Chief Constable Rupert Bone. "But we remain resolute. Ms de Tricycle died thrice. Our tests show this beyond any doubt."

Fourteen similar incidents are under further investigation. Mr Nice will be buried voluntarily next Tuesday.

Carnival Queen has best arse yet

Annelise Gullivard, the recently chosen St Eyot's Carnival Queen has "the best arse yet", according to the judging panel.

She will hold the coveted position for the next twelve months, during which time the panel will enjoy looking at her arse as she goes about her duties.

Stiffs

Nichola Logan

aged 30 years
of Onmy Parade, Whoft.
Peaceful until the end,
then kicking and
screaming.

Sadly Missed

Patient

slipped away at Whoft Hospice on July 2nd after a lengthy illness.

Not too sure what his name was actually. Lovely guy, shame about that huge purple lump on his neck, wonder what it was. He always made us laugh with that huge purple lump on his neck.

Fond memories - all the staff at Whoft Hospice. Something like that. How much would that be? £14.50?!! You're having a laugh! Oh, go on then, stick one of those crosses at the top too

DEREK RIFLEMAN, sneezed himself out of a window in his sleep, July 3rd, aged 86. A loving, wheezing parent and grandparents to Michael. Love Billy, Madge & the kids xxx Funeral to take place at St Humbert's Chapel, Wripple on 27th September. **NO FLOWERS**. Donations to the Hayfever and Asthma Research Foundation.

Acknowledgement

Florence May Sexton

The family of the late Florence May Sexton wish to apologise to relatives and friends for the last few years of her bitter life, during which time she made things extremely difficult for those around her.

Particular thanks to the more than tolerant Mr Baker next door, who received a daily letter from Bitchnanna detailing the many and varied ways in which his budgie could be made into a glove.

DANIEL ROTISSERIE quickly, at the hand of an aggrieved dealer, on Framley High Street, June 27th, just outside Boots. "They broke the mould when they murdered you." Funeral has already taken place. Donations if desired to the "He owed me 15 grand, Mrs Rotisserie. Now that debt belongs to you" Fund.

Taken From Us

Why did you do it?

Alan Ant
1987 - 2002

"Ridicule was nothing to be scared of"

Mum & Dad

HOW IS MY TYPESETTING?
01999 974 976

Peter Ointment

Died December 8th

He was a kind, loving man with an infectious smile and disease that affected all who were close to him. He will be missed, sorely by everyone whom he touched. From the patients, nurses and staff of Ward 20 Framley General Hospital. We must find a cure.

New Arrivals

It's NOT a boy!

CONGRATULATIONS
Tom and Linda Squirts

on giving birth to what you claim is a bonny, bouncing boy, even though it clearly has a sixpence where it ought to have a winkle. Call it David and dress it in trousers if you have to, but we've taken a vote, and it's definitely going to grow into a lady.

Love from the staff of St Germain's Hospital, Molford.

PET FUNERALS

Family pet dead?
Don't want to lie to the kids?
We help soften the blow.

We'll take the corpse of your late pet and place it with a loving farm family.

We have hundreds of accommodating, caring, rural families on our books, none of whom mind having the odd dead dog on the hearth rug.

Rover's gone to live on a farm
THINKS:
Must get rid of the body somehow...
Now you don't have to lie...
Rover and you can BOTH go to heaven!

DOOLITTLE'S PET PLACEMENTS
01999 388 680

IT'S A BOY!

GRUNDY

Alexander Yusuf, born 26.05.02. Announcing your wedding to Barbara on 03.08.31 and your untimely passing on 16.11.48. You will be sorely missed by Barbara, Michael and Daphne.

Grandad xxx

LOOK! GREAT VALUE!

if you'd like to take advantage of our great 3-in-1 offer, call **Denise on 01999 974 974**

BAZALGETTE A wonderful baby boy, Changing Rooms, a big brother for Food and Drink and a third child for Peter and Sir John.

IT'S A BOAR!

It's A Boar! Toctoc Erwin Born June 30th 2002, weighing 300lb to proud parents Asterix and Obelix.

Scrunch! These announcements are crazy.

GOUNOD-RELEASE 06.06.02, Reginald. A beautiful second grandfather for Adam and Jasmine.

MIKE DENNISON would like to announce the birth of baby Ella, 18lbs 6oz on 03.06.02. Martine Dennison, would like to announce that this is never ever happening again and is looking forward to being able to sit down at some time in the future.

It's a family announcement!

£35 boxed
£15 plain
£40 pop-up

01999 94 76 94

JANE & DANIEL IGLOO are delighted to announce the appearance of a smaller version of themselves, but amazingly combined into one tiny person. How on earth did that happen? Enlighten us. 01999 655 543

ELLIOT

Louise & Patrick are delighted to announce the safe arrival of Delboy Jason, born 30 June, weighing 8lb2oz.

A beautiful baby boy for either Louise & Patrick or Louise & Keith MacGowan (blood test result pending).

Thanks to all the staff at St Grandad's.

OPAL & SOFT FRUIT wish to announce the birth of Penny Chew, a beautiful sister for Bazooka Joe, Black Jack and Bubblicious.

WANT TO APPEAR on the Announcements Page? I can kill you, marry you or get you pregnant! All services performed dicsreetly in the privacy of your own home. Competitive rates. Call Vince on 0999 754 544

It's a phantom pregnancy!

Karen Delling, you attention seeking muppet, you can throw up all you like, you're never going to throw up a baby. Now do a nice big fart, and get out of that bed, someone with a real foetus needs it.

Love from the staff of St Germain's Hospital, Molford.

Adversaries

50th Anniversary

50 years ago you stood me up outside the Paragon Cinema, Mildred Witting.

"Though night draws in cold
My heart remains true
Love never grows old
I wait here for you"

Never forgotten

Oliver Dixon xxx

DIXON Happy 49th Wedding Anniversary Susan. From Oliver.

ANNIVERSARY

Congratulations, Mum and Dad on the forty-sixth anniversary of the invention of the hovercraft

"Together forever, hearts entwined on this special day"

All our love, Carl and Mandy

CRAZY-GOLF, MICHAEL & JEANETTE. Eleven marvellous years. Happy velcro anniversary. Thank goodness she never found out that you don't really work on an oil rig. From all the girls at Maxine's 24-hour Bowling Whorehouse.

Annoncements

LOOK WHAT OUR SURVEY SAID!

You've always been like a Les Dennis to us.

From William & Ffion

HAPPY BIRTHDAY TO YOU!

Happy birthday to you
Happy birthday dear
Mildred and Patty Hill
Happy birthday to you
Lawsuit pending.

GOOD LUCK DAD!

Wishing you all the best on this, your special day!

05.06.02 6am EST

"See you in hell, asshole"

LOOK who's under your bed!

Sweet dreams, Josie. Love Mr Hollyhock and "Old King Pipe"

Look who's 3 and a half!

Scott! Who are you on the phone to?

Oh, for goodness sake... Give me that. Who is this? Oh, dear. Sorry, don't listen to him. No we don't want to take an advert out. Yes. Sorry to have bothered you.

LOOK WHO'S STILL WETTING THE BED!

Is this what I have to do to make you stop, Roger?

No-one drinks 12 cups of tea before bedtime - I know you're doing it on purpose.

Eleanor xxx

CONGRATULATIONS

Josie, on finally finishing your dinner. You know you can't afford to miss that much school and dinner is good for you.

Pease pudding hot
Pease oudding cold
Pease pudding on the plate
Three weeks old !

Mr Hollyhock

LOOK WHO COULDN'T AFFORD A BOX AD WITH A PICTURE OF YOU IN IT! (Imagine that photo of you in the bath as a baby with ice cream all over your chin printed in an oval here). Happy Birthday, Simon! All our love, Mum and Dad.

ABSOLUTE-BLEEDING DISGRACE The wedding of Julie Absolute-Bleeding and David Disgrace will unfortunately take place on Tuesday the 5th despite all our well-intentioned advice.

LOOK WHO'S RUNNING OUT OF OXYGEN!

Keep shouting, Dennis! Love Chris and Lynsey.

Announcement

Mr & Mrs Vernon Elliot

Would like to announce the forthcoming marriage of their son Peter to Olivia De Steam on 12th June at Llaniog Golf Club, but we can't because he's just slept with her dad

LOOK WHO'S 208

Happy birthday, Cecil.

From Auntie Mirabelle.

Look who's 3 and a half!

I nearly four.

And rockets up the side. Please. VISA 9432 6543 764 9999 16 Fankyou.

TO ORDER a Father's Day Massage call Trixie or Vince on 01999 322 191

LOOK who's fucking my wife!

Peter, you first class turd. I thought you had more taste. And you can forget about getting your lawnmower back *- Ray*

Adoptions

ADOPTION LETTER to ADOFRM548. Dear Birth Mother. Mother Helga and devoted father Frank would be honoured to help adobt your baby. We love being parents to our adorable, adopted 2 yr. old son who's looking forward to becoming a father. We're helping him to help you. Thanks. BOX FR6988

OUR PROMISE TO ADOPT YOUR BABY

(ADOFRM085)

We promise to raise you in a home with laughter and tears. We promise birthdays with fake trees and Christmas with real eggs. We promise to create a home for you that is full of heat. We promise to remind you that without us, you'd be somewhere else.

Please help us fulfil our promises.

01999 587776

(calls charged at 50p minute. min call length 5min)

life'style

with style guru Eugenie Solids

Bodystockings are in, in and still in this year, so show off your lovely shapes with a skintight orange number. You'll certainly be a hit with some of the ladies!

Don't be shy to show a little more on the beach this *été*. Cover up unwanted hair with a hat. Can't stretch to beach-flops? Seashells make an adequate alternative.

Always be aware of your proportions. Short waisted? Wear a smile and a neat bowler hat. Petite torso? Not my problem. Fat arsed? Try dieting, Porky.

Furs are very definitely in! My Italian spies tell me that otter is in the ascendent this week. Forget those moaning namby-pamby animal rights, fur is pretty.

Wear a Newby's Fart Enhancer from Newby's Health Saloon of Molford to distract from that embarassing moustache problem. People will be falling over themselves to get out of your way before it happens again!

WITH WINTER over for another year I've been turning my eyes to Summer. I've been leafing through some magazines so that you know what to wear without breaking a bank.

Sprinkle talcum powder on used socks and twice-used underwear to mask your unpleasant odours. Prevents chaffing I'm told, but I wouldn't know about that, I'm told.

Eyeliner. Fairy Liquid. Persil. K-Y jelly. Condoms. Preparation H. Fish fingers. Bread. Clover. Econ cheddar. Frascati. 10 x Ben & Jerry's Dbl Choc. Light bulb (40w). Lunch with Darren. Pick up Jessica from school.

Hollywood stars always look their best but you can achieve this year's Gene Hackman look with nothing more than a coat-hanger and some glitter. *Time for your close-up, You!*

Low shoulders are raging on the Supermodel catwalks of Paris and Framley. If you can't afford the neck extensions, try Newby's Neck and Chin Tincture (£13) from Newby's Health Saloon of Molford.

Tired eyes? Try Newby's Cucumber Pirate Eye-patches (£5.99 a pair from Newby's Health Saloon of Molford) to flatten those unwanted retina wrinkles and widen irises.

Don't be afraid to show a little less on the beach this summer. Cover up unwanted hats with hair.

Don't be afraid to show a little less on the beach this summer. Cover up unwanted hats with hair.

In belly-buttons are out this season - if you have difficulty converting yours to an 'outie' then I usually find that a partially-sucked malteser fits nicely in my hole.

Team fuchsia lipbalm with a *The Damned* album sleeve on each knee to achieve that elusive punk look. And then try gobbing in your own face as you speak to your boss like that.

Newby's Health Saloon is open Mon-Fri 9am-5.30pm (Sat 5.30am - 9pm) for all your health and beauty needs and ladies. 10% discount available on wrong treatments.

HIGH STREET OFFERS. Newby's Pharmaceuticals are offering a 2-for-1 deal on eye-concealer make-up, for that smooth-faced look that's so popular this year. Mellard & Esst have slashed the price of organic leggings. Flammings have a promotion on eyelash perms - remember afro lashes are to die for. Ms Outside are celebrating the opening of their new beautarium by offering a free arse-wax for you and your dog.

NEW SMELLS FOR THE MEN THIS SUMMER

SPIRIT OF EDEN
£2 a bottle from Newby's Pharmaceuticals

Splash it all over with this wonderfully delicate fragrance. Used sparingly it suggests innocence, copious amounts reek of betrayal. This jolly little scent comes in 4 litre, easy to carry bottles, so you'd never need not smell of *The Spirit Of Eden*.

BODYSOCK for men
£10 a bottle from shops

There's no excuse for not pulling the ladies with this effort from the laboratories of Conq. The smell reminded this journalist of Edwin Starr, but I could have been mistaken. It's equally effective used as an all-over body lotion or mouthwash. Killer.

BEANS ON TOAST SHAVING BALM
£2.75 a gallon from 6am, weekdays

There's a whiff of the hardy outdoorsman about this ingenious combination of robust aftershave balm and hardwearing varnish. The finish is smooth and tough, bringing out chin grain in bold tones, and with the alluring fragrance of a freshly cooked midday snack, you'll be beating them off with a splintery plank, Dandy Dan!

LOSE A STONE A DAY -the sugar and water way!

Advertising promotion

We all know that crash diets can be a good weigh of losing those extra stones quickly. Much better than Sit-Ups or DanceDiets or Aerobic.

This is why a company has produced a set of simple-to- follow diet books designed to allow you to lose weight faster than you can put it on.

The Sugar and Water Diet can be used throughout the day in place of your three regular meals. Sugar for energy. Water for rehydratration.

Here are a few sample recipies to make your appetite go all whet and hungry.

* * * * *

BREAKFAST
Ice Cold Sugar with Water

Fill a cereal bowl with

250ml of cold tap water. Add sugar and stir violently for a couple of minutes or until all the sugar has been absorbed. Stir again and eat immediately

LUNCH
Sugar Glacier Lollies

Add some sugar to some water, stir, and freeze in plastic lolly molds. Using the above amounts should make enough lollies for some people. I have found that these tasty treats can keep for up to forever.

DINNER
Sugar Lumps in thick and dreamy 'gravy'

Arrange 4 sugar lumps vertically on a plate. Warm some water in a saucepan and simmer for 5 minutes or so until thickened. Pour carefully over the sugar tower. Add sugar and

water to taste.

SNACKS
Bite-sized Treats

Diets shouldn't be boring affairs with long gaps between prescribed meals. If you get hungry, munch on some sugar lumps. Thirsty? Try water.

* * * * *

By following your 3-Stop Diet Plan you should soon feel the pounds falling off and you won't miss a meal.

TIP If you haven't got a sweet tooth, swap sugar with salt.

Squatters evicted from bouncy castle

Mrs Scholes in jubilant mood after her legal win.
PHOTOGRAPH BY POGLESWOOD ADAMS

A THREE-YEAR battle to evict a group of rowdy travelling types from a bouncy castle in Molford has finally come to an end.

Residents and campaigners looked on as bailiffs arrived in the back garden of 42 Leonard Rossiter Way and served legal notices on the five badly dressed squatters.

"This is a personal victory for me," said Marion Scholes, in whose garden the bouncy castle was inflated for her daughter's sixth birthday party. "The last three years have been a living hell of loud music, marijuana and constant bouncing."

CARNABY GROOVERS

Mrs Scholes' long fight to rid her garden of scruffy hipsters has been the subject of a huge publicity campaign, and has even featured in an hour long documentary in the television.

"This must never happen again," said Mrs Scholes, "and if it does, the council should deal with it much more quicklier. I handed in a petition at the Town Hall a year and a half ago, signed by everyone in Leonard Rossiter Way and Bruce Bould Close, and no-one even rang to thank me. I'm not a complete tit, you know, but I know when I'm being treated like one."

Mrs Scholes, whose daughter has had to hold her last two birthday parties in the loft, now plans to deflate the castle and return it to the hire company she now owes £42,500.

New roadmarkings "erratic and wrong"

MOTORISTS have given a lukewarm welcome to a new series of roadmarkings in Sockford town centre. The controversial road-mounted instructions are the work of a guerilla team of town planners and civil engineers known only as "The Black Wing". This elite cadre of urban signage contractors strike by night, then melt into the darkness like gossamer upon the winds of eternity. The signs will be replaced with proper ones next Friday.

PHOTOGRAPH BY SEXTON DELICIOUS

Church minibus vadnalised

A NEW CHURCH MINIBUS has been vandalised only two weeks after it was bought with money raised by parishioners in a series of demeaning sponsored activities.

Hooligans seriously damaged the vehicle, - belonging to St Damonoutofblur's church, Molford - scratching the paintwork with cufflinks and smashing the stained glass windscreen.

The Revd Julius Pantomime, vicar of St Damonoutofblur's, told churchgoers in his sermon on Sunday that, although the windscreen was beyond repair, there was a bright side to every silver lining.

"It is a terrible shame that we've had to tape polythene over our once beautiful parish windscreen. But I have to admit that we seem to be having far fewer accidents now the driver's view of oncoming traffic is not blocked by colourful scenes of The Ascension."

We then sang hymn number 149 and ate magic Jesus biscuits.

Cruelty to dog - help wanted

The RSPCA is appealing for help after a 10-month-old bulldog was left in a sack in a hot car with concrete wheels with all the windows shut in the middle of a motorway for three weeks before being hanged by the throat from the "St Eyot's 3 miles" sign by irate motorists.

Anyone with any information about why the animal had been forced to wear orange lederhosen and a prescription monocle throughout the incident should contact the RSPCBD on 01800 PORDOG.

BUSINESS GNEWS

BUBBLE BURSTS ON CRISP MAN

TURN YOUR MEMORIES INTO CRISPS, the Framley firm that promised to TURN customer's MEMORIES INTO CRISPS, has gone into bankruptcy after only 6 months' trading.

Unlike successful businesses, 22-year-old Lee Organisn's Internet-based family-run firm has hit the financial ocean floor.

A hastily organised presconference yesterday saw Lee announcing his intention to fold the firm like a "foolscap envelope" and "post it to the receivers".

As news reached the marketplace investment men rushed to buy any stocks and shares that weren't connected to the the crisp enterprise, and to sell all of the ones that were. Something crashed.

"If there's one thing I've learnt from this business adventure", Lee told us, "is that not enough", he continued, "people wanted their memories turned into crisps"

"At first we sold some, and then we sold lots, so we thought we'd try and sell lots and lots," he explained quite clearly. "Unfortunately not as many people wanted lots and lots as wanted some, and so we found ourselves with lots left over."

The Framley Examiner's own business expert, Jennifer Oat, says that this phenomenon is quite commonemon and the news is unlikely to have a significant effect

on the worldwide crisp memories market.

What's he doing?
PHOTO BY CHICK BEAK

"There will always be a small global contingent who would like to see a treasured memory captured on the face of a potato chip,"she gasped.

But as they say, you can't bury a good man for long. Towards the end of his speech, Lee announced that he wasn't planning an early retirement bath.

"We've got to move with the times. The World Web has opened up whole new boulevards of opportunity for us. Now is the time for us to consign the crisp memento to the dustman of history and seek out brave new horizons for business expansion."

Mr Organisn pulled down a curtain revealing a freshly painted logo: "Turn Your Memories Into Shoes!" Then, with the aid of an overhead projector diagram and a pair of shoes, he outlined the possibilities.

"You can do a lot with laces," he said. "Platform soles are a happy memory, brogues more melancholy."

Trading was brisk.

Business to Business
with our businessman, Nigel Drivel

The future starts tomorrow!

ARE YOU PAYING TOO MUCH IN MANAGEMENT CONSULTANT FEES?

IT'S A SCENARIO not unfamiliar to many businesses. It's been a good few years, the company is growing, and the management consultants have started to shape your future.

And then it all seems to go so wrong. Overheads are rising, the consultants have to re-think, capital gets sold off and even headcount can suffer. Short- and short-to-medium-medium-term debt can be crippling, especially with interest rates being so low: there's always the prediction that your future debts will cost more because inflation is bound to rise.

It can be utterly dreadful being in business some times, isn't it, businesspeople?

But just when you think you're walking around in circles, you find the answer around the corner marked 'management consultants.'

Consultancy costs can be astronomical, and often chisel away at budgets that will suffer after they've borne the cost of those costs. The inside track from The City is that it's time to ditch those consultancy costs. But how?

Well, here's where you turn the corner marked 'next generation of management consultants.'

In the competitive consultancy environment, more and more companies are competing to offer more and more more cost-effective services at more and more and more affordable prices. Fortunately for those of us in the business-to-business business, the new wave of consultants are leaner, fitter and faster.

Based in a converted 20th century barn on the outskirts of Wripple, The Company Company is one such "2G" team of consultants.

Managing director (or "team stag" in 2G-speak) Steve Glibbs is roundly optimistic (and a millionaire).

"We're taking on major projects at the moment, by accumulating a huge portfolio of consultancies and consulting on all their consulting. They consult us for decisions that help them cut the costs to make their decision making more profitable."

"It's absolutely astonishing. I can't believe what these companies will pay. I'm minted. You saw the Jags on the drive?" he continued. "One of our 'team leverets' took home £13,000 last month. We're all laughing."

It certainly looks as if the future will belong to companies like The Company Company. If your consultants are costing you too much, perhaps they need consultants? The future starts today.

WJC&S
Wee Jimmie Crankie & Salterton
SALES & LETTINGS

THOXTOXETER

We are proud to announce the sale of this genuine 1960s shrinkwrap maisonette in much sought after area. The property shrinks to fit, snugly smothering the occupants every summer. Previous owner only recently escaped during unseasonal cold spell. Quick sale preferred before weather changes. **£110,395**

FIELDINGFIELD

Well-mannered Gemini property. North facing and south facing. Gregarious. Gets on well with Libran neighbours. Lucky colour: Magnolia bathroom. You will meet a handsome stranger in the cupboard under the stairs. **£210,000**

CHUTNEY LE BASIL

Compact one-bedroom magical fungal feature, convenient for all local amenities, Economy 7 storage heaters. Fully fitted kitchen. Off road parking. But still, essentially, let's not beat around the bush, a big mushroom. **£40,595**

WANTED

Due to unprecedented demand and an abundance of customers seeking a property in your area, we urgently require **YOUR PROPERTY** and no other properties in your area.
Face it, it's too big for you now the kids are at University, with you rattling around it like a pea in a skip, and frankly what you're doing with the garden is knocking a couple of grand off the asking price every time that cowboy squeaks up the drive with his wheelbarrow, so give us **YOUR PROPERTY,** Mrs Eleanor Jessop

CALL MIKE OR CAROLINE IN PRESSURE SALES
WJC&S 01999 864 722

RUBMY

Delightful 3-bed family house. Large garden. Open plan lounge. Kitchen / breakfast room. Squatters. Excellent location, near to shops & transport. Period features. Screaming headless ghost of a 9-foot nun. Off street parking for 2 cars. **£11,985**

TOLLEPHANT

Spacious church conversion. Owner must put up with loads of people turning up unnanounced once a week to sing *Immortal Invisible*, drink your wine and eat your crisps. **£495,950**

WRIPPLE*

*ON THE MOVE! One-of-a-kind 5-bed house, currently situated in Wripple. Soon to be situated in Molford. Two long metal legs extending from bottom of property, walking at 10mph up the inside lane of the FR404, heading east. Conveniently located (phone to find out for what at the moment). **OIRO £160,000**

YOPNEY ST OH!

Surrounded by walls and ditches, this charming 6-bedroom 17th Century property has been unoccupied since the 17th Century. Advances in Mole Machine technology mean this fine family home is finally uncovered. **£585,995**

WRIPPLE

Desirable bargain 2-bed property. Photograph recently airbrushed to remove toppling chimney and damp outside wall. **£85,795**

SOCKFORD

Flat-roofed house, 25' x 25' x 25'. Number of windows on opposite faces adds up to seven. Currently facing in highly sought after lucky direction, hence **£114,390**

COMMERCIAL

FOR SALE: Chocolate factory. 2 previous owners. Glass elevator (fucked). Chocolate river choked with dead midgets. E-mail Mandy at Bucket's Golden Ticket Enterprises. mandy@bucketents.com **£POA**

Excited shoppers wait along the sliproad by the DeLorean Industrial Estate, Sockford.

PHOTOGRAPH BY ST EMILLION POPDANCER

SALE MUST START SATURDAY

POLICE HAVE ORDERED that a sale at a shop in Sockford "must start Saturday".

Officers say they were forced to act after receiving a number of complaints from local members of the public.

Sockford residents had expressed concerns that traffic and emergency vehicles might have trouble negotiating the three miles of queues that have built up outside the shop since the first "Sale Starts Soon"

signs went up in March.

Local schools have reported that truancy levels are at an all time high, and no firemen have reported for duty since June.

The owners of the shop, Anna-Barbara Production, and her common-law business partner Phil Mation have both been cautioned, and the sale, at Key Cutting City on the DeLorean Industrial Estate, will start, by court order, this Saturday.

CLEARLY A NEAR MISS

by Odgar Cushion

A MAN I MET YESTERDAY told me that a cyclist was involved in a bizarre near miss in the town centre last Thursday.

At around 2.30 in the afternoon, glaziers were delivering new windows to Gossip's Florist's in Purple Passage. But as they crossed the busy four-lane Cockson Road, carrying a 3m x 5m pane of glass, a cycle courier, rounding the corner at some speed, came within inches of losing his life.

"It was shocking," said a bystander (my man), "the cyclist didn't spot the pane of glass until the last minute. He didn't have time to brake, and I saw one of the workmen carrying the glass gasping with shock."

STROKE OF LUCK

But what happened next was an astonishing piece of luck.

"The cyclist just passed seamlessly and perfectly through the glass. It was like something out of Narnia. It was so peaceful and sublime that I almost barked my yop."

A representative for the glazier's, F.H. DeSmith, declined to comment, but Colin Yaffle, a professor of physics, logic and brilliance at Framley Community College, thinks there might be an explanation.

"They may have been carrying a pane of air," he said yesterday. "No, hang on, let me think about this. Some panes of glass have huge bubbles in them. No, that's not it, either. Just a minute. They may have achieved a perfect molecular velocity and just existed within each other for a moment without any of the usual interference, like the cyclist having his face smashed to bits.

"Yes, that'll do," he said.

The glaziers were reportedly so shocked that they dropped the pane of glass and it shattered into millions of annoying pieces.

Child dies of garden

A SMALL CHILD which had a severe allergic reaction to pollen was last night lying dead in hospital, say sources.

The little child, which has no name for legal reasons, was playing happily in its mother's friend's garden when it suffered anaphylactic shock (very bad for you) after coming into contact with a flower.

The owner of the deadly garden, 38-year-old Gwynyrd Skynyrd, was the night before last said to be "devastated" at the news that magistrates have ordered her 24ft source of pride to be put down.

The mother of the tiny little child, known only as Mrs ?, last night called for dangerous gardens to be tagged.

"The Home Office," said Mrs ?, "must."

Bulldozers are already on their way.

Children missing since Saturday

By TAUNTON MISHAP

FOUR SCHOOLCHILDREN who went missing while on a hiking holiday to abroad have now not been seen since Saturday, say calendar experts.

Jolyon Hurrah, the co-owner of Higginson's Adventure Holidays - who was supervising the kids on the outward-bound course, told reporters that the children's disappearance had got everyone stumped.

"We don't have a clue what happened," he explained yesterday.

"The group was playing an innocent game of blindfold hide and seek on the brink of a precipice in the middle of bear country when it happened.

"I had been chosen to be 'seeker',

so I turned round for half an hour to count to ten thousand before going to find them.

"And when I did, I was horrified to discover they'd simply vanished into thin air."

Hurrah says he searched the area for nearly twenty minutes before giving up and walking to the nearest town to alert the police.

The four children, the only survivors of the rollercoaster accident that last week claimed twenty of their party, had been due to come home this Sunday, but their parents are now being encouraged to forget about them and have some more kids as soon as possible.

The last photo of the missing children.

PHOTOGRAPH BY JOLYON HURRAH

Railway designer killed by new Framley loop-the-loop rail link

by Jesus Chigley

INVESTIGATORS were yesterday looking into the future of Framley's new £200m corkscrew railway after a disastrous test run killed the track's designer.

Maverick engineer Christopher P. "Rice Crispy" Rice was tragically flung from the buffet car of an experimental test train as it negotiated the second of a series of loop-the-loops that were intended, in Rice's own words, to serve as the "crown jewels in the crown" of the new rail route, linking Molford and Framley stations. After falling 180 feet, bouncing from strut to strut of the superstructure of the loop and landing on a grass siding, Rice died instantly, doctors say, of lung cancer.

EYEWITNESSES

Eyewitnesses described the scene.

"It was brilliant. I don't know how he did it," said Petra Wilkommen, who watched the accident from her bedroom window. "It's definitely the most death defying stunt I've ever seen. Except for the bit where he died."

Rice's deputy engineer, Helen Belljar, said that, though the tragedy was tragic, the construction of the rail link had to go on - and studying what went so horribly wrong this time would avoid further deaths in future.

Framley Station is closed by some police tape. (Inset) The unfortunate designer.
PHOTOGRAPHS BY BESERKELEY GRENADIER (INSET POSED BY DEAD MODEL)

"Though this is a difficult time for all of us, we can learn from what has just happened," she told me and I wrote it down.

"For instance, the first loop, above Chutney Junction, worked brilliantly. People on the platform heard Christopher and the test-monkeys all going 'Wooooh' as the train went round, and there was a lot of waving. It's a blinding loop, that.

PLUNGE OF DOOM

"It's the second loop that's the problem. We need to examine it carefully to see what might have gone wrong."

This second loop was Rice's pride and joy. Using a new design never before seen in railway engineering. it formed a revolutionary "figure of six" in the track. Experts are now keen to discover what tiny flaw in the construction of the loop might have led Rice's test carriage to be flung hundreds of feet into the air at over 90 mph.

"We're going to try everything, but the rail link will be built," said Ms Belljar, "and it will have Chrsitopher's beloved loops."

Plans for a revised "figure of four" shape are already on the drawing board, and the railway should be.

Whoft Cemetery full of stolen bodies

FOREIGN POLICEMEN Interpol have raided Whoft Cemetery after sustained allegations of grave robbing.

Cemetery manager, Emily Locque, we can exclusively reveal, has definitely been pinching the graves and headstones of celebrity corpses from other cemeteries around the world, with a view to reburying them in her own graveyard and attracting tourists to the area.

Police found famous communist landmark, Karl Marx, who was stolen from his Highgrove resting place in 1994, propped up against a still warm furnace in the crematorium.

The bodies of Dustin Gee, resident comedian on TV's *The Laughter Show*, and tree/car accident victim/singer, Mark Bolam were traced by police kiff-dogs to the staff quarters, while the ashes of Lizard King Van Morrison were found in a biscuit barrel labelled "BURY THIS - URGENT."

Mrs Locque has previous.

Cannibal woman innocent, apparently

THE FRAMLEY Examiner would like to offer its most sincere and humble apologies to Mrs Emily Locque and her family. In last week's top-selling Examiner we stated that Mrs Locque, manager of Whoft Cemetery, ate partially-cremated bodies for her tea. This is not the case and The Framley Examiner is happy to correct any misleading impression that they may inadvertently have created. Sorry.

Appeal lodged to speed up treatment for mentally ill

By ADAM WRENT

THE COMPANY RESPONSIBLE for a new home for mentally ill patients next to a Sockford housing estate has lodged an appeal in an attempt to up the speed at which patients recover.

"These people aren't helping themselves," said Graham Grahamsson, CEO of WellbeingProfit plc. "We urgently need to spearhead a more efficient turnthrough in our patient-to-bed ratios. Basically our clients are going to have to get better quicker."

The company, valued at over £13bn, is hoping to see people with depression being allowed home the same day as they are admitted.

"It's not impossible," said Mr Grahamsson, "I'm no scientist, but if you inject someone with enough Prozac or electricity, say, they must get better almost immediately. I would have thought that was obvious."

The entrance to the nut unit.
PHOTOGRAPH BY DEANNA OH

The home, which is one of the company's flagship franchises, is planning to offer special one-off bargain treatments for autism, OCD and [not being able to get a hard-on] (>FLAG: whats it calld?), with same-day cures for shyness, fecklessness and jumping to conclusions.

The centre was at the centre of a controversy last year, when a former patient was found trapped in his own microwave ten minutes after being discharged.

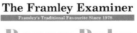

Framley's in a safe pair of hands, as long as its safe pair of hands is on duty

A safe pair of hands

by Katie Blirdsnest

THERE'S AN OLD SAYING that says "If a job needs doing, it needs doing well". Well, that could equally apply to Ron Aerosmith!

Ron has worked the lockside at Urling for over forty years, acting as Framley Barrier - a traditional craft dating back, I suppose, more than forty years. On Wednesday, after getting my hair done and buying some binbags and toothpaste, I went to see him to find out just what it is that it is that he does.

THE TIDE

I met Ron in his cottage by the lock and asked him actually what the Barrier's role involved in fact.

"The whole of Framley is built on a flood plain," he told me as he poured some tea. "Twice a day, the tide sweeps in up the river Fram all the way from Fracton.

"By the time it reaches Urling, it's a tidal wave almost forty foot high, that frightens cattle and ruins the washing. A fearsome sight, to be sure."

"My job, as it was my father's job before me, is to stand in the deepest part of the river and drink the incoming tide before it reaches the town."

I'd never heard of this before, but Ron assured me it was all true, and showed me a framed swimming certificate which had been changed to read "swallowing certificate".

£4000

It didn't take long for me to become convinced that Ron's work is clearly a job and a half! Although he recently negotiated a nominal wage of £4,000 a year from Framley Borough Council, he sees his work as more of a calling than a career.

"If I don't do it, who will?" he asks. "Show me someone else who can swallow nearly a million gallons of floodwater a day, and I'll gladly pass the job on to them."

ARMY OF ROBOT PIKE

Ron never married and has no children of his own to teach the Barrier's craft, so he fears for the town's future.

"One day I'll have to retire, when my lungs can't take the pounding any more. The day after that, you'll be pulling seaweed out of your upstairs windows, mark my words."

His job is made harder, he told me, by the actions of a woman he calls 'Kan'Thor the Evil One', who lives only to thwart Ron's good work.

"Last week I had to fight off an army of robot pike, controlled by her mind waves," said Ron. "Next week it'll be a yacht manned by skeletons." Check this.

Ron stands guard by the upper course of the Framley and Tedlingford canal.
PHOTOGRAPH BY PEASON GRATEFRIEND

Brownies reunion

HAVE YOU EVER been a member of the 2nd Molford Charlie Brownies Pack?

Current pack leaders are trying to organise a reunion of anyonewho has ever worn the distinctive yellow and black, zig-zag uniform. It'll be a chance to relive memories and there'll be root beer and chocolate chip cookies.

The Crest of the 2nd Molford Charlie Brownies'

The Second Molford Charlie Brownies, the last active group in Britain, meet on the pitched roof of the Village Hall every Tuesday evening, as they have done since the pack was formed in October 1950.

Former packmembers who wish to attend the get-together are invited to contact newly appointed Woodstock, Mrs Patrick Peppermint. The pack are particularly keen to contact that little red-headed girl, or the one with naturally curly hair.

Obituaries

Born bad

Dame Margaret Le Fontleroy Duq-de-Granmercy (née Bad)

Shockwaves echoed round the Framley social scene with the death last week of evergreen debutante Dame Margaret LeFontleroy Duq-de-Granmercy, one of the area's most respected rich old ladies.

Born in Whoft in 1909 to a wealthy family of landowners, Margaret Bad was elevated to the high life by her marriage in 1931 to Reg Le Fontleroy Duq-de-Grancmercy, the man who came to fix the boiler. Leaving her stuffy life behind, and much to the disapproval of her family, she joined the bright young set, and ran with it.

Fortune smiled again when, in 1934, while holidaying in Marakesh, she invented the device that makes the sound of a door slamming when you slam a door, a gadget that is fitted to every door in the world to this day.

Already rich beyond dreams, Margaret put the proceeds from her invention towards finding a cure for being hit by a bus, the illness that had dogged her estranged mother years before (throughout the war, Margaret drove an ambulance, picking up people who had been hit by buses during the blackout.)

Sadly, after her husband died in 1971, when he coughed up his own mind, Margaret became a recluse, only venturing off her country estate four times a week to organise parties and charity dinners and go and watch snooker.

Tragically hit by a bus, at 92, she leaves twin sons, Quentin and Um.

Local journalist and "character"

Odgar Cushion

It is with great sadness that we announce the death of one of Framley's best-loved journalists, Odgar Cushion, self-appointed chronicler of the bizarre.

Always cautious about revealing his age, Odgar was born at sometime between 1932 and 1994. He attended St Shoebingon's Grammar, Chutney, where he excelled and left before taking any exams.

Keen to make a name for himself, he began working for The St Eyot's Flugel at the tender age of either 15 or -47, and soon had his own column, *"We'll Fancy That"*, that bears his name in The Framley Examiner to this day.

Dedicating his life to the pursuit of the unusual and peculiar, Odgar made the news himself as often as he reported it. In 1961, he became the first man to ride a bear across the English Channel, and was well known locally as the owner of Framley's biggest ice cube.

He died suddenly on April 11th, after falling eight stories from the pavement to the roof of Denegate carpark. Relatives say life has returned to relative normality since his death, but were delighted to notice that on the following Sunday, all the flowers on Odgar's favourite roundabout had burst into bloom, spelling out the date, time and manner of his remarkable death.

He is survived by two daughters, Whoopi and Pin, and Framley's biggest ice cube.

an honest woman of her, Ricky! So it just remains for me to lead this toast to the happy couple. Please charge your glasses. Richard and Julie! Buyer to collect. After 6pm. 01999 387 664

BEETLE WIGS. June, Potato, Ground and Rove Beetle hairpieces. One size fit head. Also bag of Monkee Nuts. £100 the set. FR 01999 662334

OCTAGONS

GET A JOB, you bone idle waster. Excellent working order. £6. 01999 729 690

DOLL'S HOUSE. Burnt out husk. Complete with two sets of charred furniture and dolly smoke detector with flat dolly batteries. £25 01999 887265

BOY. Boy for sale. Going cheap. Only joking. Girl for sale. £2,500,000 ono. Call Mr. Hollyhock 01999 654722

BOX of early 90s memorabilia. "Vanilla Ice is Vanearly Nice" T-shirt; Picture of Mike Edwards from Jesus Jones beating Lady Miss Kier at Super Nintendo; 4000 cans of Cucumber Classic Coke®; a 22p stamp. £offers. Box FE8911

BOOK "How To Make Pencils" £5, or will swap for copy of "How To Stop Making Pencils". Help me. Please. 01999 733 291

MINDGAME GAME

STANNAH Stairlift to Heaven. "The last gift Grandma will ever need". Fits most stairs. £250. Fram 944 321

YODASTREAM. Star Wars tie in drinks dispenser. "May the fizz be with you!" £16. 01999 734 299

WISHING MACHINE. Ever wanted really expensive clothes but never been able to afford them? The new Sinussi 4500 turns rags into ballgowns, pumpkins into carriages and glasses into slippers. Comes with three refillable wishes and four mice. £599.99 from Ranfurly Electrical. 01999 646 900

RARE "RAINBOW" merchandise. Geoffrey Hayes backpack. Rod and Jane pencil cases. £10 the lot. 01999 765 409

LIGHT LIFTING. I'll take all your lamps and bulbs and raise them up to six inches higher. £12 p/hr. 01999 644 802

Last year only 6 complaints regarding
The Framley Examiner
classsified ads were upheld by the Advertising Standards Authority, resulting in a fine of only £375,000

24-HOUR DOG WALKING. I can outlast your pet. Drive hounds into the ground. Look on my walkies ye mighty and despair. 01999 403 651

SHIP'S BELL, £2. Also ship, £42m. 01999 444 864

MOUNTAIN BIKE with 400W amp and 2 Peugeot bass bins. £350. "Cycling has never been so audible" *The Grocer*. 01999 611 310

THE SKY AT NIGHT. £350. It's alright. Nobody uses it at night. Call Vince on 01999 911 055

FREE HARDCORE from damaged brick wall. Approx 5 - 6 cubic yards. Some girl-on-girl. Must collect. 01999 398 878

BREAST MILK. Vintage. Marked "HRH Queen Mother 9/6/98" with crest and certificate of authenticity. On its own, £250. With 3 Union Jack straws, £274. Call Box FE8202

SHOWER. Vgc. £30. Five minutes only. Put the mat down and remember to turn the boiler off. 01999 629 299

FRIDGE FREEZER with 3 drawers and tie rack. £100. 01999 744 347

WHIZZ-KIDS

GLASS DARTBOARD. Used once. £3, with some bits loose in Newby's bag. 01999 511 951

"ONE SMALL Step For Jazz, One Giant Leap For Satchmo" by Louis Armstrong. Autobiography of first trumpeter on moon. Rare marked up galley. £offers. Box FE8432

MICROWAVE Radiator. £60. 01999 400 958

PINE BREAKFAST BAR with pine stools, pine bacon, pine egg and eight slices of pine toast. Inedible but hardwearing. £350. Call after work on 01999 533 280

The Framley Examiner
Make your ad stand out high
light it with a box

DOES HE TAKE SUGAR? diabetic testing kit. £6. Box FE8511

400 TONS of well-rotted horse manure. 3 years old. £1 a bag (a bag holds 400 tons). 01999 971 703

CAN OF STELLA. 3cl left in bottom. Would suit smoker sitting some distance from ashtray. £350 pcm. 01999 622 924

KENWOOD CHEF. £35p/h. 4 years experience working in one of London's top stately homes. 01999 709 996

CHIP-ITES

DRUG HABIT. Also bongwimple and tonsure with an acid house smiley shaved into it. £20. Call Brother Francis on 01999 877 601

TOPSOIL. Free to collect from gardens up and down my road. Bring own spade. 01999 248 860

RAT, 50p 01999 698 787

BRIAN ENO'S Oblique Strategies coaster set. 6 designs including "Maybe this isn't your drink", "Imagine you're still thirsty". £15. 01999 710 252

MOTORISED WHEELCHAIR. 5 gears. Top speed 180mph. 0-60 in 4.8secs. Sun roof. Alloys. 3 times London Marathon winner. £18995. 01999 252 977

MY CHEQUEBOOK. 6 cheques left. All signed but otherwise left blank. OIRO £20. Danny on 01999 499 032

SPICE RACK. 1 jar each of Oregano, Lemon Grass, brown powder, something that looks like leaf litter, and a load of little sticks that taste like Blackjacks. £4. Call 01999 533 912 before I finish all the little sticks.

We now offer a FREE 24 hour voice-ad phone line.

If you want to hear any ad on this page read by the person who originally placed it, simply call 0999 974 978 and, when prompted, clearly say the first word of the ad you require.

Or, if you'd rather hear the ad read by Martin Jarvis, say "MARTIN SAYS" then the first word of the ad you require.

The Framley Examiner

CARAVAN. £2,500. 6 berth Crusader Convivial. Isobella Ambassador awning. Top of the range. In beautiful mahogany frame for wall mounting. 01999 399 629

OLYMPIC BID. Unsuccessful hence £28m. Call 0121 999 4638.

BATTERED WIFE, £3.50. Saveloy, £1.00. Mushy peas 85p. Call Cap'n Fist on 01999 486 688

HOLE IN THE GROUND. £16. Ideal for looking like you only exist from the waist up (in my garden). Buyer to collect. 01999 676 273

BOILING ice skates. Ruin the rink! Hard to put on though. But then isn't everything these days? Call Elsie on 01999 641 318 to talk about anything. I'm waiting for your call. Don't get cross if I don't have any ice skates.

SAMPLING KEYBOARD. £160. Tests your blood and urine while you type. National Food and Drugs Administration approved. 01999 749 841

UNSATISFYING SEXUAL ENCOUNTER with Michael from Data Inputting. Over in seconds, with some awkwardness at work for 3 months afterwards. Will swap for going home with Darren instead like he offered earlier in the evening and not getting shitfaced. Call Emma on 01999 616 563

YORKSHIRE TERRIERS, £65. Yorkshire puddings, £1.50. 01999 529 300

INVESTMENT OPPORTUNITY. Bring in a fiver and we'll turn it into £££££s instantly. Call Dean at the Photocopy Shop on 01999 655 855

MISERABLE ROGER™ PIRATE TRUCK. Unsatisfying toy for dislikeable children. Makes a loud whistling noise when unattended. Unbreakable. No batteries required. 01999 558888

BURTON'S TEACAKES

MARBLE ASHTRAY, £3. Doubles as spare marble ashtray for person with marble ashtray. 01999 233 954

THE FEAR OF GOD. £30. Box FE8028

UNIVERSITY CHALLENGE "Dusty Bamber" booby prize circa 1984. £offers. 01999 732 888

WAITROSE culture range / twenty tins of haiku shapes / in tomato sauce. £22

LEATHER briefcase, £10. Open-crotch PVC pantcase £12. 01999 646 119

REDNECKS

THERE GOES a nice pair of legs, pair of legs, pair of legs and other Crack-a-joke-book punchlines, in presentation box. £18. 01999 212 624

UNDERAGE deodorant. £5. Box FE8771

GIRL'S WORLD CUP. £12. Dress up the Jules Rimet trophy in a range of ribbons. Make its hair grow. Great gift. 01999 423 331

LE CREUSET pans. £45. Set of 5. Suitable for hob, oven or evening wear. 01999 498 788

RISING unemployment figures, £15. Would suit Leader of the Opposition. Also appalling record on public spending, £20. Many more available. 01999 644 842

LOTTERY TICKET. £4.3m winner. Used once. £1. 01999 659 590

COLLECTION of 1960s boardgames. Including "Backstreet Operation!" (plastic coathanger missing), "Carnabopoly", "Hungry Hippies", "Turn On Tune In Connect Four", "Ringo Bingo", "Profumo Downfall" and "Ken Kesey's Drop Out". Offers. Will split. 01999 644 372

YOU'RE BOTH WRONG

CASE OF 36 bottles of red wind. 1996 vintage. Strong, fruity bouquet. £90 ono. 01999 800 750

PIG HUTCH. 4' x 2'. Freestanding. Feeding bottle and bowl. £12. Call 01999 646 630. **GUINEA**

1500 COMMEMORATIVE Royal Wedding of Princess Charles and Prince Diana souvenir mugs. Slight factory printing error, hence £25 the lot.

Last year over 1,924 classified ads for his burst spacehopper were placed by Mr J. Ottingham in the pages of
The Framley Examiner
Well done.

FAT BLOKE. Up for just about anything. Call Tony on 01999 510 655

WASHING MACHINE REPAIRS. It's never been easier. I get in your machine. Put me through a cycle and I'll see if I can tell you what's wrong (no boiling). Also spindryers, hoovers and ironing boards. 01999 268 430

EARN £3000 A MONTH! Get a really good job, apparently. Call 01999 629 801 if you know more.

LEGO. 650,000 pieces. Makes bungalow or 3rd floor flat. £450pcm. All bills except water. 01999 733 221

3-PIECE FRIDGE £120 ono. 01999 449 374

SPIRAL HEIDI

A MAN AND A VAN needs another man to drive the other van. Call a man on 01999 302 088

SINGING LESSONS. For children and adults. No callout charge. 6 months parts and labour. Free estimates. Everything I Do (Adams) £18. Automatic (Pointer Sisters) £25. Call 01999 500 232

FANTASY FOOTBALL World Cup Video 1966. England 9, Germany 2. Geoff Hurst 8-trick. Beckenbauer killed by final penalty. People on pitch throughout. £7. 01999 543 286

1 DOZEN Gala Pie eggs in 6-foot long box. £4. 01999 522 940

POCKETLESS billiard table. No end of fun. £175. 01999 319 050

COMMEMORATIVE Mel and Kim Silver Jubilee souvenir plates, with Appleby Mint certificate of authenticity. £65. 01999 744 380

SICK 8 times this morning. Had to take day off. Pissed in a carrier bag. Lizzie bloody furious. 01999 765 488

GARDEN SERVICE. Pissing. Slumping. Shitting. Home-made compost. Call Bill on 01999 643 939

HALL FOR HIRE. Nice telephone on sidetable. Hatstand. Stairs on left leading to parents' bedroom. Call Stacey on 01999 300 843

FISH and chips tank. 4' x 1' with cabinet, filter and light. £20. Pickled egg 50p.

KIDS' POOL TABLE. 1" x 2". One ball (brown). No pockets. Possibly just a bit of baize and a Malteser. £offers. 01999 299 721

WEDDING DRESS. Size 24. Ivory jockstrap and depilator. Call Sweaty Malcolm on 01999 833 065

PARENT COSTUME. "Any time is bedtime when you look like your Dad". £15. 01999 400 211

JIM ROYLE humour destroyer. 6" plastic replica, will repeat previously amusing one-liners until rendered unpalatable Tomlinsonisms. Belches Mambo #5. Also GenuineManOfThePeople Top Trumps. £16.99. No time wasters. Call Jenny or don't call Jenny. The choice is yours. 01999 653 766

MOBILE BATHROOM. Comes to your door on time, whenever your girlfriend is spending hours and hours and hours and hours doing Christ knows what in yours. £1300. 01999 865 400

FIAT STILETTO SPACEWAGON 2.0i, one lady owner, middle-aged, divorced, WLTM mechanic with heart full of lust, £6,800. Tel Simone 01999 671444.

AND THE YEAR...? Call Noel on 01999 811 8055

ECSTASY TABLETS, Penguin logo on reverse, 10 thou., street value of up to £22,000. Doubled up order for staff party by mistake. Contact Rowland on 07999 871920

BAIL, £20,000. All donations will be delightfully received. Hopefully I won't be burning the fire station down for a third time! Box FE8510

FRAMLEY EXAMINER FLATSHARE

MAN BROKEN into millions of pieces offers room to homeloving woman who will sweep me neatly into a corner. £80p/w. 01999 754 654

ONE BED FLAT, WHOFT. Would suit one bed flat keen to convert to 2-bed maisonette. £65 p/w. 01999 844 311

ROOM TO LET in 3-story house. "Jeff's trip to Australia", "Annabel meeting Elton John", "How we got the landlord to knock £4 off the rent". Bring your own. £320pcm. 01999 622 812

CODGE - Room to let in small house in large room. Removable period facade. All original 1/12 scale fittings. Share with 5 other females of differing sizes and age. Ideally suit contortionist or professional doll. £doll

PRINCES FRESHBOROUGH - Entire second floor to let in quiet, first-floor house. No kitchen but sitting room has 'kitchen design' and smells of cookery. No time wastrels. £1200pcm

WELL-BEHAVED GHOST seeks room to haunt. No chains. 01999 399 804

FRAMLEY - Busy drawer to let in quiet Mayor's office. Stripped pine floor, high ceiling and washing machine. All bills inc. ex council tax. £85 pw.

The Framley Examiner
"So, Denise from the telesales desk of The Framley Examiner classifieds department, we meet again. You appear with the inevitability of an unloved season. Well, it would appear you've stumbled upon my little plan. But no matter. Soon it will be too late..."
Mr H. Drax, Codge

DURBITON - Flat to rent in smart 1960's terrace. Dble bedroom and 1/4 "skinny" bedroom. Kitchen/Cafe. Purple heart-shaped bed and shared back alley inc. fitted Lesley Ash. All mod cons. Would suit Shepherds Bush geezer. 12/6 pw.

SMALL SPACE available to rent in child's wardrobe. Would suit professional, light-sleeping smoker. No rent, but tenant must lurk at bottom of wardrobe in dark, rhythmically chanting "Old King Pipe, Old King Pipe! Coming to eat your hair!" for eight hours a night. Call Mr Hollyhock on 01999 482762

Terry HOLLYWOOD LETTING AGENTS AND VIDEO RENTALS

Flats, houses and latest blockbusters to rent.
£2.50 a night.
Some I.D. required (gas bill or addressed junk mail)
Weekend special - 2 for 1
Please rewind before returning.
If we're shut, just post the keys or tape through our letterbox.

01999 266 084

trapped under the chassis of the tank for over half an hour until the emergency services pulled the couple free with the help of Stromboli, the World's Strongest Man. Black coffee was served and sandwiches.

Fireman's Helmet

Musical Treat

ARTHRITIS CARE. - It was music, music, music for members who had a visit from three buskers. They sang *Kum Ba Yah*, *I Will Always Love You* and *It's The End Of The World As We Know It* at the same time and later treated their captive audience to some duets and, eventually, some solos. Everybody had a most enjoyable afternoon and members were sad to learn of the death of two of the buskers during the performance. Arthritis xmas cards were on sale and Rubik's cubes were left outside.

Silent Tribute

PARISH COUNCIL. - A meeting was held on Thursday at Whoft Memorial Village Hall. The meeting started with a fortnight's silence to remember the sixteen guest speakers who have died on the platform in the past month. As usual, the ceiling fell in on the person in the middle chair at the table, guest speaker Lollyrod Perkins (inventor of the long-forgotten Erg) on this occasion. Mr MacKenzie was again called to mend the ceiling, and arrived escorted by two parole officers.

Creme

Exciting film show

CREME FILM CLUB. - The society has arranged a film show on the village of Creme to take place in Creme Village Hall. The show will be open to local people. Viewers will be taken on a journey around this lovely village and have a chance to meet the many interesting people who live there, including themselves and each other.

Little Godley

Back To nature

RETIREMENT HOME. - Residents at Malgrave Hall were treated to a demonstration of sexual intercourse by Pammy Cum and Rocky Neville, two of America's most celebrated pornographic actors. The delighted audience were invited to go off in pairs and practise some of the exercises, including the popular double-lapper. After tea and soggy biscuit, residents were then shown Ms Cum's most famous film, *Tupelo Ass-Station Gizz Guzzler.*

Quiz Afternoon

FLORAL CLUB. - Just for a change, members of the Little Godley Floral Club were

Framley Town Plans

21 & 23 Walliams Hurrah, Friern Benedict, erection of illuminated sign "Fuck off, Dennis" along dividing fence. **Gents conveniences**, corner of Hopalong Row and Hartnell's Farm boundary, St Eyot's, construction of adjoining regional sales office, ancillary departmental offices and mezzanine reception for lavatory facility. **49 Bulgaria Tassel**, Sockford, installation of 24-hour oompah band on first storey flat roof. **11 Winton Terrace** Removal of house to make way for statue of same house being demolished. **29 Buccaneer Place**, Creme, addition of 2nd storey to garden. with upstairs pond. **38 Jalapeno Crescent**, Molford, removal of front of house to allow neighbours to see what John's done with the kids' bedroom. **112 Gotobed Vale**, lowering of entire street to make house look bigger. **102 Gavin**

Corners, Whoft, modification of front of house to let it smile again. **6 Ciconne Avenue**, Thoxtoxeter, erection of huge bow on roof to make house look like a big present. **94 Yowling Bench**, Urling, extension of back garden by five minutes. **3 Gabbitas Rd**, St Eyot's, removal of 6-foot blinking eye from cellar **19 Kevin Toms St**, Codge, transposition of house into key of B♭. **52 Glove Rd**, Wripple, removal of tennis match from television and replacement with episode of Quincy. **14 Peyote Villas**, Fracton, election of 2-storey MP. **81 Devoto Ramble**, Chutney, 2-blanket extension of existing den using pegs, beach towel and auntie's duvet, to allow extra comic storage. **32, Windsor Gardens**, removal of annoying bear. **41 Candida Rd**, Whoft, silencing of Yankee Doodle doorbell at number 43.

CELEBRATING A LONG LIFE

CANDLES APLENTY there were at the birthday party of Wripple's oldest resident, Nichola Logan, who reached the grand old age of 30 last week.

Nichola was born in Wripple during the reign of Elizabeth II and has lived there for the whole of her lifetime. At the time of her birth man setting foot on the moon was over a week away, the Titanic was just a dead boat, not a film at all, and public houses closed at 11pm to allow the armaments industry to make shells for the Great War.

Her 9-month old son, Max, described Nichola as "still on the ball and enjoying life to the full". Nichola also received the traditional congratulatory text message from Prince William and was later led away for a ride on The Carousel. **PHOTO BY FURCOAT AGGUTER**

locked into the garden centre and questioned by American intelligence experts. All members were released after 36 hours, with the exception of Mrs Buckley, and the CIA described the siege as "productive."

Coppernob

Grape Apes

A BUS STOP, COPPERNOB.- A disorganised shambles of a walking human pyramid was arranged to 'freak-out' certain elderly members of the parish. The motion was put forward by a young gentleman at the front of the busqueue who thought it a necessary step to prevent complacency during the autumn years.

Thoxtoxeter

Sweet Jesus

THOXTOXETER CHRISTIAN COVE.- A delivery was taken of 500 marzipan Jesuses as a token of friendship between Thoxtoxeter Christian Cove and Thoxtoxeter Christian Club. The confectionery Christs, depicting scenes of His life and what He may have got up to afterwards, are all over 7ft tall and of variable stickiness. A return gift of 10,000 Our Lady Marmalades is planned for early this afternoon.

Chutney

School Success

RUBMY INFANT SCHOOL OPEN DAY.- Another school open day was planned for early next year after the success of last Thursday when all 400 pupils managed to enter the school and participate in a full-day's education. The school remains closed in the interim period until the headmaster's annual 360 day adventure holiday comes to an end.

Inspirational speaker

CHUTNEY MOUNTAINEERING SOCIETY. - This Thursday, in a change to our previous plan, inspirational speaker Mohammed Al'Mutah will come to visit the Mountaineers. This is due to the continued, inexplicable failure of the Mountaineers to make the trip in the other direction, despite all our best efforts.

Sockford

Mobile Church

ST. CHURCH OF THE GREEN, QUEFF.- Repairs to the historic bell tower were once again suspended after recent structural inconsitencies caused the building to topple heavenwards. A tarpaulin, set-

up to prevent such happenings, came loose and created a 'brick balloon', which is now heading towards Sockford. The congregation are praying for clement weather and a favourable wind.

Bum's the Word

1st SOCKFORD BROWNIES.- This year's sponsored swear raised over two hundred pounds and eyebrows as the Sockford Brownie pack swore their way into the history book. The event, which coined three hundred new swear words and two inaudible to the human ear, was interrupted by an impromptu display of the effects of gravity on brick church towers.

Successful Event

PEOPLE'S GUILD - Meeting at their new venue in the car park, members enjoyed a splendid talk by Jim Twin, who entertained the assembled crowd with repeated questions about where the A999 was. He left after five minutes in a red Vauxhall Average, complaining that he wasn't their bloody guest speaker and that he didn't seem to be able to get a straight answer to a straight question from anyone in the village. Members voted by 28-3 to invite Mr Twin to return to the guild. Anyone with information about his whereabouts should join.

First stone

INTERNET CLUB - The recently-formed Internet Club, going from strength to strength, invited Mr Bill Gates, the inventor of the computer, to lay the first stone of their new website, being built on brownfield land on the site of the former air factory. Mr Gates politely declined, but did send a message of goodwill, 'GR8! b xxx :-)' which members voted unanimously to use as their mission statement. The first stone was eventually laid by robots.

Well Done!

WINNERS' CUP - The Sockford Enthusiasts were represented in this year's community riots by six suitably violent residents. Although not among the winners, all six gave creditable preformances in the bricking, the clubbing and the looting, some beating their own personal records. A special exploding prize for excellence in petrol-bombing was presented to Doug Bunnit by guest speaker Ch Con Rupert Bone.

Local hospitals and bystanders thrown into shock as
Ambulance crash happens

by Taunton Mishap

AN EMERGENCY AMBULANCE rushing to the aid of two ambulances that had crashed into each other dramatically crashed into the Accident & Emergency department of Framley General Hospital in the early hours of Thursday morning.

The ambulance, believed to have been driven by driver Gregor GitzFerald, smashed through plate glass, steel, concrete and patients at what Britain's speed chiefs have described as 45mph. Twelve doctors, seventeen nurses and 28 people in a serious condition are now either dead, dying or in a serious condition.

The patient being carried by the patently out-of-control vehicle, Julian Chaucer, who was pregnant with a child, was yesterday said to be in a stable condition. His baby is just as likely unharmed.

Emergency doctors were called several metres to attend to things like internal bleeding, as a state of emergency was declared by

What Thursday's carnage might have looked like, had our photographer not been at a fete.
ARTIST S IMPRESSION BY TAUNTON MISHAP

Framley's emergency services.

SUSPICIOUS MINDS

Framley General Hospital''s A&E department hit the headlines earlier this month when it was closed off and surrounded by police for 28 hours after a man walked in claiming to be Elvis. By the time he was released and arrested, a crowd of 20,000 had gathered to look at The

King.

Three further ambulances were called to the scene on Thursday morning, but they crashed into the other two ambulances and the crashed ambulance.

There was no survivor.

If you are concerned that a friend or relative may have been injured please call the emergency helpdesk on 01999 542 542 and ask for Maxine. Hang up if Chris answers.

I have decided to resign

By DAMIUN CLAVALIER

AFTER SOME six months here, I have decided to resign. Try as I may to get sacked or find a reason to stay, nothing seems to work. (I set fire to the editor's laptop yesterday morning and he failed to notice.)

I, 19, deny being too good for this job. "I am no egotist," I said yesterday.

"But things have got to change," I continued. "It's been an enormously enjoyable and educating experience

and I shall miss it."

And, as I also pointed out, I thought long and hard about taking this decision. Mind you, I thought long and hard about taking the job in the first place, and yes, I was wrong.

I also denied describing my job as "like being locked in a shed full of cretins" and pointed out, accurately, that my resignation would not be noticed even when I shoved it under their noses in 32pt headline, and looked forward to many more blissful and tortuous months filling time here.

Fish auctioned for over two trouthand quid

The mounted trout that is selling for
PHOTOGRAPH BY KICKASS VAN HALEN

A TROUT caught at Framley Municipal Baths in 1911 is being auctioned for £2500 at Sockford Auction Rooms next week.

The stuffed fish on a bed of stuffed wild rice in a glass case weighed 18lb when caught by S. M. Norris just before a war, and is now thought to be the most valuable fish ever caught in the pool - worth the equivalent of more than a lifetime's pay.

The auction catalogue also mentions that another trout caught in the same year by an S. M. J. Norris is valued at £300. It is not clear if this was the same angler or a father and son or even if it's the same fish.

Anyone with any information about this sort of thing should call our Vague History desk on 01999 603282.

News In Brief

POP'S POWERFUL FUTURE

A report published this week has revealed that by the year 2029, every third song will be called *The Power Of Love*. In addition, says the report in Thing magazine, every fifth song will be called *Ship Of Fools* and people will be able to download millions of mp3s in seconds from credit cards made of recycled fingernails.

NEW HOSPITAL MACHINE

Framley General Hospital continued its long-term investment in more up-to-the-minute technology this week, when it became the proud recipient of a new Flymo lawnmower. The machine, valued at £79.99, hovers above the ground while cutting the grass. Skeptics say the two may not be logically possible at the same time.

VICAR ARRESTED

A Church of England vicar who was found having sexual intercourse with part of a tortoise at Framley Museum has been released from police custody on bail. Rev Nester Thrilling, 58, yesterday said "alas, there is a beast in all of us." He now plans to wrestle with the idea of taking his own life.

CEMETERY TO MOVE

Framley's famous Victorian cemetery is, after many years, set to rotate again. A National Lottery grant has allowed the gigantic complex of subterranean machinery to be spruced up and restored to working order, and from next month, the cemetary will rotate five times daily just as it did in 1843. "It's nice," said one resident, "we get some fresh air."

AIRPORT SABOTEURS

The saboteurs of the proposed Molford St Gavin airport will meet this Sunday at the corner of Skullion Farm and Porterhouse fields. When the diggers roll up, questions will be asked but answers will be scarce. Placards.

Plans for church anger just about everyone

MISS - I feel I must respond to your article ("Church moves with the times" Examiner Aug 17th) and state the case of Wripple residents more strongly.

The plan to move St Mauve's church six inches to the right to allow the passage of an approaching snail is, quite frankly, a slap in the face to tradition. Protestors' feelings run high on this matter, as your excellent full-colour photograph of the burning verger showed most clearly.

Regardless of what so called animal rightsists may say, a church is a church. I'm sure Jesus would have turned in his empty tomb had he known what was being proposed.

TETBURY GRANDMORPH
Mittelnachtstrasse
Wripple

MISS - The scenes of violence that marred last week's protest at St Mauve's will have lodged in everyone's minds like a marble in a fallopian tube, but we should not let that distract us from the real issues.

The snail - currently on the verge by the lych gate - has clearly indicated the path it wishes to follow. It would be against nature for man to place a church in its way.

The church must be moved. It is as simple as that. Remember, if we don't inherit the earth from our parents, we steal it from their children.

MISTRAL STARLIGHT
The Wickery
Molford St Gavin

MISS - Moving St Mauve's historic 15th Century church six inches to the right for the benefit of a snail is madness.

What about the worm coming up the side of the vestry? Surely the church needs to be moved six inches to the left.

HOXTON WINNEBAGO
Non-Alignment Pact Way
Chutney

MISS - I wonder if you might help me trace the attractive woman I met at the St Mauve's church-moving riot last week? Around 5'8", slim built, pro-snail, with strawberry blonde hair and a sharpened chairleg. I was the pro-church bearded man with the under-over assault rifle. Do get in touch.

DAVID EOHIPPUS
The Gondolas
Wripple, FM6 9QT

Hear, here!

MISS - Well said! (Editorial, Examiner Aug 17th). If God had meant man to be descended from monkeys, he would have given us a tea party.

Prof. YOSEMITE VEGEMITE,
Creme

St Mauve's church, Wripple - threatened with a six-inch movement.
PHOTOGRAPH BY PERSEPHONE MAGIC

The importance of being him

MISS - I recently received a letter from Framley Borough Council asking for my comments on a proposed mobile phone transmitter mast to be erected only a few feet from my next-door neighbour's house.

I strongly object to this proposition. My neighbour, Mr Frank Holder, is a decent man who simply does not deserve to have this scabrous monstrosity located within eye distance of his immaculate patio.

However, those wankers, the Dennisons at number 67 should be subjected to any form of cancer-giving totem there is going.

For too long we have suffered their annual anniversary party and constant car washing, not to mention their three young children who, I fear, will only ever be taught not to say their bedtime prayers at 8pm every evening by a healthy dose of radiational mindwipe.

My good lady wife and I would be further delighted to witness the demolition of their house in order to build some kind of imminent motorway.

Please pass my comments onto the relevant council.

DEVON PLANXTY,
65 Sapphireandsteel Walk,
Sockford

You're all c*unts

MISS - You know who you are. Yes, you. Parking in my church reserved space. What part of "reserved space" don't you understand? C*unts, every man jack of you.

And what's so hard about not pissing in my flowerbeds? You lot. Yes, I'm talking to you c*unts. C*unts to a man. C*unts,. c*unts, cunts. The lord may forgive you, but I never will. Bunch of c*unts.

Rev OILY WINDSCAPE,
Molford St Malcolm

Police to write letter to paper about article

MISS - I wish to clarify your story "Police To Ignore Intruder Alarms" (Examiner, Aug 17th).

Your story stated incorrectly that under our new policy, Framley police would only respond to intruder alarms if there was nothing good on the telly.

As Framley Police Station is located at the base of an extremely steep hill we can actually only receive BBC2 and ITV. So we will respond if there is something good on BBC1 or Channels 4 or 5 so long as there is nothing worth watching on BBC2 or ITV.

For a copy of our pamphlet "What Your Constabulary Watches" please phone us on 01999 999899 (having first checked to make sure that Emmerdale and Ready Steady Cook aren't on).

DESK SGT JOE MOUSE,
Framley Police Station,
Framley.

Political madness gone correct!

MISS - I object in the strongest possible meaning of the word. I've been correct for all of my life until now.

Not only do I find myself having to refer to my """"intellectually different"""" son as Thicky Thicky Malcolm Johnston rather than simply Thicky Thicky Malcolm, as I have called him for years.

Now I'm told that I must call a policeman a 'personman' of all things.

And this is just the tip of my iceberg.

MRS RONETTE JOHNSTON,
The Pinny,
Whoft

Ask Captain Mitchell

The Framley Examiner's very own agony aunt answers your questions

Lawn trouble

DEAR CAPTAIN MITCHELL,
I have been happily married to my husband of ten years for ten years now, and until recently I couldn't have been happier.

My husband has always been interested in gardening, and we used to enjoy discussing his hobby, but recently his focus has narrowed to a point that I feel I no longer know him.

In the old days, we would visit garden centres together to buy plants and furniture, and I would help by maintaining the pots, trellises and ornamental features in the garden. Now he simply locks me in the kitchen every morning before going out to buy lawnmowers.

Since the weather turned in April, he has purchased over 350 lawnmowers, all of which are currently parked in the back garden, obscuring the landscaping and dripping oil on the lawn.

Sometimes my husband rides one of his favourites up and down the patio for hours, staring at me in silence as I gaze mournfully out at him through the kitchen window. When it rains, he puts a grassbox on his head, and shifts into reverse.

I have tried to show an interest in his new hobby, but every time I try and crawl out through the catflap, he just comes at me on his Qualcast, crying.

Please help me - RW

Captain Mitchell says:
Try soaking the clothes in a vinegar-water solution overnight. That should bring back the chip-shop freshness you miss so much.

Sex problem

DEAR CAPTAIN MITCHELL,
I live in a flat, and when my neighbours make love, I can see them through the wall. I don't want to sound like a fuddy-duddy, but it's a bit much, even in this day and age - PT

Captain Mitchell says:
Try applying bicarbonate of soda to the affected area until the stain lifts and becomes wearable again.

Gun worry

DEAR CAPTAIN MITCHELL,
Following a row about driving gloves, my fiancee has just fired a gun at me. The bullets are heading towards my face as I write. What should I do? - JY

Captain Mitchell says:
I'm sending you my leaflet "Duck: What To Do When Someone Fires A Gun At You". I hope its advice comes in helpful.

Whoaaaaah!

DEAR CAPTAIN MITCHELL,
I am becoming worried that my husband thinks I'm Tom Jones.

For the last four months, he has refused to go to sleep until I've sung him *The Green Green Grass Of Home.*

Now I find I've been booked in at Rockfield to record a comeback album of collaborations with contemporary indie artists, such as Starsailor and the Sugababe who looks like Nicholas Lyndhurst. I'm at my wits end. Please help me. This is destroying my marriage - Mrs G

Captain Mitchell says:
What's new, pussycat?

SPORTS extra

Cricketing idiot found

GROUNDSMEN AT SOCKFORD GREEN cricket ground, working at clearing the rough scrub from the perimeter of the pitch, say they have found a player believed missing since the beginning of World War II.

The lost batsman, a Mr Bob Jaundice from Lissom-by-Trench near St Eyot's, hadn't been seen since the summer of 1940, when he went in to bat for Sockford Second XI.

Sockford needed 48 to win against local favourites Wripple Cosmologists, who had declared for 216, but the game was never completed. Conscription was unexpectedly announced after tea, and both teams were immediately flown to the Egyptian Front, leaving the scoreline tantalisingly inconclusive.

By Stan Rubbish

However, Jaundice, who had apparently fallen over on his way to the crease, was face-down while his team mates were being loaded into the Hercules transport plane, and missed the whole thing. Not realising the game was over, the lone batsman stood his ground.

Since this time, Jaundice has been fighting a guerilla cricket match from the bushes near Silly Mid Off, making use of low ground cover and an improvised bat.

Mr Jaundice, hiding from the undergrowth.
PHOTOGRAPH BY MICHELOB PAOLOZZI

THE SUMMER GAME

Sixty years later, the grounds crew stumbled upon the batsman's nest. They ordered Mr Jaundice to leave the bushes, but he became agitated, flailing at the undergrowth with his rudimentary cricketing stick and screaming, "Not Out! Not Out!"

Experts believe the only way to remove the entrenched sportsman is to bowl him out legitimately using a vintage 1940s ball. Groundsmen are searching the shrubs where he was last spotted, to see if they can find evidence of a primitive wicket which they think he may be guarding.

"It does seem," said chief groundsman Arnold Laramie, "that until we prove to the gentleman that his marathon innings is at an end, he is going to refuse to return to the pavillion. It's like Geoff Boycott all over again."

Jaundice is currently 5004 not out.

SPOT THE BALL COMPETITION

WEATHER CONDITIONS: Oily **GROUND:** Soft / Hard
Send your entries to THE FRAMLEY EXAMINER Unit 149b, East Cosset Industrial ParkParkfields Bypass, Framley FR1 6LH

NAME:_____ ADDRESS:_____, Framley
POSTCODE: _____
MARITAL STATUS: ___ DAYTIME TEL. _____ SHIRT SIZE: S / XL / XM

HERE'S LAST WEEK'S ANSWER (01865) with the location of the ball indicated. There were a record number of corroct entries. All winners listed here get a crate of champagne, a night in the Miami Motel, Sockford and a Mini Cooper.

Mrs Elsie Remindme, Whoft; Jeremy Liphippo, Codge; R. Tumbril, Wripple; Wendy Redknapp, Framley; Stephen Missst, Framley; Wayland Smithy, St Eyot's; Youngman Grand, Framley; Montgomery Waste, Whoft; Richard Lionfoot, Whoft; Ursula Cloybeam, Molford; Dennis Cloybeam, Molford; Witchy Poo, Creme; Haris Paris, Little Godley; Hopeful Jefferson, Bad Sandal; Trebus Announce, Fracton; Paul Ryman, The Close; Whistledown Jones, Wripple; Hootie Bellend, Clinton; Ippy Pog, Framley; Messerschmitt Ouch, Sockford; Yolanda Nameagain, Creme; Outside Nugent, Lessbury Moreborough; Riley O'Riley, Frant; Mrs L. Mouse, Framley; Mr Crovenly, Slovenly, Halbatch Crowdnoise, Whoft; Flakey-Foont, Crumb; Mr Natural, Crumb; Sgt Neil Howie, Framley; Holpme Warrington, Framley; Windmill McMasterman, Wripple; Mr O. Churchflower, Molford; Aggie Legs, Codge; Pinhead McMonarchy, Framley; Ms J. Wheelarch, Fracton; Hopalong Osmond, Framley; Longman Wilmington, Molford; Cerne-Abbas Giant, St Eyot's, Michael Pikle, Whoft; Beverly Everly, Wripple; **(CONTINUED p80)**

Jazz meet their match at Framley

BASKETBALL
Newby's Amateur Shield

THE COUNTY'S PREMIER basketball team, Sockford Jazz, suffered a severe mauling at Framley Tigers last Monday.

The friendly invitation match, held in the tigers' basketball enclosure at Framley Zoo was finally halted by giggling keepers after six Sockford players and a basketball were swallowed in seventeen minutes by Sheba, a Bengali mother of three.

This week's game will be preceded by eight bars of syncopated silence for the late Sockford stars after a special request from their coach, Chick Corea. Local bookies have closed the books on a victory for the visiting Spaniards, Newcastle Basketball Players.

FOOTBALL GOALS

LONG DIVISION

	P	W	F	A	Pts
Bungalow	1	0	0	11	0
Battery Flatford	1	0	0	59	0
Wripple Wetsuits	1	0	0	33	0
Mrs J. Hargreaves	1	0	0	24	0
Chutney Gloves	1	0	0	18	0
Framley Area Referees	5	5	145	0	15

NEWBY'S PREMIER

	P	W	F	A	Pts
Tallboy Valves	999	999	999	999	999
St. Eyot's Folders	999	999	999	999	999
Fracton Crackers	999	999	999	999	999
Batley Berettas	999	999	999	999	999
Effing Ball	999	999	999	999	999
Slovenly Emcellent	999	999	999	999	999

NONE-LEAGUE

	P	W	F	A	Pts
Busy Wednesday	999	999	999	999	999
Werther's Originals	999	999	999	999	999
Delighted United	999	999	999	999	999
Bisto Impossible	999	999	999	999	999
Durbiton Unreasonable	999	999	999	999	999
Round The Block FC	999	999	999	999	999
Whoft City Slickers II (The Legend of Curly's Gold)	999	999	999	999	999

>>MIKE GET THESE STATS FRM WENDY - IVE DUMMIED THEM IN BUT NEED DOING B4 TUESDAY DDLN - CHRIS

PERSONAL ADS

to remake in the image of my dead wife. No timewasters. Box FE8433

TEACHER, 27, petite, loves teaching Sociology and PE seeks male, 25-35, with gaps in his education. 01999 281930

CAPRICORN, genuine, honest girl (Pisces) WLTM man able to believe me. I am sisters. Box FE8938.

GREEN-EYED Sockford girl, 13, seeks beautiful, strapping chestnut mare for long bouncy ride, hymen-popping and nosebag if compatible. Box FE8361.

WRIPPLE MAN, 24, likes loud music, dancing, drugs, bottled lager and night-buses, hates clubbing, seeks accommodating female with own flat/bungalow where we could probably do all that sort of thing. Box FE8482.

BUBBLY LADY, very very soft skin, lemon-scented, clean to the squeak, fell into cauldron of Fairy Liquid as a baby seeks short male with leather gourd and own helmet for mistranslated French-language fun. Box FE87ix.

SINGLE FEMALE, 35, seeks male (any) for marriage, three kids, growing old together, maybe more. 01999 714592.

POLICEMAN, 40, seeks man, 20-22, approx 5'8", shaved head, tattoos of Johnny Mathis on both forearms to eliminate him from our enquiries. Phone 01999 999899 in complete confidence.

ELDERLY GENT, 78, seeks vivacious redhead, late 20s, for one last night of messy passion. Never done it ginger before. One remaining ambition. Boxes FE8574 - 89.

I'VE GOT a cock with a 10-second trigger but I can still make you come before I do. Box FE8595.

GAY MAN, 33, professional non-smoker WLTM gay woman for sex (by gay I mean happy). Box FE8517

KIDS GROW UP so fast these days, don't they? 07999 744 355

LIKEMINDED man would like to meet likeminded woman who likes Minder and doesn't mind that I like her for her mind. Box FE8140

WHOFT FEMALE, 36, medium build, eyes, magnetic, enjoys going to gym & picking up iron filings WLTM similarly charged male for evenings of nearly kissing. Box FE8366

DESIRABLE LADY, 38, WLTMarry man called Lee in August 1985 that won't end up shagging my best friend in our own bed, you utter shit. I'll be at my mother's, the solicitor will be in touch. Box FE8048.

TOUCH ME IN THE MORNING Blue eyed Chutney female. Varied interests. Only tangible before 12pm. Box FE8137

COULD I BE YOU? 43yo widower, into submarines, cross-stitch and mango chutney seeks 43yo male into cross-stitch / mango chutney and submarines. Box FE8667

DAVID BOWY LOOKALIKE circa 1973, now looks like Shane MacGowan WLTM person. No longer fussy. Box FE8933

MAN DRESSED AS SCATTER CUSHION WLTM man able to stop man dressing as scatter cushion before wife discovers man dressed as scatter cushion. Box FE8332

BABY-FACED MAN, 48, into Art Nouveau, oil, windmills and the music of The Spheres seeks unintelligible, lanky female(?) for spoon-bending and quiet evenings in with a bottle of gripewater. Box FE8112

SHY PROFESSIONAL MALE, 29, seeks someone that might laugh at one of my jokes. M or F, I don't mind. Not that you'll be reading this anyway. I'll be over there if you want me. Box FE8709.

ARE YOU FED UP WITH friends letting you down? Look no further - I hate you & I'll let you down. Box FE8380

WELL-SPOKEN MALE, 52, GSOH, seeks like-minded person interested in current affairs who enjoys talking to literally millions of people at the same time. Must be able to pronounce Matabeleland. And now it's over to Michael Fish for a look at tomorrow's weather. Box FE8941.

LONELY POSTMAN, 19, 7'2", interests include tombolas, bisto sniffing and The Fonz WLTM broad-minded female to test the edges of possibility. Box FE8996

HANDSOME CHUNK, good-looking male, 32, enjoys going to the gym / coming back from the gym / being at the gym seeks women to impress with chunkiness. Box FE8111

INCREDIBLY BUSY MAN, 34, seeks attractive woman for 30-second relationship, possibly marriage. Box FE8127

FLAT STANLEY seeks welcoming family with spare wall to lean against. I won't be any trouble. Box FE8433

LOOKING FOR MR WRIGHT? So am I. He was my geography teacher & he still hasn't marked my essay on terminal moraine. Box FE8006

INSENSITIVE BASTARD, unreliable, bad in bed apparently, unable to commit, some baggage from previous relationship, seeks woman 24-30 for new start. Box FE8001

PLUG SEEKS SOCKET for electric relationship. I'm not actually a plug but I do have a thumb on each hip and would welcome a chance to meet someone with appropriate holes. Box FE8722

WHEN WILL YOU MARRY ME? Anybody? Tel 01999 238764

FILM-LOVING Framley male, interested in prisons / schools / oil rigs and public places seeks Simon Bates lookalike to inform him about pirates. Box FE8778

DIVORCED FEMALE, 38, likes TV, cooking, decorating, hamsters seeks rugged male with similar outdoor interests. Box FE8129.

OCTAGONAL MALES, seek smaller square females for tesselation and problem-solving. Box FE8237

SINGLE MOTHER, 23, five kids, gets drunk easily seeks genuinely caring man that won't take advantage. Box FE8873.

AFFLUENT MALE, 34, diagnosed iron deficiency WLTM meat. Last three girlfriends vegetarians, can't fucking handle it any more. Need chops. Box FE8390.

MAN WITH MOUSTACHE seeks woman with beard. You'll understand when you see me. No kissing. Box FE8119

FIREMAN seeks non-smoker for lasting relationship. Box FE8300

WRIPPLE CHILD, 5, WLTM Father Christmas. Tel 01999 200572

I CAN BE what you want me to be. I have coloured contact lenses, wigs, a prosthetic cock and interchangeable limbs. Must be able to love me for being myself. Phone Sally on 01999 835472.

CHANNEL HOPPING guy seeks ferry for safer journeys. Box FE8499

MYSELF & MY G/F are looking for compatible friends to go out on day trips to hairdressers, Tescos, work & meeting the kids from school, possibly more. Box FE8089

I'M YOUR KNIFE. Are you my fork? Let's plate! Tel 01999 000100

BREEDING PAIR of endangered people WLTM zookeeper with dirty mags, test tube, spatula and lots of patience for unconventional 3-way. Tel 01999 707278

ARE YOU A SLIM, attractive, successful blonde? Are you looking for love through the Framley Examiner personals? Didn't think so. Box FE8766

SEMI-ATTRACTIVE FEMALE, raspberry-blonde, WLTM divorced male, 55, 5'5", into the music of 1955 and the Waffen SS. Box FE8433

YOUNG-LOOKING MALE, 81, seeks slim-looking woman, 18 stone. Tel 01999 970911

SUCCESSFUL SOCKFORD BUSINESSMAN, 46, GSOS wltm very clean female with extremely diligent standards of hygiene. Box FE8646

FRAMLEY MALE, likes cinema, hates films, WLTM huge, noisy woman with tall hat and bags of crunchy popcorn to sit behind during visits to the Odeon. Box FE8993

28-YEAR OLD MALE enjoys eating, people and eating people. Seeks gregarious, hungry, delicious woman for short term relationship. Box FE8622

BOND GIRL LOOKALIKE (Klebb) WLTM a man who thinks he can do a Sean Connery impression. There must be someone out there! Box FE8992

BEN, 23. Handsome, black Escort for women. Clapped out blue Nova for men. 07999 656504

YOU CAN'T ALWAYS GET what you want, and I'm what you always wanted. Bye! Box FE8261

ELEGANT LADY, mid-30s, seeks irrationally dependent male who will fall in love on the first date, propose to me even though we've never slept together and will step in front of the 44b bus when I reveal that I'm just toying with him. And that I'm a bloke. Box FE01999.

SOLUBLE MAN seeks woman with dry skin condition, saliva deficiency and vaginismus. Box FE8087

OLD-LOOKING MALE, 21, WLTM young-smelling woman. Tel 01999 287874

I SAW

FIRST CLASS LADY, I licked the back of your head. You tasted of glue & looked like the queen. You weren't a stamp, I've already asked that once. Box FE8736

MOLFORD DENTIST. You touched my teeth. I was 36. Now I'm 38. Box FE8949

I WAS THE ENORMOUS woman on table 14. You were a roast potato on table 2. Where are you loved one? I'm stilll hungry. Box FE8207

HELP! I SAW YOU standing there, Lady Madonna. With a little help from my friends at the Framley Examiner Personal Desk we could all come together. Everybody's got something to hide except me & my silver hammer. Why don't we do it in the road? Call Frank Ifield fan on 01999 873410

I ROAST POTATO (table 2). You nice, handsome man eating with fat, ugly lady. Where you? Box FE8422

I WAS FEEDING GRAPES to Marianne Faithfull and writing the words to Jumping Jack Flash. You were writing the bassline. Who were you? Box FE8126

FANCY DRESS PARTY, March 2001. I was dressed as a bonfire. You were dressed as an invitation to another fancy dress party. Is it still on? Box FE8926

YOU TOOK THE PISS. I cried. You laughed and laughed and laughed. Want to meet for good times? Box FE8739

I WAS SEDATED. You were coming out of my twat like a sodding train. Box FE8541

YOU WERE SHAPELY, STYLISH BRUNETTE eating alone. Michaelantoni's Brasserie. I was Italian-looking 20-something waiter. What did you order again? Box FE8961

BLACKPOOL PIER, 1961. You swallowed the rollercoaster. Why did you do it? How did you do it? When will this ride end? Tel FRA308

YOU WERE LOOKING FOR a 3-bed semi in Whoft, I was working thenightshift on the Framley Examiner telesales desk. I'm pregnant. It's yours. Tel 01999 939234

I WAS 6-YEAR OLD with overactive imagination, you were 19ft blue piggybank called Mr Waggy. Please call. We could really make it work this time. Box FE8165

CINDERELLA - We met on the slopes at Montgenèvre. I still have one of your glass skis. Box FE 8419

1964 - you were screaming 16-year old girl with horn-rimmed glasses. I was Billy Crimson & The Corsairs, Whoft Hippodrome. Box FE8195

The Framley Examiner

Framley's Traditional Favourite since 1978

PRICE 45p

FOOD

Hot hot pies

STYLE

Even numbers

WIN

A lifetime's supply of spiders

Local area flattened due to planning irregularity

OUTRAGE AS DEVELOPERS DEMOLISH WHOFT

Cutting a swathe through some Edwardian cottages.
PHOTO BY REEPERBAHN GRAPE

by Adam "Peppercorn" Wrent

THE PEOPLE OF WHOFT were this week coming to terms with what might be the biggest shock of their lives. Furious residents are claiming "an act of unparalleled and shocking vandalism" after the entire suburb was accidentally razed to the ground by property developers.

The alarm was raised at 3pm on Tuesday by computer cleaner George Fazakiel, when he returned home from work early to find his house gone.

"I turned into Psittiter Circus, and round the bend by the community centre, and realised that my house wasn't there," he recounted, 38.

"Then I noticed that the community centre was also missing, and that the road I thought I was on wasn't really there either, except for a load of rubble," he recounted.

Whoft was home to 15,800 people until this week. Much of the area, which included two primary schools and five pubs, was built in the 1880s by Victorian speculator Excelsior Melon, but that doesn't matter any more.

Present-day developers Wonham Foreign de Foreigner put in a planning application to build two one-bedroom houses with car parking in January. They say that residents were given until February 30th to write to Framley Borough Council with any comments.

THIS IS OUTRAGEOUS

"This is outrageous," said elderly Noreen Twaith at a specially-convened meeting of former Whoft residents at Framley Town Hall on Thursday evening.

"The council sent us a letter asking for our opinion and emphasising that our comments counted, but then the bulldozers and the wrecking-balls go right over our heads and do whatever they want."

Developers do not need planning permission to demolish a building unless it is listed. However, they do need to agree a means of demolition,

which WFdF claim they applied for.

Unfortunately the council now admit that a "simply frightening" amount of paperwork - possibly including the demolition form - was used in Mayor D'Ainty's highly successful Grand Framley Paper Aeroplane Race at the beginning of February. Normally, if the council does not respond to a bashing-up request within a certain period of time, the demolition can go ahead. It is thought that this technicality led to Tuesday's disaster.

NOW

Now-homeless residents are now taking their fight to court, and have formed an action group to take their fight to the courts.

"Our lawyers think we have a very good case," says campaigner Curly McWurly. "And if our initial hearing goes well on Monday, we may have our houses back by the end of the week."

A spokesman for Wonham Foreign de Foreigner made no comment except to confirm that the time for the council to reply to the demolition application had elapsed several weeks ago and that "it said 'Whoft' on all the forms - what have we done wrong this time?"

Charity jailbreak goes with a bang

THE ANNUAL RAG WEEK at Framley Community College ended on Friday with a sponsored Jailbreak that raised over £900 for drunk children.

The police, who had co-operated with students of the college to help organise the jailbreak, told reporters they were delighted with the results.

"It was great to be involved with the college," said a police spokesman. "This forges ties with the community and raises money for a good cause into the bargain. The whole event was a great success, with over 38 criminals sprung from chokey. Well done.

"We advise the public not to approach these men as they are probably armed."

LETTERS P18 & 19 LETTERS P11 & 23 LETTERS P37 LETTUCE P79 - 79 THIS BANNER P1

egs as far as the ankles with
that damages the soles of
: became difficult to break
s were becoming sticky, so
:mpted to staunch the flow
hundred feet of industrial

the bite of a mountain ant
oblems they experienced,
lly the mystery will be
her ailments were studied
s, and hopefully a cure will

:tanley Lebor, whose own
:k in the field led to so
peing saved.
ime see an end to this
:ring.